W9-BTM-004

ich schreib dir ja oft sehen von Ihm, ist nicht der Typ
der aus hohlem Faß spricht — ich muß Ihm fragen
wie Er sich die Sache denkt. Jedenfalls heißt es
nun rennen, in paar Tagen mache ich den
"Fremdenführer" für München, dü rohe das gleiche
in New-York — Kind wir haben herrliche Berufe!
Aber nichts mache ich lieber als so umherzureisen.
Komische Vergnügen, was? Darunter leidet natürlich
die [...]. 2 Wochen war ich nicht dort, wie es jetzt
aussieht komme ich auch nächste Woche nicht hin.
Was du über "gänzlich aufgeben" schreibst, überlege ich
mir. Ehrlich gestanden kann ich jetzt kaum arbeiten,
meine Gedanken u. Unruhe lenken mich sehr ab.
diese Arbeit aber fordert viel Aufmerksamkeit, Ruhe
u. Wachsamkeit, sie ist trocken, kalt, bedarf eine
[...] Brille, voll eine große Portion Haß
u. Grausamkeit. Hassen kann ich nicht mehr, die Koch-
[...] in länger verschmancen, das fühle ich so
[...], abstoßend u. klein. Verstehe mich richtig
Kind, es ist nicht launenhaft von mir, es war euch
kein Strohfeuer — die Begeisterung. Bin schreibe dir alles,
aber ich weiß du und Du sind mich richtig
verstehen, dir dürfen meine Gedanken nicht fremd
sein du darfst Kritik üben ich bitte um dein
Urteil darüber!

Kisses and love Gerda.

Valparaiso Public Library
103 Jefferson St.
Valparaiso, IN 46383

The Hours After

Letters of Love and Longing
in War's Aftermath

Gerda Weissmann Klein and Kurt Klein

PORTER COUNTY PUBLIC LIBRARY SYSTEM

Valparaiso Public Library
103 Jefferson St
Valparaiso, IN 46383

St. Martin's Press / New York

JUN 3 0 2000

940.5318 KLE   VAL
Klein, Gerda Weissmann,
The hours after : letters
of love and longing in
33410005751435

Note to Reader

The letters reprinted here are translated from the original German and edited for readability by the authors.

The authors have changed the names of some of the individuals mentioned in this book. The following names are pseudonyms: Gerta Teppel, Henry, Gary, Bäumler, Tania, Ronka, Suma, Esther, Janka, Izlu, Franka, and Mario Sarino.

THE HOURS AFTER. Copyright © 2000 by Gerda Weissmann Klein and Kurt Klein. All rights reserved. Printed in the United States of America. No part of this book may be used or reproduced in any manner whatsoever without written permission except in the case of brief quotations embodied in critical articles or reviews. For information, address St. Martin's Press, 175 Fifth Avenue, New York, N.Y. 10010.

Except as noted in the insert, all photographs are courtesy of Gerda Weissmann Klein and Kurt Klein.

Digital collage art used on the title page and on page 33 by Marc Yankus.

Endpapers: Front, letter from Kurt Klein to Gerda Weissmann, December 4, 1945; back, letter from Gerda Weissmann to Kurt Klein, December 1, 1945.

ISBN 0-312-24258-1

First Edition: February 2000

10   9   8   7   6   5   4   3   2   1

Book design by Fritz Metsch

As we pack up our bundles of old letters, we realize with deep gratitude that most of the sentiments contained in their faded pages have withstood the test of time. Having lost our parents at a young age, we looked for direction in the building of our marriage and the raising of a family in the legacy they left us. We therefore dedicate this book to the blessed memory of our parents, Ludwig and Alice Klein and Julius and Helene Weissmann. Added to what they imparted to us in their unfulfilled lives are also the values left to me by my beloved brother, Artur Weissmann. Acutely aware of our past, we entrust our family's future to the next generation, with high hopes:

Vivian, Jim, Alysa, Andrew, and Lindsay Ullman
Leslie, Roger, Julie, Melissa, and Jessica Simon
Jim, Lynn, Jennifer, and Alexa Klein.

With all our love,
Gerda Weissmann Klein
Kurt Klein

Acknowledgments

When we were faced with the question of whether we should share our intimate thoughts with strangers, and whether those musings would be of interest to the general reader, a number of people greatly bolstered our confidence in the pursuit of this venture. Thus, our profound thanks go to:

Dick and Ree Adler, Kary and Karen Antholis, Bob and Barbara Blashek, Judge Susan Ehrlich, Margaret Goetz, Naomi Goodell, Rick and Beth Reisboard, and Kit Weiss. Our gratitude must also go to Ted Weiss, for the countless hours spent poring over our just-completed translations of hundreds of letters and for helping us to select those of merit. We greatly appreciate his perspicacious suggestions in regard to our efforts. Warmest thanks as well to Michael Berenbaum— generous, treasured friend of long standing—for graciously introducing us to Ron Goldfarb, who became not only our literary agent but advisor, mentor, and caring friend. It was he who delivered our ungainly stack of paper into the hands of Diane Higgins: No author could ask for an editor with a more discerning eye and feeling heart. Thanks, too, to our copy editor, Susan Llewellyn, for her many insightful comments and suggestions.

Lastly, acknowledgments are due to our children and grandchildren, all of whom assured us that they are not too embarrassed to read their parents' and, as the case may be, grandparents' love letters.

Kurt Klein
Gerda Weissmann Klein

The Hours After

Prologue

The dusty, battered carton Kurt lugged from our garage was vaguely familiar. The jagged gray waterline around its bottom attested to its narrow escape from one summer's flood in our basement in Buffalo. The brittle, dented lid bore the marks of the odds and ends that had been carelessly heaped on top of it in the crowded crawl space of the attic to which it had been relegated decades ago. It had become one of the discards that accrue over a period of forty years, and had survived a moment of indecision about its future value before our move to Arizona. As usual—and because we always lacked time to sort things out—it came along on the journey west. There it was, crammed into the far corner of a low shelf in the garage, among similar items awaiting ultimate disposition. Now, when Kurt came upon it while searching for a ball of string, it saw the light of day.

I remembered that the box contained our letters to each other, written right after the end of the war. Almost from the day of our first encounter in that small town in Czechoslovakia just before the end of World War II, they represented our tentative probing of unfamiliarity and separation, then served to bridge the distance until our ultimate reunion and marriage about a year later.

Once, many years earlier, searching for something in the attic, I pulled out one of my letters at random. Not having read German for decades, I found some of it archaic, if not pompous, and was embarrassed by what I had written. Thereafter I never looked at it again.

This time I was prompted by a combination of amusement and curiosity. I reached into the depths of the carton and, with Kurt next to me, flung myself into these fragments from our early years. Opening the tightly folded pages revealed my youthful angular script, standing out bare and vulnerable in the Arizona afternoon sun.

Suddenly I found myself back there, in the spring of my freedom, in the spring of my life. There was the moment when I first laid eyes on my liberator in the abandoned factory building in Volary, Czechoslovakia (today the Czech Republic)—emaciated among my dying and dead friends, standing in rags, I beheld this handsome young American from what then seemed a faraway, strange world of freedom and again heard his words, "It's all over—don't worry!" spoken compassionately, sorrow and outrage reflected on his face.

That night, in the field hospital his unit had hastily established, I lay on fresh sheets, as I had not done in years, and began to pray again, for my parents, my brother, and for that American whose name I did not know. Since then, I have prayed for him every night of my life, for him, my husband.

I spent the next two months lying on my hospital bunk, hovering between life and death—between slavery, degradation, and my newly won freedom—trying to come to terms with the turmoil within me. His visits connected me to a vital self I was trying to recover. Uplifted by the presence of this handsome young American officer, I slowly made my way to the beginning of a new life.

Reading those letters, I remembered how all his gestures and mannerisms had exuded gentle power. The only uniforms of those in authority I had known before were those of our oppressors, Nazis with brutal, often smirking faces, reflecting only self-righteous arrogance.

Soon, though I was in awe of him, he no longer seemed a stranger; rather, he had become a caring friend. I felt bereft every time he had to leave; the fear and horror of my recent past would engulf me again, and so it seemed natural to take refuge in my letters to him. In them I could share with him the memories of my sunny childhood, of my parents and my brother, my home and garden and all that had been mine until I was fifteen, when the Germans marched into my hometown, Bielsko, in southern Poland. I was able to pour out to him the loss of my entire family, the years in the ghetto, then in the camps, capped by the death march to which our guards subjected us toward the end of the war. He shared his memories with me, and we learned how similar his environment and upbringing had been to mine, although he had grown up in Germany.

With each letter, remembering how private and reticent both of us had been, I marveled at how much we had nevertheless revealed to each other from the very beginning. I recalled my attempts to picture the world of freedom he came from: It all seemed like a planet in a distant galaxy, and he, who was so close, so accessible to me, belonged there. He was solicitous, treating me with gallantry and respect, and I could not picture his life there.

Reading on, I wept for that innocent, lonely girl, who tried so valiantly to conceal how deeply and desperately in love she was, never daring to hope that he might love her in return. As the afternoon lengthened into early evening, we reached out to each other, our hands touching, our thoughts back in that far-off time. Feelings of boundless joy emanated from the pages written when I found that he loved me and wanted to marry me.

Reflected also was the pain of parting after our engagement and his departure for the United States, where he would be discharged from the army. This was followed by our long separation and desperate struggle to be reunited. I realized again that I had vaulted from childhood to adulthood virtually without transition, with no one to guide me. Instinctively, and because there were no psychiatrists or support groups, I had turned to the anchor that had helped me to survive before, and on which I was now to build my future: love.

Pulling out a letter at random, I read this sentence: "I pray that we will have children who will inherit the best that is in us: the legacy of our lost parents, and that through them we will be reunited with those we lost."

The shrill ring of the phone interrupted my musings, and though I was tempted not to answer it, force of habit never lets me ignore such a summons. I was on the verge of tears, but they changed into laughter when the caller turned out to be one of our granddaughters, informing me that she was faxing her homework for Grandpa to look over and correct.

Once again the present had put the past into proper perspective and provided a consolation for which we are immensely grateful.

    Ꮼ   Ꮼ   Ꮼ   Ꮼ   Ꮼ   Ꮼ   Ꮼ   Ꮼ   Ꮼ   Ꮼ   Ꮼ

How often is it given us to relive a part of our lives, step by step, exactly as it unfolded, with all its anguish and ecstasy, in a far-off, dim past?

Unexpectedly coming across letters Gerda and I had written each other more than a half century ago, at a time when we were trying to cope with the profound losses we had sustained in our personal lives, afforded us the chance to illumine with piercing clarity an aspect of our formative years that would otherwise have been obscured by the passage of time.

We initially regarded this retrieval with a combination of wry amusement and some trepidation, not knowing what the letters would yield, considering the youthful ideals and ardor we knew they must reflect. We were also apprehensive about the potential discrepancy between recollection and reality.

On closer scrutiny what we found was an almost perfectly preserved record of the time following our encounter under extraordinary circumstances, as well as our tentative attempts to get to know each other in the aftermath of the harrowing war years. In the process each of us had tried to support the other in specific ways. Finding this cache of letters transported us back to that time some fifty years ago.

When, in the waning days of World War II, I approached the small Czech village of Volary, then known by its Sudeten-German name of Wallern, I could hardly have imagined that in a sense I was keeping my own "rendezvous with destiny." White flags were flying from the rooftops of houses, indicating that the largely German-speaking population of the town was ready to surrender to our unit, the Second Regiment of the Fifth U.S. Infantry Division, part of General Patton's Third Army.

My driver and I were two of a small force of six specialists assigned to take the surrender, each two-man team dealing with a different aspect of the formalities: civilian, military, and medical. What we did not realize was that a very special situation awaited us in town: One of the last Nazi atrocities of the war had been played out in Volary, final stop along a route SS guards had marched one of two groups, each comprising two thousand young Jewish women slave laborers, a distance of 350 miles, throughout the bitter winter months of 1945. We now came face-to-face with the pitiful remnants of the one contingent, the other having taken a different route. Of the 120 survivors, more than 30 were to die in the days to come. They had been locked up in a vacant factory building, and their tormentors had tried to destroy the evidence of their inhumanity in an abortive attempt to blow up the structure.

The following morning, amid a scene of surreal horror, I had an encounter that was to change the course of my life. Approaching the factory building, accompanied by a full medical unit, I became aware of the slight figure of a young woman standing next to the doorway that led inside. Trying to absorb the scene before me, I saw that she was completely emaciated, her hair matted and grayish; nevertheless a spark of humanity had somehow remained that made her stand out among her companions, those hollow-eyed automatons I had just seen shuffling across the factory courtyard. We had an exchange in German, and as she led me inside, she pointed toward the figures of her skeletal and dying companions, and I was stunned by the words she uttered next: "Noble be man/merciful and good. . . ." In that place, and at the end of her physical strength, she had been able to summon the lofty words the German poet Goethe had written almost two centuries earlier, admonishing humanity to retain the divine that is innate in us. They lent their own irony to the depth of deprivation and degradation to which these young women had been subjected.

From that point on I was to be continually impressed by this young woman, by her bearing, her composure under those unspeakable conditions, and later by all she expressed, verbally and in writing, even after she fell critically ill and hovered between life and death in the makeshift field hospital in that small Czech town.

What I witnessed at Volary, shocking and unprecedented as it was for me, did not come as a surprise; rather, it was the confirmation of my worst fears, based on my own understanding of the Nazi mentality.

I was born and grew up in Germany, amid the turmoil and strife that marked the Weimar Republic in the era between the two great world wars. I was witness to the spread of Nazi ideology until it assumed proportions that proved unstoppable. After Hitler's assumption of power, we, the Jews of Germany, slowly came to the reluctant conclusion that we were outsiders for whom there was no future in that country. In my case I had the good fortune to be able to leave two years before the outbreak of World War II, when the Nazi machinery of annihilation was still in its incipient stages.

It was in June 1937 that I made my escape to the United States. Then, together with my sister and my brother, I was compelled to stand by impotently as our worst fears were realized step by step, carried out by a nation that had always prided itself on its cultural achievements. We could only watch in horror as our parents were inexorably drawn into the maelstrom of the Nazi design, to become a statistic—two of the six million Jews who would perish.

In due time I was inducted into the American army and, having taken part in the campaigns that followed the invasion, now found myself at the border between Germany and what had been Czechoslovakia.

In view of my own experience, it was only natural that I should take a special interest—aside from a humanitarian one—in this young woman, Gerda Weissmann. It occurred to me much later that instinctively my reaction to the barbaric treatment to which she had been subjected must have been tied to my images of my parents' fate, and my guilt at being unable to rescue them. Thus it became a personal triumph for me when, despite the physicians' prognoses, she surmounted her "night of crisis" and gradually made a full recovery. During the period immediately following my transfer from the Volary area, I would contrive to return to the hospital whenever my duties permitted, and it was a joy to watch this remarkable person blossom and once again become the positive, compassionate, and creative young woman she really was.

Although fate was to play a trick on us by consigning us to long periods of separation, the ensuing series of letters that bridged those gaps shows that Gerda had made her way back to normality in the face of great odds. In a larger sense they show the trauma and obstacles most Jewish survivors had to face in postwar Germany in the course of rebuilding their shattered lives.

Starting with the very first letter, written only ten days after we met, there emerged from our outpourings profound insights each of us in our own way had tried to wrest from the wreckage of our former lives. Our instincts at that time proved to have been pure and keenly focused, and they did much to see us through a critical and difficult period.

Soon after our encounter, my army unit was transferred to another area, but I was able to stay in touch with Gerda Weissmann not only through correspondence but through occasional visits to the field hospital in Volary where she was convalescing. In the course of those visits I was able to extract an important promise from a captain of the division that had replaced ours: We knew even then that this Czech territory would be ceded to the Russians in the very near future. The officer assured me that he would see to it that Gerda and her companions were evacuated to points inside the American zone, provided they were able to be moved.

By July 1945, Gerda had been discharged from the hospital, and with the Russian takeover now imminent the captain was as good as his word. Once Gerda and her companion (the others had gone elsewhere) reached my army post, I was able to arrange their move to Munich, as well as to obtain jobs for them with the American occupation forces.

Only a minimum of correspondence exists for the following two months, because, to my delight, I could now see Gerda most evenings and weekends. Ironically, those visits had to be conducted in a clandestine manner, necessitating that I hide my Jeep from the watchful eyes of roving MP patrols, who at that time were indiscriminately enforcing the nonfraternization rule, as far as associations between GIs and the German population were concerned.

It was during those frequent visits that it became quite obvious to me that I had found a soul mate who shared my background, my likes and dislikes, my love for literature, and my specific *Weltanschauung*. Finding her most attractive, I became sure that I was falling in love with this remarkable girl and wanted to share my life with her.

At the point in mid-September when my orders for discharge from the service suddenly came through, I drove to Munich to break the news to Gerda. I was awed by the realization that I had returned to Europe with the army to fight the immense evil that had prevailed there. I had come there harboring feelings of bitterness and hatred for those who had caused so much gratuitous carnage. In the course of the scourge that the Nazis had visited on our people and the world, I had suffered much personal loss and anguish; I had not been able to save those dearest to me. Nevertheless, out of the tragedy of those times had come the key to my future. When Gerda and I went for a walk in the nearby woods that evening, it wasn't difficult to ask the question on which our destiny hinged. When we returned from that stroll in a mood of high elation, my heart was full of love.

As it turned out, we were laboring under the somewhat naive assumption that, as the fiancée of a serviceman, Gerda would soon be able to follow me. Neither of us could have foreseen the interminable obstacles that would block our course before we could be reunited.

This correspondence, which goes well beyond the scope of love letters, covers the time from our first meeting in May 1945, to the seemingly endless period of unexpected separation, to our marriage in Paris in June 1946. It reflects the postwar trauma and harsh realities Gerda had to cope with in the chaos and ambivalence that prevailed in Europe in the aftermath of the war. Throughout, it illuminates one survivor's struggles along the road back to normality, at a time when no countries were ready to afford those survivors a chance to rebuild even a semblance of their former lives.

Also reflected in these writings are my own encounters with bureaucratic red tape and my readjustment to civilian life after having passed through the crucible of events that had molded me. During the years of searching for the woman who represented my ideal, I had come to believe that perhaps I was pursuing an unattainable goal. Once I got to know Gerda I was stunned by the fact that I had found my dream, and that she surpassed anything I could have imagined. Once her shell of suffering and endurance had come off, what emerged was a very pretty, high-spirited, intelligent young woman of extraordinary sensitivity and compassion. Not the least of her attractions were those limpid green eyes that, together with her dimpled smile, could completely disarm me.

These letters, then, are blueprints of the people we were and all we were to become in the fifty-three years of marriage we have been granted thus far. What emerges from them is the redemptive power of love in the face of tragedy and loss.

I was waking up, my hand brushing over something soft and smooth. What could it be? I opened my eyes and saw a blanket, under it something snowy white. A sheet! No, it was not a dream; I was lying in a bed on a sheet under a blanket. I closed my eyes, then slowly opened them again, only to realize that the vision had not evaporated. I stroked the blanket, touching the sheet with my bony fingers. Sunlight was streaming through a window near my head. It was difficult to grasp. How had I come here?

Images flitted through my mind, fragments of an incomplete puzzle. When I concentrated hard, they began to fall into place. I remembered having been on a truck or some other vehicle, then someone carrying me in his strong arms. We had entered a room with wooden tubs on the floor. It came back to me that I had shed the rags that had hung from my body, then felt the incredible luxury of warm water engulfing me. Oddly, I had noticed that the water was green and sunlight was dancing on its surface. Gentle hands were lathering my body, and I was sitting in a tub for the first time in more than three years. Warm water had cascaded over my head from a pitcher, and someone had dried my hair.

Yes, there was this pretty girl in a long peasant skirt gathering up my rags, and I overheard someone else saying that they needed to be burned. It was when she reached for my ski boots that panic had set in. My ski boots? Those boots that Papa insisted I wear on that hot day in June just before I saw him for the last time? Oh, God, no, they can't take my boots! In the lining of the left one were the photos I had hidden for such a long time. Had they been burned? My memory became more acute, and suddenly I knew, was aware of what had happened.

Yes, I had removed the pictures before blacking out. I reached under my snowy pillow in a frantic search for them, then found with immense relief that they were there. Picking up the dirty, threadbare piece of rag, frayed but dry, I opened it slowly, reverently. I had not looked at its contents since that icy day in January when we started the cruel march that had lasted through the bitter winter months and had decimated our numbers. Now it was spring, and my treasure was safe. I clutched the sturdy small cardboard rectangle on which I had mounted them so many years ago. The tiny photos that I had cut out in the shape of hearts: Papa, smiling, sitting on a boat that was cruising the Bosporus. That was taken when he attended my uncle's wedding in Turkey in the summer of 1937. Then there was Mama in Krynica, the Polish resort to which I had accompanied her in the summer of 1939. I remembered when she had bought the silk for the dress she was wearing in the photo: black patterned, with raspberry-colored flowers. "If the flowers were red, they would be too harsh, too loud," she had said. "See how beautifully the colors blend?"

She had the milliner put the ribbon in the same raspberry color around her wide-brimmed black straw hat, demonstrating as always what great style she possessed. The ribbon was detachable, and there was a white one as well, and still another one with polka dots and a yellow silk rose she would attach to complement what she was wearing. Each time she wore it, the hat looked distinctly different. Mama! Mama, where are you?

And there was Artur, sporting a tie, all dressed up. Where was he going that day when he posed with his insouciant smile, leaning against the garden fence? And Abek, my special friend: I can't tell when or where his picture was taken.

My thoughts were interrupted by a commotion, the dreaded sound of marching boots outside. Quickly, automatically, I hid my treasure under my pillow, the old fear overtaking me. From my upper bunk near a huge window I beheld a sight that filled me with awe and immense relief. A column of German soldiers was being marched down the road, their uniforms bedraggled and dirty. They were unarmed, and their faces reflected exhaustion and dejection. It was with a sense of joy and gratitude that I saw them being guarded by Americans who looked like the proverbial knights in shining armor to me, although I noticed that they wore that armor with a rather casual air. Love filled my heart, and clutching the tiny bundle under my pillow, I began to cry softly. Yesterday? Was it only yesterday that we had been given freedom? And then I pictured again the nurse coming down the aisle of the ward, holding a tray of mugs filled with milk. One of them had a crude flower painted on it. Oh, how I wanted that mug, and as if I had willed it, she handed it to me. Taking a sip of that warm, sweet milk unleashed something tremendous within me. It was a hard, bitter knot coming loose and making me break into convulsive sobs as never before. At the same time, I found prayer again. It was a prayer of thanks for the gift of life, for seeing Germany defeated, for the Americans who had liberated us. Sorrow swept over me, sorrow over the fact that not one person I had loved was with me at this hour, sharing this miracle for which we had prayed for six long, bitter years. It was a grieving, not yet fully defined, for the loss of all that had been dear to me.

An American doctor was approaching my bunk carrying a pad. He looked at me and asked in German about my vital statistics. When it came to my birth date, he broke into a smile and exclaimed, "May 8—why, today is May 8, your birthday! And Germany capitulated today. The war is really over; did you know that?" No, I did not know it. "To me the war was over with my liberation." "Yes," he allowed, "that was yesterday, but today it's official." He touched my hand and tenderly touched my cheek. "Your birthday," he spoke softly, compassionately. "You will always remember your birthday." I lay there, unable to absorb it all. To think that this was my birthday: I was twenty-one years old; the horror had begun when I was barely fifteen.

A little while later the doctor who had shown such kindness returned, handing me something wrapped in paper. "For your birthday," he said and left abruptly. As I was to learn, it was Dr. Aaron Cahan from Chicago who gave me my first birthday gift after the war. What I found was a piece of chocolate, something I had not tasted in many years. I let a tiny morsel dissolve on my tongue, savoring its exquisite taste—soft, sweet, and soothing—stirring memories of a thousand dreams.

I always got chocolate for birthdays during my childhood. It invariably consisted of *Katzenzungen,* literally, "cats' tongues." My parents knew only too well how much I loved chocolate and my cats. At one time I was the proud owner of eight, all black, and only I could distinguish among them. Schnautzi had given birth to seven black kittens on a snowy, cold afternoon and had carried them in her mouth, one by one, into the kitchen near the warm stove. I named them Frutzi, Schmutzi, Stutzi, Kuba, Mruczek, Tygrys, Ziobak, my terms of endearment, which ascribed to them certain character traits in a combination of German and Polish. How strange that I could again remember all their names now, whereas I could recall only six of them as I stood in line, waiting to be shot, at one point during the death march. While I was frantically searching my memory for the missing names, our guard's mood changed arbitrarily and we were spared. No, I did not want to think about that now—only about the happy birthdays of my childhood, with all their attendant feelings of well-being, about the gifts from Papa, Mama, Artur, and Omama (my maternal grandmother). Linked with it also were memories of Niania, my nanny. It was always on my birthday that Niania would solemnly intone: *Gottes Finger zeigt den Weg* (God's finger points the way). Then she would point her finger at me, "Because you were born, we came together." I knew the tale by heart because she repeated it so often—and invariably on my birthday.

Niania to me only, because I was the only one permitted to address her in the familiar *du* form. To everyone else—and that included my parents, brother, and grandmother—she was Frau Bremza. Her first name was Sofie, in honor of Emperor Franz Josef's mother, as she would proudly point out. She considered Sofie to be the "real" empress, dismissing the emperor's beautiful wife, Elisabeth, as "a bit of fluff." Niania revered the imperial family, even though her only child, a son, had been killed during World War I in the service of the emperor, who was dead too by then—as was the Austro-Hungarian Empire.

In April 1924 another great tragedy befell Niania. Her house burned to the ground, along with most of her belongings. Blessedly, she and her granddaughter, Irma, were saved. Irma's mother, Anna, worked as a cook in a small nearby town. Clad in her late husband's postman's coat, the only garment that survived the fire, Frau Bremza had come to see my grandmother, whom she knew slightly. On hearing her story, Omama immediately came up with a suggestion. "My daughter, Helene, is expecting a baby soon. She is in delicate health and we could really use some help. Perhaps you and Irma could come and live with us for a few weeks? It would be a big favor." For the hundredth time Niania would shake her head. "God works in strange ways." So Niania and Irma, then approximately seven years old, came "for a few weeks" and stayed for thirteen years.

When I was very young, Niania would tell me that my parents found me in a *Maiblume,* those demure, bell-like lilies of the valley that always burst into full bloom around my birthday. I was skeptical and pointed out how small those flowers were. "You were little, too," Niania would say in a tone that did not invite any further questions.

As the hours wore on and the defeated columns of German troops kept passing by my window, I let my thoughts take me back to my childhood, my birthdays serving as counterpoints to the shuffling feet below. Memories crowded my mind, fragments that brought certain events into sharper focus. As if in a viewfinder, an image presented itself: a chocolate torte reposing on the kitchen table, as only Mama could bake it. She had a special knack for coming up with the most wondrous confections: homemade marzipan, which she would sculpt into various forms— animals, flowers, and many more. And her *Vanillenkipfel,* those delicious vanilla crescents, and *Pariser Stangen,* lemon-glazed nut bars, were the most delectable creations imaginable. Now it escaped me for which birthday she had adorned that special torte with symbols of good luck: a tiny horseshoe, a jolly little pink pig, and a four-leaf clover. Artur immediately interpreted the pig as representing my table manners, and I tossed my new red ball right into his face.

The four-leaf clover now took on a different meaning. It reminded me that Ilse, Suse, Liesl, and I had called ourselves that—*ein vierblättriges Kleeblatt.* But the others were not as lucky as I. Ilse died in my arms only a week ago, making me promise that I would go on for one more week. Ilse, oh, Ilse—just one more week! If you could have held out that much longer! You made it plain that you were a *Pechvogel,* an unlucky bird, and, yes, you were. And Suse, it couldn't have been yesterday that you died! Suse—yesterday? No, it was a hundred years ago. We had made a bet on the train that took us to the first camp three years earlier, a bet for a quart of strawberries and whipped cream. I said we would be liberated, and you said we would not. How could it have been only yesterday? Why am I here while you are not?

But where was Liesl? Her leg had been hit by a bullet from a strafing American fighter plane, an injury she had dismissed as inconsequential.

I knew she was hurting because I had seen the wound, but when I took that first American to see her, she only smiled as if she were unaware of what was happening. She must have been running a high fever, her eyes were so strange. Thank God, she is here in this hospital, getting the same good care that is restoring me. I must ask about her right away, I resolved. In the camp we had perfected a game of make-believe. Her bunk had been next to mine, and I remembered how after one night shift I had awakened to hear the rain beating down hard on the roof panels over our bunks. I noticed that Liesl was up too and impulsively blurted out, "I will get up soon and go to the garden. I know the grass will be wet, and I will pick up the apples the storm has blown down." Without missing a beat she would come back, "Nothing tastes better than a real cold, tart apple. But we'll have to hurry; remember, we have an appointment later for that new dress. . . ." We would go on and on like that.

Liesl was one of the most beautiful girls I ever met. Oh, I can't wait to see her, I thought. I made the nurse promise to find out about her. A few days later I learned to my utter dismay that Liesl had succumbed to her wounds on the very day I turned twenty-one, just a day after we were rescued.

I let my recollections drift back to other birthdays. The most memorable one was my fifteenth, in 1939. That May was unusually warm, so my party was held in our little gazebo in the garden. It was green-latticed, with a roof over it, through which the lilacs that grew in profusion had forced their branches, infusing its interior with their fragrance. I thought the purple ones exuded a more intense fragrance than the white ones. My girlfriends were crowded around the small table. Mama had baked a marble cake in a fluted pan, heavy on the chocolate side, and made her divine vanilla ice cream. I wore my new short-sleeved navy blue dress, with an enormous white pleated organdy collar, stiff like a clown's ruff. And my own first real silk stockings, along with another first: navy blue shoes with heels. My friend Thea had the same shoes, but hers pinched, she remarked, while handing me the most wonderful present: a rather large brooch, made of wood, in the shape of a heart. In its center a small cottage window, flanked by shutters, brightened by dainty white flowers. The overall effect was of a little chalet-type house, and when you opened the shutters, there was a portrait inside of our movie idol, Shirleika (Shirley Temple). I instantly pinned it to the center of my large, white, pleated collar. Papa and Mama presented me with a small rectangular watch, its face bearing roman numerals. It goes without saying that I would check the time every few minutes.

I remember that Artur's gift was a bottle of eau de cologne that I used only for special occasions. Up to that time, I had furtively sprayed myself with my mother's Tosca or 4711, but this was my very own Chat Noir "so that you can smell like your cats," Artur teased. This was accompanied by a big hug and the bell-like timbre of his mischievous laughter, which was reflected in his warm brown eyes and his smiling lips.

Attl—as I called Artur, while I was Gertl to him—Attl, where are you now? You must be thinking of me, because you know it's my birthday and, of all things, my twenty-first. Can you believe that? And you are twenty-five. We are all grown up, both of us! When will I see you? Soon, soon, I hope; after all, the war is over. Oh, my beloved brother, will I see you soon again?

I let memory overtake me, fixing on my fifteenth birthday. It was the last one before the war, before everything fell apart, was irretrievably gone. I drifted back into the golden sunlight of my untroubled childhood, when I had felt cosseted, secure, loved, and protected. But it began to fade, and I knew I must go on.

I was sixteen in 1940, and a memory came to me in a flash, that of running into the garden with Artur's letter from Russian-occupied Lvov in my hand. His letters were sparse and infrequent, and this one, addressed to me, came on that very day, as if by magic. It contained a photo, Artur looking very serious and much older, almost like a stranger. He wrote, "I know that you are as brave as you promised to be," and that's when I threw myself onto the young new grass and wept. I cried with a mixture of happiness and sorrow, happy to see Artur's letter, yet sad, so sad. Something was awakening in me, a feeling I couldn't define, but they were tears for the loss of my happy childhood and all it had held.

A few days later, an ugly sign went up on the gate to our garden: JEWS NOT PERMITTED TO ENTER, making it official that we had been dispossessed. I abided by that prohibition for the next two years, with one exception: I "trespassed" for a final good-bye on the day we left our home forever.

Try as I might, I could not remember anything about my seventeenth birthday, but my eighteenth loomed up in my memory like a monument, like a gravestone: hard and bitter.

I wake up in my bed in the ghetto, Mama and Papa standing at the foot of it. It strikes me how nearly gray Papa's moustache is, only traces of reddish hair glinting in the morning sun. He touches my tousled hair, his hand gently brushing my cheek before kissing it. Mama's face is gaunt, her cheeks sallow; though she smiles a wan smile, there is no merriment in her large dark eyes. Somehow it has escaped me until now how much she has changed. Yet her voice is high and full of the old upbeat ring as she hands me an incredibly precious gift: an orange, a real orange! Imagine, an orange in the ghetto! "Mama, where and how could you have gotten it?" Her smile widens. "It's a secret." She shakes her head. She knew what it meant to me to get an orange. I peel it slowly, its aroma enveloping my bed. Mama carefully gathers up the peels. "I will boil them with a little saccharine and crisp them into a confection." On my insistence she tastes a tiny slice, claiming that the acid really bothers her stomach, something it had never done before. Papa, too, declines my offer of a slice, saying that he was not overly fond of oranges, which also leaves me puzzled. I finally persuade him to have a sliver, and he allows that this particular orange is very tasty.

After a while a few of my friends appear, and Mama has baked cookies from hoarded oats. They taste exactly like macaroons, we declare. Then Abek shows up with a portrait of Artur that he has painted from a photo. Somehow it fails to give me the pleasure I would normally derive from such a gift, because it painfully underscores Artur's absence. I am trying hard not to show my disappointment, knowing how much time and devotion Abek has spent on it. He had been trying to please me in so many different ways, ever since he arrived in town among a transport of Jewish men. He enjoyed a special status and, due to his artistic gift, was able to move about freely to restore paintings for the German occupiers.

Long after I had devoured the orange, I found out that Mama had gone out of the ghetto and somehow managed to acquire it in exchange for a pearl ring. It was the last present I was to get from my parents. A few weeks later we were brutally separated.

I recalled that I dreaded my nineteenth birthday in the Bolkenhain camp in 1943. Yet it proved to give me some unexpected pleasure. My friends had prepared a surprise. On the table was a white paper doily, made from the wrapper for yarn we used on the looms. It was intricately cut into a lacy pattern, and my slice of bread for that morning was spread with margarine! Truly a treat, for only on Sundays did we get that delicacy. Ilse had scraped it from her bread to save it for me. That year I received precious gifts that I had considered impossible to obtain under the circumstances. Yet, my friends had managed to improvise them: shoelaces made of factory yarn; three bobby pins, fashioned from wire on which spools were suspended over the looms; a kerchief, cut as a triangle from a square. The girl who gave it to me kept the more bleached, torn half for herself. And a few green leaves on which reposed a flower plucked through the barbed wire that separated our compound from the director's garden. Finally a package arrived from Abek, containing clothing, some food, and dried flowers, and I couldn't believe it had come on that day.

I was overwhelmed. How could I possibly repay my friends? And then an idea struck me. I set to work over a period of time, usually by the feeble light of the washroom bulb, to write a rhyming skit, poking fun at camp life and predicting a brilliant future for all. The performance was a rousing success when we put it on during the two-day Christmas holiday when the factory was shut down.

May 8, 1944, was a black day. Orders came for us to be transferred to Grünberg, also in Silesia, a factory/camp rumored to be especially harsh. The following day vividly stood out in my memory. At first the train had created a welcome sense of isolation. My thoughts could roam freely, my dreams not hemmed in by the myriad restrictions of camp life. It was a May morning in all its glory, and I was twenty years old. Around midday we had to change trains and were herded to another platform. It was particularly bitter to note how, although a war was going on, people all around us were walking about briskly, pursuing their busy lives. Only we were the slaves. I was clutching my meager bundle of threadbare belongings, waiting to be shipped to some dreaded destination, the yellow star ablaze on my chest, back, and head.

Then there was a moment I instinctively knew I would remember all my life: It was an instant branded into my consciousness. A girl my age, followed by a porter carrying her luggage, strode purposefully toward a train compartment. She was wearing a light gray suit, accented by a fresh white blouse and a matching beret. My eyes followed her as she entered the compartment; I saw the porter lifting her suitcase into the net luggage rack above the seat, observed her giving him a tip, after which she leaned out of the window, as if searching for someone. And then I spotted a man approaching the rail car, heard her call out, *"Hier bin ich, Papa!"* (Here I am, Papa!) That's when I felt the stabbing pain. Some time later, after we were put on the train, I let my mind replay the scene I had witnessed, but when I came to the girl's joyful exclamation, I couldn't go on.

Now I was twenty-one, was free, but where would I go from here? What would my life be like in time to come? Who was that girl on the train I had so envied? What turn would her life take? I dimly perceived even then that the scene had been a kind of confrontation with myself, a realization that despite everything that had happened, I had been blessed with my family early in life. Instinctively I knew that somehow I should never want to exchange my life for someone else's. Thus my first day of freedom, my twenty-first birthday, was coming to an end. Where would I be on my twenty-second?

My encounter on the last day of the war with the pitiful remnant of a group of Nazi slave laborers, young Jewish women from Poland and Hungary, had a profound impact on me. One of them in particular stood out because of her bearing and her aura of dignity, despite her deplorable physical condition. Her words extolling human dignity and goodness, as unexpected as they were stunning under those circumstances, added new fuel to my own torment regarding the fate of my elderly parents, who had disappeared from their deportation camps in France into the great void of the unknown a few months before I joined the army at Fort Niagara, New York. All we knew of this, the second deportation they had experienced, was that it had taken place in the summer of 1942, from the South of France to an unknown destination in Eastern Europe. The first such upheaval had burst upon my father and mother two years earlier, on an hour's notice in 1940, tearing them from roots in Germany that could be traced back to the early seventeenth century. It came as a consequence of the Nazis' vow to make Germany *judenrein*, to "cleanse" it of all Jews. Nevertheless, along with my sister and brother, I had clung to the irrational hope that somehow they had survived, perhaps in the Nazis' "model camp," Terezin (Theresienstadt), Czechoslovakia, set up to dupe the Red Cross inspection teams that occasionally made an appearance there. In the sober light of the war's end, it became unequivocally clear that I would not see my parents again, although it would take another year until we could get confirmation of the facts of their deaths.

What was the life from which my father and mother had so brutally been uprooted? I can only think of it in terms of a curious blend of cultured middle-class life, with the many hardships imposed by the economic climate after World War I, which had begun with the unchecked inflation of the early twenties and turned into the Great Depression, lasting well into the thirties. Similarly, life in Walldorf, my hometown, could be regarded as an amalgam of provincial outlook, infused with the sophistication that lay just beyond in nearby Heidelberg, that seat of great learning. Geographically, Walldorf belonged to the Province of Baden, and its claim to fame was that John Jacob Astor, born there in 1763, had gone on to become its best-known son and benefactor. (As some good-natured scuttlebutt still had it among the town's citizens, John Jacob had acquired a cow in a less than legal way in order to pay for passage to the New World, but had more than made up for that by donating a beautiful orphanage to the town in later years, for which the grateful town fathers had erected a monument in his honor.)

Throughout my childhood, all of life was underscored by the discordant voices of political dissent that wracked the Weimar Republic, leading to the inexorable march of Nazi ideology, which reached the heart and soul of the German people. Along the way it intoxicated the masses, sweeping aside everything in its path, in a single-minded effort toward the achievement of its aim: Hitler's assumption of power as chancellor of the Reich in 1933.

When I think of my parents' fate, the question that comes to mind is how they coped with the hardships that followed them all their lives, testing them to the limit. Mother was an orphan, having lost her parents and brother to an influenza epidemic at an early age. She considered it a stroke of extraordinary luck that from that point on she was able to spend her formative years in the cultured home of a loving aunt and uncle, getting the type of basic education that other young ladies in her circle were accustomed to. In 1909, at twenty-six, she heard through family members about a thirty-four-year-old man in Heidelberg, not far from her hometown of Grünstadt, whose wife had recently died in childbirth; he was looking for a mother for his infant son. His name was Ludwig Klein, and once he and Alice Nahm met, a marriage was arranged in short order.

As my parents were fond of relating, their honeymoon was one of undreamed luxury, taking them to the enchanted city of Venice. And Mother confided how she had been so abashed when asked by Father what memento she would like to take back to Heidelberg from this fabulous trip that all she had managed to blurt out was the suggestion of a hatpin—and how Father, much to her disappointment, had fulfilled her simple request to the letter by presenting her with precisely that gift. Considering that necessity brought them together, it was a blessing that their union turned into a nearly perfect match. Mother was modest in her demands yet a model of industry, shirking no duty that came along and resolute in trying to help solve any problems that presented themselves. She was humble and compassionate, at the same time displaying a sense of self-worth. She was generous to a fault, and always mindful of what "they" would think. She liked people and gossip, could be judgmental, and had a good sense of humor, loving fun pursuits, though ready and willing to take on the job of bringing up an infant stepson. She had a simple, steadfast faith in God that was to be sorely tested in time to come and, although not rigid in the observance of her faith in the sense of Orthodox adherence, never lost her belief in the divine. In the face of the worst tragedy that could befall anyone, she had a way of downplaying the gravity of her and Father's situation, even under the direst of conditions, to minimize our anguish.

Two years after her marriage, Mother gave birth to a daughter, named Irmgard, or Gerdi, as she would be known. She was the second of my siblings, my half-brother, Max, being my senior by twelve years, whereas there was a nine-year gap between Gerdi and me. In retrospect those years before the beginning of World War I were the only somewhat carefree ones Mother was to enjoy in the course of her married life. The hostilities that led to World War I broke out in 1914, and that precipitated a move to my father's childhood home in nearby Walldorf, because it was thought safer during wartime to live in the countryside, where food was more abundant. My father, meanwhile, was called up for army service. No doubt this move was also dictated by economic necessity on Mother's part, considering that there was little money to pay the rent on the apartment in Heidelberg. As it happened, Grandmother Babette, by that time a widow in her sixties, still ran that household and needed a helping hand. The war had left the simple country home in Walldorf without men; Grandmother's seven sons had all been called up for service. She also had three stepdaughters, one of whom was still living with her, so it wasn't easy for my grandmother during those four war years. At best Grandmother and Mother eked out a minimal subsistence. To be sure, there was enough to eat, but little or no income.

Mother pitched in right from the start, learning to take care of Grandmother's assortment of farm animals, mostly poultry, as well as the two vegetable gardens that helped to make them largely self-sufficient. Later it was quite natural that, after the death of the matriarch of the house, she should take over her mother-in-law's many household duties.

For most of her life Grandmother had run this household of twelve single-handedly and resolutely, setting an example as the epitome of thrift while adequately catering to her family's needs. As it turned out, the only one of her sons who was able to go on to higher learning was her youngest, Fritz. Fortuitously, he had been named after the Archduke Friedrich of the Province of Baden, his birthplace, and so could avail himself of a university scholarship to which he, as the seventh son of a family and the archduke's namesake, was entitled. He went on to become a civil engineer.

I never knew Grandmother Babette, having been born two years after her death, but family lore about her abounds. Throughout her years of marriage, and despite her arduous duties, from caring for family and land, to feeding of chickens and geese, even milking a cow, she had always retained an intellectual curiosity that led her to study Latin along with her son, Fritz. Some of her letters survive, attesting to her love of language.

Fortunately, all seven sons returned from World War I unscathed—and unaware of what had happened meanwhile. Just days before the first ones made it back, she slipped on the cellar steps and tumbled to her death. One of her sons, Eugen, would recount how he had been returning from the war when the train stopped at a siding where a gypsy fortune-teller offered to read his palm. She gravely shook her head and with a pained expression predicted that he would not see his mother again.

The end of the war in 1918 had brought some return to normality, but hardly any stability. It fell to my father, Ludwig, and his brother Heinrich to try to revitalize the family business, which had lain fallow during those years of global conflict—in the face of the harsh economic climate that prevailed during the Weimar Republic.

The two brothers had had to take over their father's hops, tobacco, and grain brokerage business after his death in 1902. In Father's case it was unfortunate, because he would have been much more inclined toward an academic career, but of course that was out of the question for economic reasons. It was simply taken for granted that not many choices lay open to young men in that time and place.

Unlike Mother, Father was much more reserved, seldom showing his emotions. However, he, too, possessed a good sense of humor and was known among family and friends as a dry wit who could be counted on to come up with many a bon mot. He was widely read and could explain any situation in a lucid and logical manner. His experiences had taught him to be skeptical of others' motives, although for himself he would adhere to the strictest of standards. It was as though he had made one of the ubiquitous German proverbs his life's motto. *Üb' immer Treu' und Redlichkeit,* the admonition always to follow the straight and narrow, was something he would practice in business as in his private life, often to his detriment when up against others who were less scrupulous. Because he was a realist, he did not—unlike so many others—delude himself about the Nazi menace toward Jews. My brother, Max, brought to light a most telling memory, in the course of an encounter we had when we were both serving in the American army on maneuvers in Louisiana in the summer of 1942. It dealt with the time, five years earlier, when he and my father had accompanied me to Hamburg and Bremerhaven at the point of my emigration from Germany. My last view of Father was of him and Max standing at the dock, waving farewell. After which Father turned to Max and said, "I don't believe I will see my boy again."

For me, watching the receding figures vanish from view and unaware of what the future would hold, the pain of parting was tempered by thoughts of the great adventure that lay ahead. Nevertheless a jumble of impressions took me back to the blurred image of Mother's tear-stained face in the hallway of my childhood home, where we had made our final good-byes two days earlier.

It was in that house that I was born in the summer of 1920, a place in which education and culture were valued, although in retrospect it appears to me that we always felt on the fringes of "bigger things" that were going on in the world, especially in cities that were deemed a *Grossstadt,* in short, a metropolis. Still it was a house that exuded warmth and caring—despite the economic woes I was to become aware of during the first decade of my life—and a great deal of laughter would echo from its walls, especially when my older sister's friends and classmates would spend the evening or occasionally stay overnight.

In the early twenties inflation ran rampant, wiping out any gain my father and Uncle Heinrich had made since the end of the war. I remember M. Klein & Söhne (M. Klein & Sons) as a business that required constant struggle to keep it afloat, creating a great deal of insecurity and uncertainty. By the time I was old enough to comprehend what financial havoc the inflationary period had wreaked during the Weimar Republic, I found myself playing with drawers full of "funny money"—bills whose denominations ran into the millions and billions of marks. My parents had somehow held onto them, I suppose in the vain hope that someday they might be declared legal again.

As was the custom in most middle-class families of that place and period, Mother had some live-in help during my formative years, although I remember that there was a certain turnover: When one of those maids got married, they would recommend someone else from their family or hometown to take over their duties. Most of the maids came from an area known as the Odenwald, where people lived a backwoods type of existence that would manifest itself in the superstitions they all harbored. The maids would regale me with stories of "witches" in their town who had given the "evil eye" to those who had crossed them, to the point of causing horrible illnesses—even death—in those they disliked. What had also gained currency in their town were the many instances of people who had apparently died while in a state of suspended animation. Thus they had been buried while still alive, as was proved in the case of those who through some twist in the maid's story were exhumed in time to be saved.

Tales of that nature were not conducive to untroubled sleep on occasions when I found myself alone at night and in the darkness of my bedroom would hear all sorts of strange noises, from creaking beams to weird animal sounds. But those were "the good old days." Having maids in Jewish households came to an end with the issuance of the Nuremberg Laws in 1935, along with many other restrictions that disenfranchised Jews at that time, above all depriving them of their citizenship rights.

I do remember that from my earliest childhood I had a love for books, and thereby hangs a tale often recounted by Mother with great amusement. It seems I was sitting in a playpen at a tender age, trying to get her attention about an urgent matter. Because my cries went unheeded for a time, I apparently banged my fist on the toy before me and, in anger and frustration, exclaimed, "One doesn't even get books around here!" I was able to make up for that deprivation later in life, and some of my fondest memories go back to my childhood illnesses, when I could read to my heart's content without feeling guilty about neglected chores. I remember times when after lights-out I would continue with whatever saga absorbed me at the moment, reading with a flashlight under the blanket. Only with great reluctance would I come to the last page and the end of my companionship with the characters I had gotten to know and love—or hate, as the case might be.

I clearly remember reading many of the tomes that were classics in the English-speaking world, such as *Treasure Island,* Kipling's *The Jungle Book,* and, yes, the Tarzan series. From these I soon gravitated to James Fenimore Cooper's *Leatherstocking Tales,* and it wasn't long before I discovered *The Last of the Mohicans.* Once my interest in the American Indian had been sparked, I became utterly fascinated by a German writer of tales of high adventure, Karl May, who was everybody's boyhood idol. Many of his writings dealt with American frontier life in an astoundingly authentic way (especially in view of the fact that he never set foot outside Germany and wrote a great many of his stories in prison). Although his tales were set in exotic places around the world, in all those exploits there was one constant: His protagonists always gained the upper hand over their adversaries through measures as cunning and resourceful as they were innovative.

Inevitably the stories dealing with the American West led to an obsession my friends and I developed about everything to do with our romantic notions of American frontier life. This was greatly enhanced by watching the movies of American Westerns featuring Tom Mix or Tom Tyler, or reading the likes of Zane Grey, and we would try to emulate those heroes by dressing up in Western garb (as closely as we could imitate it) and playing "Cowboys-and-Indians." It was always my fervent wish to explore those mountains and prairies depicted in literature and on film, and I could not have imagined then that the American West would become my own stamping ground in later life.

My boyhood years until 1933 were spent freely intermingling with classmates and friends, in one another's homes and fields, helping to harvest crops, threading tobacco onto string for curing the leaves in attics, and similar pursuits. Father's warehouse served as a playground for building secret hideouts among the bales of hops he would process and sell to breweries. In addition, tobacco and sacks of grain were stored on several floors. In turn my friends' barns and haylofts would serve similar purposes, when we were not engaged in playing soccer or a variety of "street games." In fact, the whole town was our playground: Woods, fields, or a simple sand hill would become a popular spot, especially in the spring, when we would roll Easter eggs along channels that snaked down the hill under bridges we had carefully built to cross the paths the eggs would take. Those diversions were in no way inconsistent with our own Passover observances, but rather such activities took on secular aspects, like those during celebrations of a national holiday.

In the winter there were ample opportunities for ice-skating and sledding, but whenever weather permitted we would find ourselves engaged in "war games," in the course of which the French inevitably were the enemy. This was an outgrowth of the indoctrination we received in school and our reading in national magazines—stories drawing on the ancient feud with France, always depicting the French armed to the teeth in comparison with the Germans, and making clear that their Maginot Line was impregnable. At the same time there existed a peculiar double standard: Everything French, especially the language, exerted a certain fascination and snob appeal and was much sought after.

Even at thirteen I could sense that there were forces at work determined to settle a score after the inglorious defeat of World War I. I often thought that the country might be involved in another war before too many years would pass, a prospect I contemplated with horror.

For their part my parents, brother, and sister participated freely in all social or communal activities that befitted their age and standing, as did Jews elsewhere in the country, in other strata of public and private endeavor, or so it seemed to me. It was hardly surprising then that I felt my childhood to be an absolutely normal one until the Nazi takeover in 1933.

Having lived in nearby Heidelberg, our parents still retained many connections there, and much of the family's social life, aside from the children's education, revolved around the much broader horizons available in that cosmopolitan city. Thus, individually or as a family we would frequently avail ourselves of all that Heidelberg had to offer, be it social, cultural, or its scenic splendors that abounded everywhere. There would be wonderful walks and hikes all around the city and in its mountainous environs.

Because all this was such a natural part of the structure of our lives, and because I, along with everyone else I knew, considered myself to be an integral part of the fabric of German society—in no way different from others—the feeling of betrayal after the Nazi takeover was all the more acute. Although initially my friends and classmates tended to be apologetic about their gradual estrangement from us, Nazi propaganda eventually took hold, and those apologies changed to derisive taunts that promised a trip to a concentration camp to any Jew stepping out of line. It didn't take much longer until most of my former friends and classmates broke off all contact with us and a completely hostile attitude set in. For a while there would be isolated instances here and there in which a former friend would still speak to me, but as time went on that too ceased.

In the course of the first year after the Nazi takeover, I had been able to watch up close, during mandatory class attendance at films such as Leni Riefenstahl's *Triumph of the Will*, how that masterpiece of propaganda was taking effect, leaving me to wonder how I, at fourteen, had suddenly become an outcast. One of the greatest shocks came when one of my teachers, until then a favorite of mine, addressed the class about the "guests among us," who had better toe the mark if they didn't want to suffer most unpleasant consequences.

Of course we should have been prepared for such attitudes by then. The early days after Hitler's assumption of power come to mind. At school in Heidelberg we had a free period once a week, devoted to religious instruction for the various denominations. Our religious teacher addressed us regarding the latest events. His words still ring in my ears: "Well, we have seen a momentous upheaval in recent times, whose outcome is unalterable. I do not know what I can tell you about what lies ahead for us. The only thing we can hope for at the moment is that no one comes to our doorstep and slits our throats." That particular projection of what might happen was hardly a random figment of Mr. Durlacher's vivid imagination. Rather, it was based on a line from a marching song the SA storm troopers timed to perfection so they could bellow it as they tramped by Jewish homes: ". . . and when Jewish blood splatters from our knives—yes, then all will go well!"

While all of us, adults and youngsters, were waiting for what would happen next, an incident occurred that gave us some inkling of what might be in store for Jews. On coming home from school one day and getting off the streetcar at its terminal station, which was at the only hotel in Walldorf, I became aware of a great commotion surrounding that building. Not daring to ask any questions, I made my way home and found that some facts had already come to light in the meantime. My parents had heard from neighbors that in the course of the morning, a contingent of SA men had rounded up all known Communists in the town, had herded them into the courtyard of the Hotel Astoria, a pallid imitation of its renowned namesake in New York, the Waldorf-Astoria. There this gang of thugs had beaten them in an unheard-of orgy of brutality. In order to show the extent of their "humanity," they had summoned the town doctor—before the beating—to attend and to minister to their victims' wounds.

During the ensuing weeks, the town's Jews waited for the other shoe to drop, but when no further excesses took place, they lulled themselves into a false sense of security that let them rationalize that perhaps the worst of the revolution had passed, that as law-abiding citizens who had lived in those surroundings for generations, they would be spared any further anguish. The human mind is ever ready to deny the unthinkable.

In the years leading up to 1933, the number of the town's Jews hovered around sixty, as against the general population of five thousand, and those numbers steadily declined to nineteen by the time of the 1940 deportation of that remnant—among them my parents—to the Camp de Gurs, in the South of France.

Perhaps because the number of Jews in the town was so small, they formed a close-knit community with a conservative adherence to religious services and, in general, a lively interest in the arts. As time went on it became increasingly more difficult to get the required minyan of ten men needed for any official religious service, according to Jewish stricture. That meant that often the missing number of men had to be brought in from a neighboring village. Although Walldorf had provided two rabbis of note to temples in large cities within Germany, our small congregation could not afford one of its own and so had to make do with a prayer leader, Mr. Hahn, the father of one of those spiritual leaders. During my early teens Mr. Hahn was in his seventies, and it may be said of him that he wore many hats. In addition to conducting services, he served as religious schoolteacher for the handful of Jewish youngsters, and with great determination tried to imbue us with a sense of our Jewish identity. Within the span of my recollection, there were only two births and one wedding on record among the Jews of Walldorf, leaving Mr. Hahn to officiate mainly at funerals, as far as those aspects of his duties were concerned.

Until 1933 the Jews of Walldorf enjoyed an active social life. On weekend afternoons a group of men would meet at someone's home or in a restaurant for their popular card game of *Skat*, while in the evenings families would visit one another for regular social get-togethers. On such occasions there would be an abundance of food, much easy banter and gossip delving into the foibles of members of the community not present at those "soirées." The conversation could and often would take a more serious turn, especially as the position of the Jews became more precarious. Parallels were established with France's notorious "Affaire Dreyfus," which still weighed heavily on people's minds. Before Hitler's assumption of power, this was often regarded as a bellwether of what could happen in Germany as well when it came to anti-Semitism. I remember a distant relative by marriage, Louis Weil, a confirmed Francophile, perhaps because there was in fact a French branch of his family. He subscribed to various French journals, and I remember him holding forth on the subject of anti-Semitism, and coming to the conclusion that, as in the Dreyfus case, in which someone of Émile Zola's stature had helped stem the tide of anti-Semitic sentiment in France with his famous *J'accuse*, so in Germany, too, justice would prevail in the end. So, the Jews of Germany deluded themselves that they were part and parcel of the German nation and that it would always remain that way. It was Louis Weil, incidentally, who told me somewhat wistfully at the time of my emigration that the one thing he envied me about going to the States was the fact that I would soon know enough English to be able to read Shakespeare in the original. Alas, he himself, who spoke no English, was never to get the chance to learn it. Before 1937 was up, he succumbed to a sudden illness, one of the lucky ones to die of natural causes.

Because with the passing of each month it became increasingly clear that Germany represented a dead end for Jews—a fact that we, the young among them, understood and seized more readily—we gave a great deal of thought to where our future might lie. Within my family, the focus became the United States, where we had a number of relatives, some native born, others who had gone there before the turn of the century, and still others who had made their way to those shores more recently.

The ever-increasing restrictions regarding Jewish businesses were achieving their aim of curtailing and eventually halting all commerce between "Aryans" and Jews until the owners of Jewish enterprises either went out of business or were forced to sell to Aryan firms.

As Father's hands were being tied more and more, and income from his hops brokerage business dried up to minimal levels, Mother, in her resourceful, industrious way, jumped into the breach. She pursued several small ventures. She would ship to clients in cities far and wide the specialty of our region—asparagus—when in season. Or she would provide out-of-the-ordinary sweets and confections to family members and friends in nearby cities, along with specially prepared goose delicacies or poultry from our backyard.

It took only one year after the Nazis came to power for my father's business to suffer to the extent that he could no longer provide tuition for my pursuit of what I had hoped would be a professional career. That meant that at fourteen, along with other Jewish boys, I began to cast about for avenues that would eventually lead to emigration. In the meanwhile we felt it was important to acquire some sort of training that would stand us in good stead, no matter where our paths would take us. In my case the choice of a trade seemed fairly obvious. Having always been enamored of the realm of books, I chose the nearest thing to that predilection: printing.

In short order I was fortunate enough to begin an apprenticeship at a local stationer's whose expanded business comprised printing as well. I had barely moved beyond the basic training stage when the authorities got wind of the fact that this "Aryan" shop was employing a Jewish apprentice, and so my career as typesetter came to an abrupt, if temporary, end after only a few months. That left me with few job prospects and emigration still looming in an uncertain future.

At that point there existed a few Jewish businesses in Walldorf that had not yet been adversely affected by events, and as luck would have it, I found employment in a cigar factory, then still under Jewish management. Of course it was hardly what I had aspired to, but considering the options, it was a good job. It also helped bring in some funds in the face of my parents' steadily declining income. This change of career kept me in greater isolation from my friends in Heidelberg, save for weekend excursions to attend the meetings of the Jewish young men's club for as long as that was still possible. Having only two other friends in our small circle in Walldorf drove me increasingly toward the more unfettered world of books, which let my fantasies soar toward other horizons. I remember the three years between my leaving school at age fourteen until my emigration at seventeen as a time of great uncertainty—and of the erosion of most of our civil liberties. For the time being I had my work and filled my spare time with books or music from the radio, or both. Often I found myself playing a game of solitaire, well aware of the fact that I was doing so in more ways than one. Although I always craved the companionship of my contemporaries, the constraints of the times helped to intensify a natural tendency toward introversion.

Meanwhile my sister completed her nurse's training, and—the wheels having been set in motion—her prayers were answered when she received the necessary legal papers from one of our American relatives that provided an escape from the untenable situation in which we all found ourselves. Thus, in the spring of 1936, she was the first of our immediate family to make it to the safety of the United States. Because most of our relatives lived in Buffalo, it was an obvious move for her to settle in that city. In due course she was able to prevail on another relative to furnish a similar affidavit vouching for my support, making it possible, to my immense joy and relief, to follow her a year later.

Transportation provided no problem in 1937, inasmuch as my brother Max was then still working for the Hamburg-America Line, and so I was able to leave by mid-June on one of the SS *St. Louis*'s sister ships, with a happier outcome than that liner was to have two years later. The atmosphere on board was pleasant, and despite its name and the flag under which the SS *Deutschland* was sailing, there were few outward manifestations of the terror I was leaving behind, much of that no doubt attributable to the international clientele aboard.

Among the shipboard friendships I formed, one stands out in particular. It was with an American student, my senior by a few years, who had just concluded two semesters at Heidelberg University, a subject that led to many insightful conversations. We talked about his impressions of the country, and he went on to try to depict certain aspects of the American way of life that lay ahead of me, including, I still remember, some of the sophisticated humor from the pages of the *New Yorker,* a magazine to which I would become addicted in due time. What Fred Irvin was able to convey to me in his flawless German, picked up in the course of his year in Heidelberg, were his feelings about Germany. By and large his experience had been a most positive one, and he had encountered much that he liked a great deal. On the other hand he had not been blind to what he had seen all around him, as he made clear to me. What he enlarged on in subsequent letters, which reached me in Buffalo from his home near Philadelphia, was his observation that a great many of the German people were far too militaristic and in time to come would have to pay a steep price for their excesses, among them those directed at Jews.

. . .

It took eight days at sea to reach the safety of the American shore, and the sights familiar to me from photos and films inspired a feeling of awe and wonder. It was thrilling to actually glide by the Statue of Liberty and to see the New York skyline from this vantage point. All of it filled me with immense gratitude. Everything was new and exciting and held out a promise of unlimited possibilities. Above all I felt safe. In 1938 my brother, newly married, made it to these shores as well, and within another year, Max was able to have his wife, Sue, follow him before the entire immigration picture for Jews took a decided turn for the worse. Throughout the late thirties the economic outlook was far from ideal in the United States, as elsewhere in the world. Because we were aware that Father and Mother's situation was deteriorating rapidly, my siblings and I struggled to hold any kind of job, no matter how menial, that would allow us to bring them to this country. To that end I took a number of supplemental evening and weekend positions that ranged from working in the fast-food restaurants of that day to part-time employment in a tobacco and dry goods store. Apart from that, it was nearly impossible to convince anyone of the precariousness of our parents' situation. Soon thereafter a chain of events was unleashed that forced us to stand by in paralysis and frustration, witnessing developments that, predictable as they were to us, seemed to take most others by surprise.

On November 9, 1938, the outrage that was to be known as *Kristallnacht* became a watershed in the Nazis' treatment of the Jews. It represented the start of Hitler's "Final Solution," the elimination of the Jews of Germany, to be followed later by that of the rest of Europe's Jews. From that point on, most avenues of escape would remain blocked to my parents, although we came excruciatingly close to rescuing them on several occasions.

The scene most vividly associated with my realization that I would not see my parents again is one that linked the forces of nature to the inexorable movement of catastrophic events in Europe. Engraved on my mind is the evening of September 3, 1939, the Sunday when—in the wake of the German invasion of Poland two days earlier—England and France declared war on Germany. The news of the expected war had burst on the airwaves early in the day, and one of my oldest and closest friends, Otto Kahn, also a recent arrival in the United States, had persuaded me to join him and a few other young people on a visit to Niagara Falls. I remember standing at the foot of this monumental natural wonder

as twilight was falling, absorbing the thunderous rush of water silhouetted against a still-blue evening sky. I tried desperately to convey to
my friends that this day spelled the end of all hope regarding my parents.
Somehow I grasped at that moment that it was the ominous foreboding
of the deluge to come.

Peace! Peace! That great word that holds within it the meaning of life, the breath of freedom. Freedom! I welcome it in the rays of the golden sun, and I salute you, brave American soldiers. To us you are not ordinary men, but mythical heroes who fight to liberate us and who meet us with outstretched arms. Your sympathy is great, but we cannot speak the unspeakable and you might not understand our language. You are a people of freedom—and we? Are we human still—or again?

They have tried to drag us to the lowest level of existence, demeaned us, treated us worse than animals. Yet something has remained alive within us, for it stirs anew. It is a soul sensitive to the beauty of blossoming spring. The heart that beats in our breast pulsates with feeling. Slowly the petrified shell under which cruel barbarians have cut deep wounds is breaking, leaving a vulnerable, newly healed heart.

Words of farewell for you were whispered by my friend's dying lips: "Welcome them, welcome our liberators. I won't live to see them so greet them for me, they who liberate you!"

—Gerda Weissmann, May 10, 1945; read by Fifth U.S. Infantry Division chaplain at the funeral of Gerda's companions.

Field Hospital, Volary [Czechoslovakia], May 16, 1945

Dear Kurt,

You are probably surprised to hear from me now—but, to be honest, your abrupt departure today, almost in the nature of flight, gave me reason for concern.

You might say, "You could mention that the next time we see each other," but the desolate atmosphere here seems to have reached a nadir. Perhaps that has triggered my feelings that you heard something that upset you. I do not wish to pry into your privacy and your memories. Yet if you feel the need to share your anxiety, you will find full understanding on my part. Somehow it is easier for me to convey these thoughts in writing rather than in the course of our conversations, which are so often interrupted.

You assured me of your honest interest in my life and thoughts, and if that is the case then I can claim that you should share your concerns and pain with me as well. Your army friends who were visiting the other girls seemed in a more rambunctious mood as their laughter filled this ward. But I don't believe those interruptions caused the wounded expression on your face. So, my dear, brave liberator, I hope that you nevertheless had a pleasant evening, which certainly is not possible here right now. The fact is, I am happy to escape the noise around me and in that way find refuge by writing to you.

You said that you had not read much German "literature," aside from military dispatches, since you came to Europe. So it is irresponsible of me to confront you with this lengthy missive. Enough of that, and certainly enough about me. Just one statement: It was your understanding, your caring, that so enormously helped over the first, most difficult days. I shall be eternally grateful to you.

Always,
Gerda

Eleonorenhain, Sudetenland [about five miles from the Volary hospital],
May 20, 1945

Dear Gerda,

You can perhaps understand why this answer might turn out to be a rather clumsy one. I'm out of practice and feel as though I'm skating on thin ice.

My emotions must have been on full display in order to have aroused your concern to that extent. That's why I'm ashamed to admit that those pensive moments you believed you noted can only be traced back to cumulative reasons. They might best be described as a reaction to the feelings you know so well.

It is only now that the finality of my parents' fate is fully dawning on me, after all the years during which I grasped at the slightest straw of hope. And I'm saying that because I recognize the unselfish way in which you are attempting to spare me the incontrovertible facts. Does that sound too pessimistic? After all, you said yourself that we have to be honest with each other.

It is gratifying to hear that my lame attempts to divert you from your bitter experiences were at least partially rewarded by success. Now, however, you have switched roles, and it is I who am in your great debt for your exchange of ideas that betrayed a rare insight into my life. Is it your custom at all times to give without thinking of yourself? I can well imagine the protest on your part that I have triggered. Guess I ought to set your head straight, whether you like it or not.

I could best become reconciled with German literature by letting you take me back into it again. May I say that, thanks to your lines, along with a fantastic broadcast of Liszt's *Les Préludes*, this evening proved to be nearly as stimulating as if I had spent it with you in a certain ward of a field hospital with restrictive visiting hours. That feeling of having a conversation with you is constantly being reinforced, because not a minute goes by that I'm not being disturbed by a thousand trivial disruptions.

Oh, well, I promise that from now on I'll wear only cheerful expressions on my face. And you can help achieve that by writing soon again.

Your Kurt

For a few days following the armistice, I had been prevented from returning to the field hospital in Volary by the details of processing thousands

of surrendering German troops. We had been compelled to improvise prisoner-of-war enclosures of a scope that defied all our previous experience, a task that demanded all our concentration and efforts.

Although the mood among the prisoners varied, we had had some prior inkling of the crumbling morale among the German troops. Generally they seemed relieved that they had fallen into American hands rather than having had to surrender to the Russians. I remember one German officer offering me a cup of wine, because the entire crew of the vehicle he was riding in was "celebrating" the end of the war. When I declined, having spoken German to him, he insisted that he knew me and that in earlier years we had played tennis in Vienna, a city I had never set foot in. He went on to suggest that we should team up with the German army to fight the Russians henceforth. In other words the whole war had been a game, and now it was time to be friends, switch sides, and have a go against another opponent.

Later the irony of that situation, which was so repugnant, further hit home. I hardly needed to wonder how he would have reacted had the case been reversed and I had been one of his hapless Jewish victims. In the course of our sweep through France, Luxembourg, and Germany, those feelings had always intensified whenever I would come across SS troops, knowing a measure of their crimes even then, although the full extent was yet to be revealed. At such times it was inevitable that thoughts of retribution would cross my mind, but I soon realized that I could not stoop to their level, quite aside from what I perceived to be my military responsibilities. It was with bitterness that I realized how futile my personal feelings of vengeance would be if I were allowed to cross the bounds of humanitarian behavior—and that none of that would ever bring back my parents, or anyone else.

Volary, May 24, 1945

Dear Kurt,

I'm writing this letter although I foresee no possibility of sending it at this point. Yet I'm hoping that somehow an opportunity will present itself later. Inasmuch as the insignia of the division that replaced yours bears the color blue—the color of hope, I believe—perhaps I will manage to get this to you. *In optima fidelis* [trust in hope].

Can I assume that you have gotten used to your new place? Are the surroundings beautiful? Has your feeling of homesickness for America subsided after viewing "beautiful" Germany?

I can't report much of great interest, because everything seems to revolve around the same pole for me. Tomorrow is a red-letter day for some twenty girls here: They will be moving into a lovely villa, where, I hear, they will have access to a freer and less restrictive life than in the hospital.

I have not lifted a finger yet to give direction to my own life—instead, I will play for a little more time and let fate take over. After all, it smiled so kindly at me two weeks ago at the liberation.

Somehow my thoughts are directed toward writing my life story. Honestly, that idea seems to occupy my mind more and more, and I'm unable to dismiss it. I want to go back, way back, perhaps to the time when I was racing across meadows with a huge bow in my disheveled hair and joyfully climbing trees in my garden. I see it as going back to my sunny childhood only, up to—well, I would like to eliminate six years from the book of my life. No doubt they will be adequately covered in many other volumes.

But you know, Kurt, more and more often I believe that I might try to make the daring leap from my enchanted childhood to the sunny reality of freedom. You also gave me the privilege to share with you good as well as bad memories and thoughts. There is only one promise I must exact from you: It's one you *have to keep.* If I tell you something sad, it must evoke in you only understanding, never pity! Of course I can't forbid that—but I would be able to move and act more freely in your company knowing that you think of me as an equal. Please, Kurt, understand and promise.

The last few days have been pretty sad. It is the first time I can look back in freedom to the years of horror. Memories wash over me like waves, mounting to heights of total recall and then receding. Unfortunately I have time now, lying on my bunk, not doing anything. Entirely too much time! Still too ill to be allowed to get up. I wish I could already walk. Instead, I think, remember, observe, and try to visualize the future.

I'm not too happy with what I see around me; I feel bewildered and isolated. After the first flush of euphoria at freedom, some of the other girls don't seem to be reflective at all, or particularly grateful, but rather assertive and demanding in an unbecoming way. Somehow I feel wounded, alone, and sad to have to stay in this environment. But I have not lost the desire for the planned leap toward my future.

If you have arrived at this point of my ramblings, I admire your patience. I hope we will meet again.

Until then and always—my best wishes,

Gerda

∞   ∞   ∞   ∞   ∞   ∞   ∞   ∞   ∞   ∞   ∞   ∞

Kurt, by now the most faithful visitor to the hospital, was commonly referred to as "Gerda's lieutenant." The other girls couldn't understand why he didn't provide the clothing and food I needed, which he as an American could obtain. No one really understood our relationship, nor could I explain it. He instinctively understood my needs. By not bringing me clothing, he made me feel that he did not see my pitiful need of them, that I appeared to him as a normal girl, briefly confined to a hospital. His gifts of flowers and reading material were appropriate. Thus he helped me to regain self-confidence. Mine was a top bunk, and he often stood beside it for lengthy periods of time, just talking to me. I remember once glancing at the gun on his belt. Fear or anguish must have been reflected in my eyes, because from then on he would slip it under the bunk as unobtrusively as possible. Before he left, he would retrieve it, and, if I was watching, would usually make such offhand remarks as, "That darn thing is so heavy and useless anyway."

Kurt's visits were the highlights of my existence. One day, checking the thermometer the nurse had given me, I confirmed my suspicions that I had a high temperature. Fearful that I might not be permitted to have visitors, I shook it down before the nurse returned. In due time Kurt came but seemed ill at ease. After a while he told me that he was being transferred to a town in Bavaria, Pfarrkirchen, approximately 160 miles from Volary. He showed me photos of himself that had just been taken, and I desperately wanted one but was too shy to ask for it. After I repeatedly looked at one in particular, he realized what I wanted. An idea struck me, and I asked him to go out into the hall and write something on it. The thought of his leaving threw me into a panic. I was sure that I would never see him again. He was going off to some distant place, and after that they might send him farther yet, perhaps to Japan, now that the war in Europe was over. From there he would no doubt return to the United States and I would never see him again. All he would remember of me would be his encounter with a girl who had been desperately ill.

I have to get up, I resolved, I just have to. I pleaded with the nurse to help me get out of bed and put on the blue-and-white cotton dress I had been given. He must think of me in a normal way, no matter what the cost.

Seeing me in such a desperate state, the nurse relented. I had not been able to walk at all since liberation, and each step caused me excruciating pain. With her help I made it to the door, where I met Kurt, just about to reenter. His amazement at seeing me out of bed compensated for the great effort every step required. Supported by his strong arm, I walked with him into the yard amid trees in full bloom. Suddenly one of Hans Christian Andersen's fairy tales came to me: "The Little Mermaid," which I had known as "Rusalka" in Polish. It was about a mermaid who was in love with a prince. Her most ardent desire was to walk with him just once. A witch sold her a brew that changed her fins into legs. The price she paid for leaving her element was steep indeed: Each step was like walking on knives. Now that fairy tale had become my reality. Kurt was my prince, the knight who had slain the monstrous dragon. But he was about to leave for his own world. And I—how had it ended for Rusalka? Had she gone back to that other world, and would that be my fate as well? But this was real, and he was here. He was the only real part of the fairy tale, the only dream that would not fade in the light of reality. Now he was leaving, and in all likelihood I would never see him again. The pain of walking was nothing compared to the pain of parting. But he must never know my true feelings; that much I must do for him. He must never know my pain.

We said our good-byes at the door, Kurt assuring me that he would try to return as soon as he could. I could just barely manage to thank him, then crawl back to my bunk, where I took out the photo he had given me, to read his dedication: "To Gerda, at the start of a new life." What new life? There was nothing left now. There was nothing to look forward to tomorrow, and he would not come again. What then—was I to go back home? What home? That place no longer existed. I had been trying so hard over the years to hang on, to dream, to make believe. Ilse, Suse, Liesl, and I had sustained each other, bolstered each other's hopes. Now I was the only one left. Why? It would be so easy to let go, much easier than to hang on. Those were the thoughts I can remember before everything turned black.

I had no concept of time and place, no pain, only some dim awareness that I was very ill. When I opened my eyes I was looking at Kurt and also became aware that a nurse was putting ice on my lips. Kurt was real, not a figment of my fevered imagination. Taking my hand, he "scolded" me about getting sick the minute he turned his back. In a teasing way he called me a foolish little girl, using the familiar du form of address for the first time. He stayed for most of that night, telling me that I must get well, and I fell asleep with my small bony hand in his strong one. The crisis was over. Later I learned that I had been unconscious for most of a week, suffering from pneumonia and typhoid fever. Kurt had appeared at a critical moment and had disregarded the danger of my contagion.

Where Papa had once been my figure of strength and authority, I now loved to watch how politely yet forcefully Kurt dealt with the nurses in the hospital, how casually he returned the salutes of GIs, how much he teased me, as Artur had. Every time he appeared, it was as if a window opened onto a view suffused with sunshine—and when he touched my hand, an indefinable ecstasy enveloped me, depriving me of all reason. He was the only reality, a bridge of remembered happiness over a river of pain and loss, taking me toward some hitherto unknown shore. But he was bound to leave sooner or later.

I was convinced that Kurt would visit me on his birthday, July 2. After all, he had promised that we would celebrate it together, and in turn I had assured him I would be sufficiently fit to go for a walk with him by that time. I was diligently practicing my steps, slowly regaining my balance, despite some pain along the way. No question, I was making progress, and could hardly wait for that special day. Thinking about what birthday gift I could give him, I decided to write several essays touching on some childhood and more recent memories.

All that day I was waiting in great anticipation, groping for a logical reason that would explain his absence, but I could find none. I agonized over that, turning over all possibilities in my mind. A terrifying thought occurred to me that he might have caught my typhoid fever. Was there a way to contact someone to get information about him? Finally I realized that I would have to wait for word from or about him. What it made me fully realize, though, was that he had become everything to me and that I was deeply in love with this handsome young man—only he must never, never know.

Kurt's twenty-fifth birthday was almost over. It was evening, and he had not come. Again my eyes went to his photo, as they had throughout the day. Reading his inscription about the start of my new life made me *infinitely sad. I was certain now that it was meant to be a message of farewell. Feeling alone and abandoned, I wrote a bitter letter to my uncle in Turkey.*

❧   ❧   ❧   ❧   ❧   ❧   ❧   ❧   ❧   ❧   ❧   ❧

Volary, July 2, 1945

My dear ones—my beloved uncle,

It is in a welter of overwhelming emotions that I write these words to you. The first lines to my nearest relative! Uncle Leo, can you possibly perceive what this means to me? To be able to say, "I have survived the war!" I can't believe it. It does not ring true that all the suffering is over. Can it be so? Now my thoughts focus on you, my closest family, though you are far away in Turkey. Are you, dear aunt, and the sweet children all right?

I cannot and will not attempt to convey even a fraction of my experiences—that would take years and reams of paper. Three years of concentration camps and a march on foot of 550 kilometers, starting with 2,000 girls, of whom fewer than 120 survived, I among them. Not even in depictions of medieval torture and horror can one find crimes such as the Nazis committed.

I don't know how and why I survived. On May 6 we were liberated by American forces. I was at the end of my strength, physically as well as emotionally, and collapsed. Since then I have been in a makeshift hospital. I was critically ill until two weeks ago. I am feeling better now.

During that time I have asked several kind people to write to you. I hope that you have gotten news about my survival from several sources—especially from Lt. Kurt Klein, who has become a good friend. I owe him a debt of gratitude, for he helped me regain my mental balance during my most difficult days. Unfortunately he was transferred to a different post after that, but I hope to hear from him again.

Today's letter is sent through the kindness of an army chaplain. My beloved uncle, I have tried to put off the question that is burning on my mind since the first line of this writing, but can no longer do so. Although I fear the words, I am compelled to ask them: Oh, God, do you have any news from my beloved parents? I cannot think, cannot conceive that fate would be so cruel to me. Oh, please, God, please. Since the day of our parting, I have heard nothing but rumors of a tragic fate. But I hoped and prayed and believed in miracles. I still do.

I have not heard from Artur in two years. The last news was that he was in a camp in or near Lemberg [Lvov]. Then all mail ceased, and we were cut off from the rest of the world. We heard of the horrors that took place in those parts. I worry so and tremble at thoughts of the worst, and pray. I am trying to establish contact with Bielsko, hoping to find him there.

You remember me only as a child, but the past few years have accelerated my transition to adulthood. It was not easy, and I always tried to act in the manner that my beloved parents would have expected of me. Now that I can write freely, I must also tell you the truth. Both Papa and Mama were very ill, at home and in the ghetto. Papa had a heart attack and we had terrible, worrisome days and weeks. Everything we owned was taken from us, everything. My heart breaks at the thought that they might not have survived to experience the beauty of freedom. Why? Why?

Now I am turning to you, Mama's beloved only brother. I need your advice for my future. I stand here, alone in a strange world. I want to go home—the dream of going home sustained me—I want to go home to people who are close to me. I yearn for a bit of warmth and calm after three years of hell in the camps. What is going to happen now? That question occupies me day and night.

I have met some people by the name of Knäbel; they own the factory in which we were locked up the night before liberation. Herr Knäbel claims he knew some associates of Papa. He and his family have been very nice to me. His daughters, who are considerably older than I, have also been very kind.

Some of my friends are planning to go home when they get well. I want to wait to hear where my family is, for I won't go back if they are not there. I won't go back to the ruins of my happy childhood, to the place where we were so brutally separated. My thoughts and emotions are in total turmoil; one moment I want to go back, the next I say: Never! What should I do?

I am not afraid of hardship or work. I have learned to work hard. Twelve hours a day and many nights we worked on spinning machines and looms. Nothing will be too difficult for me, once I regain my health. I only want peace, quiet, and some kindness. My education is nil. I am twenty-one years old. I want to learn, I want to learn languages, particularly English. I want to understand art, because I always had an interest in it.

Please forgive this chaotic tone. In this flood of thoughts and words I am trying to convey what has worried me for years and caused so much anguish. I confess my heart is heavy; I can't lie about that. I am still weak after that long, debilitating illness. I have just learned to walk again. Although everyone is very nice and helpful to me, I am alone; none of my closest friends survived. I am without means and won't take anything from strangers. There is no one close to me. I am so homesick, so lonely. I want Mama, Papa, Artur—I want to go home.

[The rest of this letter is missing. I found it among my uncle's possessions after his death.]

Although I was in the process of recuperating, my newly won freedom left me feeling isolated from what was going on around me. I could only marvel at some of the other girls' resourcefulness in taking charge of their lives, hatching plans to return to their former homes, or moving into local quarters, acting totally adult. By comparison I felt inadequate on all fronts. I seemed to have survived by marshaling my imagination and at times through denial. After my separation from my parents, I managed to wipe the three years of anguish and deprivation from my mind. When I thought of home, and that was all the time, I thought of it as it existed before the war, realizing on another level that it could not be so. Nevertheless I lulled myself into a feeling that through the miracle of liberation everything would be restored. It was a crutch that had worked for me, had seen me through those harrowing times. Now the war was over, and what would become of the dreams that had nourished me? What of the reality of the situation? Somehow I had to face at least that of which I was certain. I knew that my parents had been sent to Auschwitz, yet had pretended to myself that they were young and strong and could survive. Now I realized that I had superimposed on their images the ones I remembered from happier times. I did not want to picture my father as he looked after his heart attack: gaunt, gray, and weak, or my mother as the emaciated, frail, worn-down, aging woman she had become by the time of our separation. In my heart and mind they still lived in the familiar childhood environment, notwithstanding the fact that I had been witness to its destruction.

.   .   .

44

When the dreaded notice came for the Jews to leave their homes, we were "allowed" to sell our belongings. My mother was close to a nervous breakdown, and Papa directed me to sell everything. The townspeople, most of whom I didn't know, descended on us like vultures. One man took a pink goblet from the liqueur set Artur and I had bought for our parents' twentieth anniversary, in April 1939. He grabbed the slender stem and let it tumble to the floor. "It's not worth much," he said. "After all, one glass is missing." With a smirk he handed me a few dirty, crumbled bills. I would never tell Papa what really had happened, I vowed to myself, swallowing tears of frustration and bitterness and then proceeding to sweep the shards from the bare floor.

Nothing remained from the home I had once known and loved. It had not been luxurious—far from it—but in its untroubled days it had a nurturing quality about it. It was a warm place in which my mother was born and my grandparents had lived ever since their marriage in the late 1890s. The years had seen it filled with objects of special significance to the family, cherished mementos of a more carefree time. The dream of returning to it had been the crutch to my survival, underpinning my conviction that it would be mine by the very magic of freedom. Now that the walls of brutality had crumbled, I needed to face the reality I had known subconsciously but had managed to push from my mind.

How I longed for the days when I had been die Kleine, "the little one," cared-for and protected. Only there had been a role reversal, and it was I who had learned to protect my parents. It was I who would stand in line at the store day after day, clutching our meager ration cards bearing the huge J that identified us as "enemies of the state," in the hope of getting a little bread or a tiny bit of margarine. I had taken on that task after Mama came home in tears one day, humiliated by the treatment she had received. People she had known all her life either rudely ignored her or at best had whispered a furtive hello. I picked up the net shopping bag, declaring resolutely that I needed some fresh air and from then on would assume that chore every day. It also fell to me to open the door whenever there was an ominous knock and Mama would shepherd Papa toward his hiding place in the wardrobe, initially over his vehement protests.

If I decided to make it back home, what would I find? Who would live in our house? The garden must be in bloom, and certainly the sign prohibiting Jews from entering must have come down. Would the former neighbors still be there? Frau Prosner, she who brought the first letter from Artur, which he addressed to her, not knowing where we might be.

Thinking of Frau Prosner triggered another image, that of a hot summer's day: I am out in the yard, and through the garden fence branches hang heavy with gooseberries. I go there and pick some, then see little Erwin Prosner. He runs up to me, then toward the house, his piercing shrieks assaulting my senses: "Mutti, the Jewess is devouring our berries. They are only for us Germans! Mutti, come and slap her face." Frau Prosner comes scurrying out of the house, her face flushed, and quickly yanks him back, his face contorted with hate. She walks up to me and takes my hand. "I'm so sorry," she whispers. "You must know, I don't teach him that. He learns it in kindergarten about people who wear the yellow star. I don't dare punish him; he would tell his teachers and we would be in trouble. I'm so sorry."

What of little Erwin? I used to wheel him carefully in his baby carriage, and one time gave him one of my favorite toys. I see the green pump and how I used to fill it with water, pumping it into a tiny pail, endlessly, over and over. What would little Erwin say if he were to see me entering my garden now? Did I ever want to see him again?

It was a lovely afternoon, and I was feeling a little better. Looking up from the book I was reading, I saw a woman enter the room, hesitate, question a nurse, then approach my bunk. At first shy and diffident, she inquired, was she intruding? No? Handing me a bouquet of flowers, she ventured that they might cheer me up. She had heard what I and my companions had gone through and explained that she knew what it was to be away from home. Her home was really in Germany, she said, she too was a Flüchtling, a refugee, and knew what it meant to be away from the Heimat. You miss your homeland, especially when you are ill like that. It was hard, she allowed, and that's why she had decided that the least she could do as a German was to visit someone like me. She let on that her best school friend had been Jewish, although she didn't know what had happened to her: One day she simply disappeared. Did I have a best friend like that?

The question she had posed would not go away after the woman left and set me to thinking of my best school friend.

Gerta! Gerta Teppel! Knit four, purl two . . . five rows, then switch. Heavy white wool . . . knit four, purl two. Gerta Teppel, my best friend, from way back in first grade. We had walked to and from school every day. Gerta and Gerda, the inseparable duo. She had blond hair with bangs that stopped just above her eyebrows. Naturally I had copied her style with my dark bangs. Every morning we would greet each other with "Servus!"* then fall into step and walk to school in animated conversation. Our classroom desks were designed for two, so we sat next to each other throughout the elementary grades. She was very neat and accomplished in so many things I felt inadequate about. That made me want to emulate her in every way possible, and it had gotten to the point where, after considerable effort on my part, it was indeed difficult to tell our handwriting apart. She excelled in music and voice, areas in which I drew an almost complete blank. On the other hand, I compensated for that by getting good marks in language and poetry classes, subjects that were difficult for her. Our respective grade averages were nearly always close.

Inseparable as we were during school hours, we would rarely meet afterward. Whenever I would broach the subject, she would be noncommittal and make some vague excuse about mysterious-sounding activities that somehow kept her from seeing me. That only heightened my interest in her, and I resolved that there was nothing, but nothing, that I wouldn't do for her.

At that time I had a crush on a boy named Henek. He had two younger sisters with whom I was friendly. My idol had the bluest eyes, the darkest hair, and a small, upturned nose. He paid no attention to me whatsoever, until one day, during a table tennis game with his sister Lola, I beat her. "You play well for a girl your age," he complimented. "Want to play a game with me?" Flustered, I accepted the challenge and promptly missed every ball, dropped my paddle at one point, then stumbled and was forced to crawl under the table to retrieve the ball. I was mortified, and to make matters worse, I hit my head coming out from under the table. That provided an excuse to break into tears. Henek, realizing what was happening, gallantly dismissed the incident. "Oh, too bad you hurt your head. We must play another time."

I took my departure through blinding tears and ran home as fast as I could, replaying in my mind all the mistakes I had made and how I could have avoided them. I found Mama in the living room, busily knitting a ski sweater for me, made of heavy, white wool, in an intricate braid design: Knit four, purl two. Four rows, then reverse. It promised to be beautiful.

Later that afternoon Lola arrived at my house to announce that a group of her friends were going skiing that coming Sunday. Could I come

*A greeting that can mean either "hello" or "good-bye," particularly popular in Austria.

along? she wanted to know. Henek would lead us, take us to one of his favorite spots on the mountain. I could hardly believe the fortuitous turn of events. And better yet, Henek would see me in that fabulous sweater! Could I? Would I? "Mama," I begged, "could you finish that sweater by Sunday, please, please?" "I think we could give it a try," she agreed with a smile. After that the needles fairly flew: Knit four, purl two. Wait till I wear that sweater with the navy blue ski pants! And Henek will be there!

Saturdays meant that school let out at noon. Gerta and I were walking home from school. A light snow was falling, the prayed-for powder snow. "You know, I've been thinking," Gerta said, "wouldn't it be nice to get together tomorrow? We could play Tivoli." I was thunderstruck: I had tried in vain to get her to come to the house to play that Polish variation of a pinball game. "Sure, why don't you come over right now. We can have lunch first, then spend the afternoon doing fun things." "I'm sorry, I can't make it right now, but I'll come over tomorrow afternoon. My parents will be at a wedding then, it so happens."

For a fleeting moment it occurred to me that she might have heard about our ski plans, but then I remembered that she never went skiing because of a leg injury. The request she had tossed off presented a terrible dilemma. I was dying to go with Henek. He would be impressed with the way I skied, and when I wore that new sweater, he had to notice me, just had to. On the other hand, how selfish of me to want to be on those slopes while my best friend had to stay home alone. No, my sacrifice for her would certainly cement our friendship—or would it? I vacillated, but in the end Gerta won out.

Sunday came, and the snow had improved overnight. Its crystal grains were glistening in the sun like a coating of sugar. Mama was delighted I had decided against going skiing. She viewed any sport with a great deal of apprehension, fear of accidents being the predominant factor. Mama possessed that rare quality of treating her children's friends as she would her own special guests. We devoured the marble cake, drank the cocoa, and thus fortified, focused on the intricacies of Tivoli for a while. To my acute disappointment Gerta left much earlier than I had antici-pated. Although it had been a nice enough afternoon, I felt that it had not been wholly satisfying. Aimlessly, I went up to my room, lay on my bed in the darkness of the winter afternoon, staring moodily at the barely discernible shape of my white sweater on the dresser.

A few years later, during the sweltering summer of 1940, well into the war and the German occupation of Poland, an errand took me to the post office, the yellow Jewish star prominently affixed to my blouse, as decreed by the occupying Nazi forces. Just then, coming down the brown sandstone steps of the building, I spied Gerta. She was wearing a blue dress with a mushroom print pattern. Looking around furtively and finding no one in sight, I kept my voice to its lowest: "Gerta!" She looked straight at me. "Gerta!" I repeated, a note of urgency and trepidation creeping into my voice. Her eyes looked straight through me, and without stopping she said, "I don't talk to Jews!"

Now I could hear Gerta avowing to someone that her best friend had been Jewish, and she would have been telling the absolute truth.

Pfarrkirchen [Bavaria], June 27, 1945
[to field hospital, Volary, Czechoslovakia]

Dear Gerda,

It's not my intention to disappear from the face of the earth without any trace whatsoever. So I'm offering a few words of explanation, if not outright apology. Yes, the army has once again lived up to its reputation by removing me from the site of my weekly pilgrimage just as a new phase of our acquaintance was opening up. That's how it happened that we each had to take our first real walk along separate roads. Actually, that may have had a beneficial effect on your state of health. Despite that, I consider myself deprived of a breathtaking event, your first attempt at mobility just now, when I could have reaped the fruit of weeks of patience—or was it impatience? Oh, well, matters must have run their course smoothly, even without the dubious pleasure of my company. In all likelihood I would soon have gasped for breath anyway.

I hope that I'll be able to convince myself personally of your total recovery in the very near future. Unfortunately I didn't remain in your area and presumably will not get a long-lasting assignment in these parts. Be assured that my occasional visits may be expected.

Meanwhile, please do pour out your heart and let me know how I can be of help. No answer yet to the letter I sent your uncle in Turkey, but it will come!

Kurt

P.S. As proof of my extraordinary mountaineering feats, permit me to enclose a flower (*Alpenrose*), which I plucked at an altitude of 2,500 m.

I have always been attracted to mountain scenery, and that love had its origin in an experience I had when I was thirteen. The summer of 1933 still allowed us some vestiges of a normal life because the anti-Jewish measures were then only in their incipient stages. For me those months held some pivotal events, starting with my bar mitzvah—in that place and time a low-key rite of passage—when, according to Jewish law, I attained the status of manhood. That milestone was a combination of solemn religious significance, along with a certain amount of fun with friends and family.

Among the largely simple gifts I received, one stood out. It was an invitation to visit with my relatives in Munich, "Uncle" Richard and "Aunt" Klärle, as I called them, although, to be exact, Richard Mayer was a cousin of Mother's who had found his wife in my hometown. The Mayers had always held a certain fascination for me, part of which no doubt stemmed from the fact that Uncle Richard was a regional representative for one of the well-known brands of chocolate, Waldbaur, which made us the beneficiaries of generous samplings from his inventory. It was tremendously exciting for me to think that this would at last afford me the chance to break out beyond the confines of my environment, the realization of much that my dreams had centered on. At the same time I would be touring the scenic beauty of Bavaria, far beyond anything that had ever been open to me. Those were in fact some of the sights that had always lain so tantalizingly inaccessible in that other world I could only read about or see in books or movies.

The Mayers exuded a sophistication to which I aspired. Auto travel with Richard, in the course of which he would make the rounds of his clientele—and on weekends with Aunt Klärle—taking in spectacular mountain scenery and actually climbing some of those formidable peaks, represented the ultimate thrill to me. Along the way there would be advice on what books to read, what plays to see, or what classical music to listen to; pretty heady stuff for a small-town boy. It opened up vistas, spectacular and real, along with those of the mind. The experience was to trigger a lifelong love of high mountains, and an appreciation as well of the heights that could be reached by exploring classical music, to which Uncle Richard introduced me.

That summer I matured in many ways, and began to grasp some of the political realities that confronted us as Jews, which Uncle Richard would explain in an attempt to help me better understand them. At the end of that period I returned home, no longer the youngster inclined toward playful pursuits Mother had cautioned her cousin and his wife about before my visit. It was indeed a farewell to childhood that nourished me for much of my life.

A decade would elapse before I would see my relatives again, by which time there had been a change of scene. The locale: Cheltenham, England, in 1943, where the Mayers had found refuge just in the nick of time before the outbreak of war. I was stationed nearby, amid the gentle, rolling hills of the Cotswolds, in an army camp that held some of the ever-swelling ranks of American troops in the British Isles. As it happened, Klärle worked at the USO club, her name now being Clara. We mused over the events of the immediate past and the prevailing uncertainties as to the progress of the war. Richard's predictions during the summer of 1933 had turned out to be all too accurate. Despite the fact that he had foreseen the situation as it in fact developed, frighteningly close to his conjecture, concerns about his mother, who was too old and ill to emigrate, had nearly made them miss the last exit from Germany. Nevertheless they had made their escape, although it meant that, once hostilities between England and Germany began—and despite the fact that they had just fled the Nazi horror—they were initially subjected to all the restrictions imposed on Britain's "enemy aliens." Richard would relate the bitter irony of being interned on the Isle of Man with German nationals caught by the outbreak of war in England. Most of them were outspoken anti-Semites who received better treatment than did the Jews in the camp.

Volary, July 6, 1945

Dear Kurt,

Thanks for your letter, which finally confirmed that all is well with you. In all honesty, I was very concerned and could not imagine what had happened. I diligently practiced my walking, and by Sunday my hopes were totally dashed, for I had anticipated celebrating your birthday with you. But please accept my belated congratulations and wishes for all that is good and happy and for the fulfillment of all your hopes.

I gather that you spent the day happily in the breathtaking surroundings of the Alps. It fills me with envy—only your lovely rose brings forgiveness. As I held it it opened up new vistas, and I felt that I too shared the magic of nature's beauty.

Not only am I walking now, but I am able to run. So I take long walks in the fields and think of the future. I've had the good fortune to learn something that is beautiful as well as practical, and am very excited about it. Frau von Garnier (Herr Knäbel's daughter) is a talented artist; she fashions jewelry in fine metals and is letting me try my hand at it. It is exhilarating to work with my hands, giving my imagination free rein. My first "masterpiece" is a tiny star meant for you. I will send it to you at the first opportunity that presents itself. Please forgive the primitive form and, without a doubt, the many mistakes, but I pray it brings you good luck.

At your urging, I must report that there were several false alarms concerning the duration of our stay here. At one point we were told that we'd have to leave, and then that was rescinded. In light of our immediate past, this does not seem tragic, and I feel that in the end all will turn out well. Of late some people surfaced from the vicinity of my hometown, but so far I have remained firm in my resolve not to go back. I don't understand my ironclad aversion to it, especially when you consider that during all those years my dreams were of nothing *but* going home. But I have made some inquiries and have some contacts in case I were to go. May God grant me my most fervent wish to find Artur there. If only word would come from Turkey soon.

It is good of you to console me. Yes, I do hope that we will get news soon. That should be enough for today, at least about me. I am delighted by your promise that we will see each other soon.

Please continue to write and describe the beauty of your surroundings. Nature can bring much solace. Do you believe that it was as beautiful there when the bloodthirsty monster prevailed? Or is everything doubly beautiful and fragrant now that it is relieved of the oppressive presence?

Stay well—I look forward with renewed joy to seeing you again.

Gerda

∞   ∞   ∞   ∞   ∞   ∞   ∞   ∞   ∞   ∞   ∞   ∞

The following day, Saturday, July 7, I was invited to the Knäbels' and spent the afternoon in their pleasant garden, so reminiscent of my own. Just as I was about to leave, torrents of rain came down, which kept me from returning to the hospital. At that moment the doorbell rang. The maid opened the door—and there stood Kurt! Not even in my wildest dreams had I dared to think I would see him on this day. He had quite obviously made the journey from his army post in an open Jeep, for his uniform was completely drenched. He had used his free time over the weekend to undertake this long trip and had to be back at his base by Sunday evening. Meanwhile he gladly accepted the Knäbels' invitation to stay the night.

While he was being shown to his room, I stood alone at the living room window watching the diminishing rain. The room felt cool and comfortable, the furniture, although from another era, was well cared-for. I noticed that the curtains were freshly starched, the drapes a bit shabby. It all was so much like my living room at home, only this home had survived the onslaught of war. I felt so alone, so longing to go someplace I could call my own.

Kurt came back into the room, standing next to me in silence for a while. Could he sense my thoughts? Then, in a reassuring gesture, he put his arm around me. I shivered at the first protective touch I had experienced in years, and the tears came. Without words he kissed me gently, giving free rein to the flow of my emotions.

It was time to return to the hospital, and we walked through the deserted streets of the picturesque town in Bohemia, the scent of grass and flowers sweetening the air after the rain. The dilemma I was facing about the next step I should take once I was released from the hospital dominated my thoughts. I resolved to ask Kurt's advice in the morning; there would be time then. When we said our good nights, my mind was a tangle of emotions.

Kurt promptly presented himself at the hospital the following morning, and I suggested that we take a walk in the fields and up a gentle hill that had intrigued me for days. After some easy banter, I posed the question that had occupied me the night before. His tone changed instantly. Should I try to go back to Bielsko? No, he didn't think I was ready for that physically and emotionally. Why not await an answer from my uncle in Turkey? Quite probably that would give me some guidance. I listened to him, infinitely glad that he was confirming what had been in the back of my mind all along: that I really feared what I might not find at home. In that way he relieved me of the burden of an imminent decision.

Although I had promised to visit Gerda, still convalescing in the hospital in Volary on my birthday, July 2, my duties delayed that trip by several days. Arriving there I found her much improved, if somewhat disappointed by my failure to show up on the day she had so anticipated. She couldn't wait to present the gift she had crafted with great care: a group of essays reflecting her musings on her happy childhood, overshadowed by subsequent events, pages bound between two beautifully finished wooden covers. The dedication read: "A few episodes from my life, to Kurt." I had time to glance at the opening sentence: "It is perhaps a daring venture to take note of a life such as mine, knowing that a life can, after all, never be fully explored. . . ."

In time to come I would have the opportunity to explore other aspects of that life in great detail, but for the moment I was immensely moved by the thoughtfulness of the gift and what it revealed to me about her. In retrospect I realize that much of it was meant to assuage the pain of my own losses, just one of the many selfless gestures on her part that I was to experience.

In the essays Gerda recaptured her sheltered upbringing and those reflections turned into a moving paean to her parents and her brother for having provided everything that helped her to weather the storm and instilled the values that saw her through her trials. There also were her recollections of camp life; her interaction with others; a dialogue with the moon during a sleepless night; a poem, written to bolster morale in the camp on the occasion of Hanukkah, in which she expressed a simple, childlike faith that, just as the Maccabees had prevailed over a much stronger enemy, so she and her companions would in the end overcome their suffering at the hands of their adversaries. Finally, thoughts on the coming of spring ended this way: "Winter was a bad dream . . . but spring restores. . . . God metes out suffering. . . . God grants consolation . . . life is beautiful!"

Absorbing it, I could only marvel with increasing admiration how she had retained her indomitable spirit in the face of insuperable odds, always keeping restoration in her heart and poetry in her soul. I felt singled out and especially privileged to be allowed this insight into the mind of a rare and sensitive human being.

Dear Gerda,

You must be in suspense about how our all-too-early return trip went: Actually it was pretty unexciting, considering the reluctant start by the old jalopy. In spite of that, the confounded Jeep insisted on getting itself a flat hind leg on the way. Oh, well, the damage was easily fixed, and some of the other bugs are out of its system as well. So you see, everything is okay; only, to be candid, my thoughts are not yet directed at my work. I wonder if this will be a week of decisions for you? I believe that if you let your choice be guided by impulse, the right decision will present itself.

You know, I'm immensely grateful for the profound insights that you gave me in your gift of the essays. They made for a most meaningful postbirthday contemplation. In the assembly of the fragments of your life, even the darkest shadows seem to reflect a wonderfully bright childhood. Love of people and nature are so evident that they force out all the loathsome events that happened subsequently. At the same time the enjoyment of everyday occurrences comes across so genuinely that things one has overlooked or taken for granted appear in an entirely new light. How often we avoid what is really important or look at it from the wrong perspective. Now I found it here, distilled in its crystal clear purity. So what I owe you is that I can reexamine all that appears half-hearted or insipid, only to find it bathed in rich, vivid colors. I value your creed all the more, inasmuch as your unshakable faith in the purely ideal, which my skeptical indecision considered nearly nonexistent, has brought it to the fore again. That is why it is I who have gained the most benefits from this friendship, without the hope of ever coming close to balancing the scale in any way.

How quickly the hours fled, and how little we could tell each other. But that will have to be made up soon, don't you agree? Incidentally, it will interest you that the army postal service has conspired against me; your letter has not yet arrived. The suspense is mounting, and if that should sufficiently stimulate your empathy, then do write to

Kurt

Before the end of July, orders came through that transferred me from Pfarrkirchen to an army base in Freising, approximately twenty-five miles north of Munich. Two months earlier, before leaving Volary, I had made arrangements that would assure Gerda's and her friends' safety. Because we had heard rumors that this part of Czechoslovakia would be ceded to the Russians in the future, I had tried to provide for just such a contingency. That meant that I had extracted a promise from the captain of the military government that replaced our unit that, in the event of an American pullout, he would facilitate the young women's evacuation—in Gerda's case to wherever I was stationed. During one of several trips back to Volary, I had been able to inform the captain of my latest transfer to Freising, and that was how Gerda and Mala* turned up in that town in due time.

My work in Freising consisted of interrogating key Nazi personnel and collaborators caught in the American net at the end of the war. While some cases could spell drudgery, there were others of immense fascination, such as when a tall, handsome man came to our lines because, as he said, he didn't want to fall into the hands of the Russians. His name was Erich Kempka, and he had been Hitler's private chauffeur.

The story he told was one of historical proportions, which came across all the more astounding for the matter-of-fact manner in which he recited it. As I saw it he had been a participant in a great drama, played out in true Wagnerian style. He had been in the Führer bunker in Berlin, and toward the end of the Russian siege had been called in by Hitler and told that his leader and his eleventh-hour wife, Eva Braun, were about to commit suicide. Fearing that their remains would be found by the Russians, Hitler had given explicit orders how to dispose of their bodies.

Kempka went on to describe how he had indeed helped carry the two bodies to the bunker courtyard, had doused them with what the British had dubbed "jerricans" of gasoline—the equivalent of five-gallon cans, used by the German army—then had ignited them. Here was an immolation scene right out of Wagner's Ring cycle, which Hitler had so greatly admired. Only this Götterdämmerung should have been renamed Twilight

*She was among a group of young women sent from Auschwitz to join the death march. Gerda and Mala met in the hospital in Volary.

of the Self-styled Gods. It made me shudder to have this brush with history, and raised the obvious question: How many millions of people had to die before the cause of their deaths vanished from the field of human endeavor?

By the middle of July, I learned that the Russian takeover of Volary was imminent. Feeling well enough, I obtained my release from the hospital and made preparations to leave. Transportation would be provided by the American army to take those of the girls who wanted to leave to two points in Bavaria that were under American control. Now that it was upon us, I had ambivalent feelings about leaving this place of my liberation that held some pleasant memories, despite everything else it represented.

By morning I was in a state of excitement as my friend Mala and I were gathering our meager possessions: in my case, a few items of clothing, a prayer book, Kurt's letters, his photo, and finally some provisions. We had heard that some of our girls who had recovered earlier had gone to a certain town in Bavaria, and so we told the captain who drove us that we would initially like to join that group in Cham. Although I had promised Kurt to come to the town of Freising, where he was stationed, I was reluctant to do so, fearing I might become a burden to him.

Once we arrived in Cham after a long Jeep ride, no one seemed to know where the other girls from our group could be found. Following a GI's lead, we made our way to the house where they supposedly were staying but were rebuffed by the owner, a woman who dismissed us with the words that they had moved on. We were at our wits' end and very, very tired. It was getting dark, and we were beginning to wonder whether we had made a mistake in leaving the security of our quarters in Volary. This town was hostile and its people suspicious of us.

We heard the tolling of a bell, and that provided an answer. We would seek refuge for the night in the church. When we found it, the portal was open and we could dimly make out the interior by several candles burning *at the far end of the nave. Wrapping our belongings around us, we curled up on the seats and mercifully fell asleep.*

When I awoke I could see sunlight streaming through the stained-glass windows. Where do I go from here? What do I do now? I turned to prayer, asking my parents to help me find my way. Kurt—I still had the option to go to Freising, as he had suggested. Luck was with us, and the American Military Government office in town promised to provide the necessary transportation.

A ride in an ambulance van got us to Freising by late afternoon, depositing us at Kurt's army base. I conveyed to the guard at the entrance just whom I had come to see, and to my immense relief saw Kurt hurrying toward us after only a short while. "I had been hoping you'd come around this time," he greeted us. "I can put you up in a doctor's residence for the time being. You must be hungry, tired, and all worn out!" I could barely thank him.

Two days later, in the course of a long walk, punctuated by what I felt to be an uneasy silence, Kurt told me of his impending leave, which he would spend on the Riviera. He asked that Mala and I stay in Freising until his return.

Freising, July 20, 1945

My friend, my good friend,

I owe you an answer, Kurt. I owe you many answers. I *must* write now, knowing that I shall never be able to articulate all I want to and must tell you before we part.

Tonight, when we had our long talk, many things crystallized for me. Your concern about my future, immediate and distant, is well-meaning. You told me that within a few days you will get a leave that will take you to the Riviera, and you asked me to stay here in Freising, assuring me that you could take care of my stay here for a pack of American cigarettes. You even made light of the fact that you don't smoke and suggested I take it as a brotherly gesture.

Forgive me for being selfish, for surely you have earned that relationship, but I couldn't call you my brother. Yes, a deep, caring friendship sprang up between us the instant we met. I shall be eternally grateful to providence for putting you in my path at that precise instant. Now please try to be objective for a moment; forget yourself, me, the war, even peace—everything. Please listen to the story as if it were a confession. I ask only one promise: Give me your understanding *without* pity.

It seems in retrospect that my life until fifteen was of fairy-tale dimensions. I was indulged, pampered, and came close to actually believing that my father's nickname for me, Princess Sunshine, was my due. But there is a price to be paid for such privilege. The war turned this heaven into hell, and my childhood ended on October 19, 1939. That was the day on which Artur left, when the person who until then had been an all-knowing figure of authority, my father, collapsed and cried helplessly. I put my arms around him, comforting him for the first time in my life, taking on the responsibility Artur had charged me with: to look after our parents. I found solace in being able to spare them at least some pain.

When I was almost seventeen, I met an intelligent, sensitive, artistic young man by the name of Abek. I thought it was a special friendship, but for him it was much more. And I could not reciprocate that feeling, for my ideal of love is something sacred. I only want to be totally honest about what has happened in my life, aside from the camps.

And then I met you at the very moment of my total mental and physical collapse. A few days before that I lost Ilse, who was like a sister to me. After the separation from my parents, she became the focal point of my existence. She needed me, and I had to live for her. That was my objective, as I had lived for my parents when I was with them. Maybe I had used that as a crutch, but with Ilse gone there was nothing else left for me.

As long as I live I shall never forget the expression on your face as we entered the factory and you came face-to-face with what they had done to us. I saw your horror, your rage, and your compassion, and at that instant, when I had known you less than ten minutes, I was overwhelmed by an uncontrollable desire to save you from pain. It is a feeling that only increased as our friendship developed.

During the weeks that followed, while I hovered between life and death, you often stood at my upper bunk for hours while others were going about happier pursuits. And then there was the evening when you so miraculously appeared after hours of riding in a Jeep, only to be told that I would probably not survive the night. It was, of course, past visiting hours, and I heard you through my raging fever, heard you argue with the nurse, taking full responsibility for your presence. Yes, you knew I had typhoid fever; nevertheless you stayed the night, holding my hand in your cool, strong one. That's when you called me *du* so tenderly for the first time. If my parents and Artur survive, they will have to thank you for my life.

I remember your unabashed joy and elation when my fever broke; I only want to give you joy! You became the only person who really cares, who understands me. And I am so deeply grateful for that. It is not surprising that I was seeking your company, as I felt you were seeking mine. You always came back when I thought I might not see you again, and I believed that you came because you wanted to be with me, because we enjoyed being together, in the process discovering how much we had in common. Or did you come out of some feeling of obligation? Did you take responsibility for my life because you *saved* my life?

I never asked you what obligations you had toward anyone at home, and you never mentioned it, but Mala apparently heard from your friends that there was someone. I feel something is wrong. You must never think you have *any* obligation toward me—never! You don't owe me anything. I don't think anybody could object to our friendship, not even to that evening at the Knäbels' when you took me in your arms and kissed me for the one and only time. You did not ask me why I was crying; you must have sensed that this was the first affectionate gesture toward me after so many hard and lonely years, and I craved affection so much. I cannot bear to hurt you; that is why I cannot stay here any longer.

You do not need me, Kurt. On the contrary, I might be a burden to you, and that is something I never want to be. If I stayed, I could not promise never to weaken and seek solace from you. You would give it to me, and I would lack the strength not to be dependent on you. I might be saddened by something, and you would sense it, as you so often did, and comfort me, gently stroking my hair. And I would feel that comfort and keep on seeking it. In the end you would grow to resent me.

I shall never stand in the way of your happiness, never. No one, certainly not you, shall suffer on my account. I assure you again that you bear neither responsibility nor guilt for the development our relationship has taken. I often feel so lighthearted in your company, so good, that I forget at times that sooner or later we will have to part. I know you well enough by now to be sure that you will never initiate it because you don't want to hurt me, so let me do it for you. It seems that your impending leave is a sign. You know that I am willing to bring any sacrifice on the altar of our friendship, even the one which I desire but know to be wrong: to stay here as you suggested. It is wrong for both of us.

Now, about my future, which worries you so much. Short range, I would like to go to Munich, because we hear that I can find work there. They are looking for people who speak German and Polish and are considered anti-Nazi. I believe I will qualify on both counts. I want to work rather than go to a DP camp, although I may have to if all else fails. As you know, my uncle can and will do everything for me, but I don't want to go to Turkey. He thinks of me as a little girl and will make all decisions for me. He loves me very much, and I realize how lucky I am, but it would be like living in a gilded cage. The bars are confining, and the golden glitter can be very cold.

I don't want to go to Bielsko either until I know that, with God's help, Artur is there. I will consider going to Palestine if the opportunity should present itself, and I pray that it should. It would be the only right place for me after all I have experienced. So you see you need not worry about me; I do have some options, I am free, grow stronger each day, and my illness seems behind me.

It is almost dawn, and I feel that you, too, have not slept. But I had to say what I did, for I sensed something unspoken between us, an unease that I can't bear. Again, please do know how much you mean to me and always will. Take pride and joy in what you did for me, but don't assume any responsibility.

May God give you the happiness that you so richly deserve, and if I should one day find mine, you will be the first to hear about it. No doubt, we will talk more in the morning. May only good things happen to you in your life. I am enclosing a little parting gift, a tiny mezuzah* along with my ardent wish that it may protect you from all evil. Please keep it with you, with all good wishes from your ever understanding

Gerda

I remember crying bitterly after I wrote that letter, feeling hardly as brave as I had pretended to be. Yet at the same time I was satisfied that I had

---

*A capsule containing a parchment scroll or portions of Deuteronomy and the name of God, it is usually affixed to doorposts of Jewish homes in order to protect its occupants from evil.

pulled it off. It was some sort of comfort, and not least a matter of pride. I knew that what I had written was far from the truth, that my feelings ran in quite the opposite direction. I did not want to go to Turkey, but not for the reason I had given. I remembered only too well some remarks my uncle had made during one of his visits to Bielsko: "Die Kleine hat lange Beine und schöne Augen. Wir können eine gute Partie für sie machen." *At the time my uncle's matter-of-fact statement did not sound strange, and I did not question that, according to him, a suitable marriage could easily be arranged for me, the "little one" with "long legs and beautiful eyes."*

Uncle Leo, in his authoritative way, had hatched plans for Artur as well, not only insofar as his career was concerned but also when it came to matrimony. Though ostensibly in jest, he was dead serious. In Turkey alliances with influential families were regarded as business mergers. I knew that my uncle loved me and would never force me to do anything against my wishes; nevertheless he would have no qualms about taking over parental authority. And it wasn't far-fetched at all that I might succumb to such entreaties in memory of my parents. The reason for my reluctance vis-à-vis those prospects was Kurt, and the fact that I was desperately in love with him.

The reference to Palestine was genuine. It was something I did yearn for and was the most logical place for me. The way I saw it, in order to go there I would have to make a permanent commitment to live in that country. How would I handle that once Artur returned? Where would that leave him? Would he join me there? Above all, I must be with him. In those days I could not imagine the great mobility the future would hold. In my heart of hearts I had hoped that Kurt would offer a cogent reason to stay where I was and await further developments.

I can only vaguely recall the conversation I had with Kurt after he received the letter in which I had tried to clarify the situation between us. I do remember that his reaction wasn't excessive, rather making it clear that he had no commitments and that my source must have been misinformed. He readily admitted to corresponding with one girl in particular back in the States, but assured me that no promises had been made on either side. Beyond that he did not elaborate.

I confess that I suffered pangs of jealousy when I thought of some of the wholesome American faces I had seen on photos and among the army nurses I had come into contact with. Next to them I felt at a great disadvantage, as far as my physical condition and appearance were concerned.

Kurt did promise to take me to Munich, though, before going on leave on the Riviera, so that Mala and I could find lodgings and jobs, presumably with the American Civilian Censorship Division.

While it was true, as Gerda had heard through her friend, that I had carried on a correspondence with one girl in particular back in the States, she had assumed that I might be bound by a commitment, which was not the case.

Her lines made me realize all the more what a fateful encounter we had had on May 7, and how she surpassed all that I had been searching for in the woman with whom I would want to share my life. Each time I was able to see her, I would discover more that attracted me about her mind, her demeanor, and her appearance, until it became clear that I was falling in love with her. What I found irresistible was her quick wit, her unwavering principles, and that fire in her radiant green eyes, coupled with her dimpled smile, which was more and more in evidence as time went by. She was possessed of an inner as well as an external beauty that became a powerful magnet for me, and the thought of this special and rare person leaving my life became intolerable.

Despite all that drew me to her, I was still hesitant about my right to tie her to me in view of the many uncertainties I perceived as looming in the immediate future. For one thing, the war with Japan was as yet unresolved, and there was always a chance that I would be sent there for the expected invasion of that country. Once that war ended, I had no idea what job opportunities would exist for me. All I knew was that I could not support a wife, and possibly a family, on the salary at which I had left my job three years earlier. I reasoned that in the normal course of events I would not have felt ready for marriage at that juncture. But these were hardly normal times.

Before boarding a flight for my leave at the Riviera, I had spoken to Captain Presser, who was in charge of the American Censorship Division, about the possibility that Gerda and Mala might work for that agency. Gerda had a job interview there the day after I went on leave.

Munich, August 7, 1945

Dear Kurt,

I'm so glad about the work I'll be doing, now that I seem to have qualified for the job at the American Civilian Censorship Division. It will give me a lot of satisfaction. I'm working against Germany! I know I was not chosen for a noble calling, and I won't be able to do too much, but it means a lot to me to search and perhaps ensure that some of those snakes will not slip back into their skins again.

You know, I can't thank you enough, Kurt. I think you know far too much, but this gives me a new purpose in life and, hopefully, some peace of mind.

Everything went swimmingly, and I take it as a good omen that you too had "happy landings." I'm really in high spirits today and am fully aware that it's all thanks to you. In my mind I'm still giving you some more details. I'm sure you're glad it's only in my mind, aren't you? But you know, I have to tell you everything, and glad tidings right away, so relax! You told me it's your wish to help me, and I don't like to accept help, but yours? Yes, it's a beautiful gesture. In turn, however much understanding I can come up with regarding everything that concerns you is meant to put your mind at ease.

I'm looking forward to an early reunion,

Your Gerda

I was delighted when Kurt returned from his leave on the Riviera sooner than expected. He looked devastatingly handsome, his blue eyes and blond hair in sharp contrast to his deep tan. The reason he gave for his early return was that a severe cold had kept him from enjoying the amenities that verdant, aquamarine paradise had to offer. I had my own thoughts on that, but managed to convey how sorry I was that he had missed a few days of fun by cutting his stay short. It was hardly a true reflection of my feelings, however. "I shouldn't get near you as long as I have this miserable cold," he was saying even as the next moment found us in each other's arms, and I felt his lips on mine.

෩   ෩   ෩   ෩   ෩   ෩   ෩   ෩   ෩   ෩   ෩   ෩

While this brief period of R and R had seemed like the exciting fulfillment of a long-standing dream, the reality was that it pointed up the emptiness of seeing these fascinating sights without the girl I had had to leave behind. My thoughts were back in Munich, and I had time to contemplate the events of the preceding months and the importance they had assumed in my life. While there were unquestionable moments of discovery and enjoyment on the Riviera, what I discovered most of all were my true feelings toward Gerda. The conclusion was inevitable that anything I experienced without her at my side was not being fully lived and that, no matter what the future might hold, I must not lose this person who had become the center of my life.

Munich, August 14, 1945

Dear Kurt,

I am writing to you again because I don't know when you'll be able to free yourself for a visit, and I have such a burning desire to share with you what I am experiencing and feeling.

Do you remember when your friend asked how we celebrated the arrival of the Americans? Can you believe that? What a concept! *Celebration?!* Of course I know he was wasn't there—but didn't he have any idea what it was like, what you found? Do I really have to bare my soul to everyone from the start?

Today was a great and meaningful day, one that might constitute my entry into this new, huge, and unfamiliar world. I am so filled with a jumble of turbulent thoughts and emotions that I simply *have* to share them with you, though I know how lame my descriptive language is.

65

What I glimpsed was a world of true freedom, a world that I have always dimly perceived, of which I dreamed—and it was put into words of reality for me. Kurt, never did I more fully understand your homesickness for America, your yearning for everything American than today. I know it cannot be only a "land of milk and honey"; I realize that even there, pain and disappointment and sorrow must exist. But I have noticed that Americans seem to emanate a type of radiance, perhaps born of the pride that is in their hearts, and nothing inflicted on them can totally eclipse it.

How can I faithfully convey the overwhelming emotion that I experienced as I sat among twenty Germans listening to the words of an American officer? He was trying to clarify the concept of what democracy means in America. Here I sit, alone, the only non-American, the only non-German, caught between two worlds, the one I so desperately wish I could be a part of and the other to which I am relegated.

The voice from the podium was strong, self-assured, full of conqueror's triumph, underscoring again and again: *We* Americans and *you* Germans. Because you did not believe in human freedom you had to settle for unconditional surrender. Tears of joy sprang into my eyes. I found a type of strange understanding I have not been seeking: the joy of those words, yet the pain of being alone to rejoice when hearing them.

Captain Presser is so terribly nice to me, but even she seems to have misunderstood, for she assures me that that message is not meant for me—that I should know that a broad division lies between the civilians here and me. Of course I know that only too well. My body is here, as is my language, but my soul is in America, the country that liberated me and gave me freedom.

Gerda

Once I was living in Munich, Kurt would visit me frequently at the comfortable house that had been found for us nestled at the edge of the Perlacher Forst, inviting woods on the outskirts of Munich. Sometimes our evenings would be spent just talking, a great deal about the past, starting with early childhood. On some occasions we would be joined by some of Kurt's friends as well as Mala's and mine. We were becoming very close, especially those of Kurt's friends who had been present at my liberation. It seemed that the experience had forged a special bond. Most often, however, Kurt and I would leave the others and walk alone in the woods. We would exchange details of our respective workdays, in my case about the letters I had come across or the people I had met in the course of the day. That could set off some lighthearted banter, especially when I would do my impersonations of the characters I had encountered. At other times we would fall silent, holding hands and remembering our families and friends who had been lost. Usually by the time we walked back, it would be under a star-studded sky.

One evening stands out: August 15, 1945. Kurt arrived earlier than usual, exuberant and in a jubilant mood. "The announcement just came through that the war with Japan is over!" he shouted, brandishing a bottle of anisette. Filling me in on the scant details that were available, it was nevertheless clear that the war had truly ended and that he would not have to participate in an invasion of Japan, which had been my main concern.

That marked the first time I tasted "real" alcohol, except for the occasional sip of wine I had been permitted during my girlhood, and the evening remains with me as a heady, delirious blend of joy and relief.

꙾   ꙾   ꙾   ꙾   ꙾   ꙾   ꙾   ꙾   ꙾   ꙾   ꙾   ꙾

Munich, September 6, 1945

Dear Kurt,

It would not be right to express good wishes for the new year only, because good wishes for friends should not be seasonal but permanent. Anyway, without breaking with tradition, I am sending you all good wishes at Rosh Hashanah, now and always. But today, Kurt, is a difficult day in a different sense. It is my beloved mother's birthday, the fourth on which I can no longer put my arms around her.

There are many flowers in my room, and soft music fills the air, evoking her gentle, tender image in an almost sacred word: *Mother.* So many obscure incidents crowd my mind; small, insignificant, everyday childhood memories, taken completely for granted, now becoming legends veiled in the mists of a bygone era. How wonderful it must be to have a mother, to be a mother, to have that unique title that can only belong to one in each family. There can be many children, but they can only call one "Mother." My thoughts go to the one who gave me life, and I think it is symbolic that she was born today, at a time when we are on the threshold of a new year.

I do feel that in all likelihood the year ahead will be the beginning of the most important chapters of my life. I recall this time last year and think of all those eyes looking up to the heavens, and I see Ilse's, moist with tears, as she whispered, "This will be the year—this surely must be the year!" For us in the camps and on the march it was a question of who would live and who would die. Although we tend to measure life within a span of years, the events that chart our course have nothing to do with the calendar. And as far as that is concerned, it surely was a most important year. It finally brought peace and security to the world. For that I am deeply grateful. Above all it was a most important year when I think of you. You have escaped the dangers of an enemy intent on destroying you, and, thank God, you came away whole.

The new year then stands swathed in veils of unforeseeable events. What will it bring? For you the certainty of a return home, of going back to a normal life, no matter what will have changed. Surely the war must have changed you, too. May you find all you hope for, and may the hand of God protect you and shield you from evil and give you peace and contentment, which I believe to be the cornerstones of happiness.

For me, too, it should be a decisive year, a new beginning. What does it hold for me? I wonder. Life—and, I pray, some kind of return "home." Most important, the inferno of the war is over. I am grateful that I can share my thoughts with you, as you keep assuring me that I always should. I do so gladly, with gratitude to have you as my friend.

Gerda

September 13, 1945. I had just returned from work at about six o'clock when I spotted a Jeep in front of the house. It could not be Kurt, I thought. He never comes before eight in the evening except on a Saturday. But then I saw him jump from the vehicle and stride toward me. "Can we go for a walk?" he asked, and I happily agreed. We sauntered through the woods, and for a time there was a strange silence between us. I sensed that I must contain my curiosity. Finally Kurt broke the spell and in a very low voice said, "I won't be able to come on Sunday."

We had planned to attend a piano recital, and I had been eagerly looking forward to it. I asked if he was going to be on duty that day. The reply was unexpected and stunning. "No, I'm going away." Tears began to sting my eyes, but I managed to ask how long his absence would last.

"I'm going home," he said quietly.

Had the earth opened beneath me, I would not have been more startled. The forest around me seemed to sway. I stammered something meaningless about being glad for him, but my throat tightened and my heart beat wildly. I wanted to thank him for all he had done, telling him how much our friendship had meant to me, but instead chose to remain silent, realizing that my voice would betray me.

"Is that all you have to say to me?" His voice was hoarse. This was cruel. Why must he prolong my torture? After what seemed like an interminable pause, he picked up the conversation: "I want you to come to America!" That was the final blow, but I managed a tentative "What should I do there?"

"Be my wife!"

I could only stare, dumbfounded. Had I heard right? Taking my face in his hands, and looking straight into my eyes, he said simply, "Don't you understand? I love you. I want to marry you."

The words penetrated my mind, and a radiance filled my being, waves of happiness, calm, and peace. I heard a bird flutter in the branches of a nearby tree. From far off a horn sounded, while I clutched my precious happiness as though it were a dream about to fade on the border of wakefulness.

I heard Kurt whisper, "I love you. And by some miracle, you love me too. I went into the war to fight, expecting only ugliness and pain, but I found love. I discovered feelings within me that I didn't know existed. I had dreams of an ideal, impossible to attain. I thought it must always remain only a fantasy, yet I found that you surpass all my dreams."

Suddenly I was in Kurt's arms, drinking in his words, oblivious to my surroundings, feeling tossed about like a small vessel on a tempestuous sea, making port at last.

A question rose to the forefront: Is he proposing because he feels sorry for me? Shyly I gave voice to those doubts, but he assured me that although he did feel a responsibility toward me initially because of my suffering, it didn't take long for him to realize that he was in love with me. At the same time he wanted to be sure that I could be happy in his kind of life and with all he could offer. He went on, "But when my orders came through to go home, I knew that I didn't want a life without you."

We both had been reluctant to tell each other how we truly felt during all those weeks. But now the floodgates opened, and the dam holding my joy was about to burst. I could no longer contain my happiness.

It seemed that both of us were like ribbons tossed into the wind, floating through the years, through places unrelated, through incidents significant to each, through this all-consuming, cruel war that had just ended. Was it predestined that we must meet, love each other, and merge our lives?

Kurt broke my musings by offering to sign up for another tour of duty in the occupation forces, allowing us to get married sooner. Another option for him would be to proceed to the United States and send for me as soon as the consulates were in operation. He pointed out that going home now meant finding the right city to settle in and getting a job, all of which would finally allow me to leave Germany sooner. If, on the other hand, he stayed it would have to be for two years.

To let him go, take leave of him, now that I had him for my own? How could I do that? What would my life be like without him, even for a day? I could read in his eyes how much he wanted to go home. I whispered faintly, "Go home," and was unable to say more. Kurt tried to console me by convincing me how much better it would be for our future if he could go to the United States and settle all the uncertainties that loomed ahead.

Before he left that night I had to ask Kurt the question that had been burning on my lips for hours. Standing at the garden gate in the luminous night, I managed to inquire, "When?"

He knew that was coming and was loath to tell me. "Day after tomorrow," he said with a pained look. In forty-eight hours he would be gone!

Unable to fall asleep, I sat at the open window, staring into the velvety night. The moon appeared to beam knowingly as if it had heard my unspoken words of happiness. I could see the twinkling of stars, myriads of them, stretching into infinity. It was a magic night, full of promise, and rich in the possession of love returned.

Before long, though, cold fear crept into my heart, the familiar dread of again losing someone I loved, just as I had lost everyone I had loved in my family. It was a fear of being alone again, of my beloved departing forever.

"Kurt," I called into the night, "Kurt, I love you."

And somehow I felt my cry answered. I knew he must also be awake, that his thoughts were meeting mine, and that there, beyond the sphere of human vision, we met, embraced, and would never be alone again.

The next day, when I arrived home, I found the house filled with flowers. My landlady told me that Kurt had brought them earlier. Champagne *was being chilled in a bucket. The landlady had brought out her best china for the occasion. Several of our friends were present, and they proposed a round of toasts, although I remember none of them. The only reality was Kurt's arm around my shoulder and the clock on the buffet ticking away our final hours together.*

We left the others behind and walked away from the house, seeking to be alone. So much to say, so little time left to say it. The conversation centered around the States, Kurt's family, and the kind of life he envisioned for us. I listened earnestly, but soon my own thoughts began to spin.

Feeling the protectiveness of Kurt's arm around me, I drew my own pictures of our future life together. It still seemed like an unattainable dream: being together and never having to part, his name becoming mine. We would watch the autumn leaves fall, the wind and snow would be at the windows, and we would laugh, have fun, be secure together, much as it had been long ago when I had enjoyed watching storms outside through the windows of my childhood home, safely ensconced amid my family.

In time to come we would be at a party, and I would hear someone say, "That's Kurt's wife." His wife—I shall be his wife!

Kurt posed a question: How many children did I think we should have? I was stunned and overjoyed at the realization that he wanted children, my children. How could I tell him that had been my most ardent wish? Long ago, in the Landeshut camp,* we had spun fantasies about what we would look for in a husband, once the war was over. Much to the amusement of my companions, I told them I would merely ask myself, Do I want him as the father of my children?

I could only marvel at that thought now. There was an incredible joy in knowing that I would soon be married and have children—his children. My happiness was so complete that for a moment I didn't even mind the inevitable separation.

For me children had always been a distant but important dream, the pinnacle of fulfillment. I had always loved babies, even when I was perhaps no older than eight or nine myself. I would quite naturally prefer to play with and care for my younger cousins rather than follow other pursuits. In the slave labor factories I constantly dreamed of some day having children, the ultimate horror being the sterilization programs that we knew

---

*The textile mill/camp, also located in Silesia, to which Gerda and Ilse were transferred after Bolkenhain.

were being carried out in other camps. I would rejoice every month that confirmed that I was still capable of bearing children, while others complained at still having their periods. The camps taught us to improvise, and we would furtively collect dusty textile waste from under the looms, wrap it in whatever scraps of paper we could find, and carefully wash and hoard those treasures for use as sanitary napkins.

Now barely able to believe that he loved me too and wanted to marry me, I could hardly grasp that I might have children with the man who had become my universe. Of course I had known all along that he was fond of me and enjoyed my company, although neither of us had dared to show overtly our true feelings for each other. Although I was still somewhat in awe of him, I found that we truly connected whenever we spoke of our childhood. Then there were the times I felt that we were worlds apart. His was an environment of power and privilege, whereas I was restricted in many ways, coming under the countless regulations that applied to civilians, such as the evening curfew. Frequently, while we were conversing in German, some GI would ask him a question in English, and that always made me painfully aware of my failure to understand what was being said. The gap seemed nearly unbridgeable. He was a citizen of a distant land, where he had a family and friends, enjoyed freedom, while I had no one and belonged nowhere. He was wearing his immaculate uniform while I had only a few hand-me-down items of clothing.

When I looked at the exquisite creatures that stared out at me from the pages of the issues of Life magazine he would bring regularly during those visits, I agonized how I could possibly measure up to those American girls with whom he spoke English, flirted, danced, and apparently carried on a lively correspondence. I felt sure that he must always remember me as he had found me at liberation, weighing sixty-eight pounds, with gray cropped hair, in rags, and not having bathed in three years. How could he then have fallen in love with me? I felt grateful to be on the periphery of his life and could hardly comprehend that he wanted to elevate me to its center.

We walked on, talking, spinning dreams, each climaxed by the miracle of our reunion, that magic day when we would be together again. It must have been long past curfew for me, but we didn't care. I inquired about the time, and Kurt dismissed it by claiming his watch wasn't working.

On the path that led back to the house, we sat down briefly at the edge of the woods. That's when I found the courage to ask how long it would be until I would see him again, and words of reassurance came back: "Short or long," he said tenderly, "my thoughts will always be with you. All my waking hours and my dreams will be about you."

Kurt urged me to think of him whenever I was lonely and to visualize him doing the same. Hesitating for a moment, he said haltingly that perhaps it would be better if he stayed on after all. Everything within me cried out to plead with him to stay, but I found myself persuading him to take the opposite course of action.

Back at the house, we sat on a couch, amid the heavy fragrance of roses in the living room and the scent of candles wafting from the wrought-iron candlesticks. I dreaded these last moments so much that I wanted them to be over. I wished that he would go quickly, knowing it was inevitable anyway. At the same time I was afraid, terribly fearful. I wanted to cry out that I had noticed the second hand moving on his watch, but remained silent.

The night wore on, and Kurt got up several times, once getting as far as the door, but then turning back again. Sitting up from time to time, I dozed in his arms. Now and then I would look up to him, he would kiss me, and I would fall asleep again for a few seconds.

Dawn crept in, gray and ugly, heralding a new day, the day on which we must part. Kurt's driver, Walter, and my friend, Mala, had kept the night vigil with us in a corner of the room, understanding our need to be together until the very final moment of departure.

The time was approaching, and Kurt walked slowly to the window, looking out into the garden. A fine drizzle was falling. Walter embraced me wordlessly, then walked out. In the stillness of the morning, I heard the garden gate squeak, at which point Mala left the room, and we were alone. Kurt put his arm around me, and together we walked down the stairs.

We stood in the doorway during those final moments, and I could see his chin quiver. "Can I take a rose along?" he asked. I tore myself away and ran into the house, snatching a few red roses from the table, then glancing around the deserted room. I couldn't bear the emptiness and hurriedly ran back to Kurt, clinging to him in desperation.

Walter had started the engine, and its noise ruptured the morning silence. I felt tears welling up, but told myself I mustn't cry. I must not cry.

Kurt gently kissed my forehead, my eyes, and my lips.

"I love you," he whispered, smiling, then got into the Jeep, its taillights *blinking sadly, becoming dimmer and dimmer as it faded into the distance. And the damp misty sky cast a shroud over my landscape.*

      ∞   ∞   ∞   ∞   ∞   ∞   ∞   ∞   ∞   ∞   ∞   ∞

Munich railroad station, September 15, 1945

Gerda dearest,

The day which dawned so gray for us is now nearly over, and I am sitting in the waiting room of "Hotel America" [Munich railroad station], meeting your thoughts halfway, while unseen hands are busy setting in motion the wheels that will carry me away from you! Since the same city still harbors both of us, your proximity is yet palpable. It would be easy to imagine that the evening will see us in each other's company, but it cannot be. In a very short while I will take the first step, the relatively short part of the journey: Munich to Paris, which we should reach in approximately thirty-six hours. What happens after that is not clear.

Thoughts come to the fore, a retrospective of the hours that have passed since our farewell. The rain-shrouded dawn that matched our mood, the ride through the sleep-enveloped landscape, its cloak gradually dissolving in the morning light, the golden raindrops hitting the headlights of the vehicle and, growing ever paler, disappearing altogether.

On arrival, a notice awaits me at my quarters, fixing the time of departure for 3 P.M. There follow preparations: trivial, even petty matters that appear ludicrous: yes, mocking challenges that attempt in vain to lay claim to my thoughts. After that everything goes quickly, and before I realize it, the vehicle is waiting in front of the door. Now I am writing this, in the factorylike surroundings of the station's huge hall, turned into a typical staging area for military personnel. It bears quite a bit of resemblance to the USO recreation rooms that serve similar purposes in the States. The ceiling is swathed in huge strips of red-white-and-blue bunting, reminiscent of the American flag, the "Stars and Stripes." And colorful lanterns hang down from the ceiling, while the walls are plastered with cartoons depicting typical GI humor.

A few of the boys are huddled around a piano, and in the center of the area is a "bar," offering the inevitable coffee and doughnuts. The men are either casually sprawled over green folding chairs, or are playing Ping-Pong, or are loafing from one end of the hall to the other. Some even write letters. What a drastic contrast to last night! I see the radiance of your eyes by candlelight, and it sets me to thinking.

This is the second time I am leaving Germany, having to leave behind what is most precious to me. The first time I did not fully perceive the gathering storm. Was it the pain or the anticipation or both that kept me from clearly recognizing the coming peril? Meanwhile the terrifying drama has taken its inexorable course; I have witnessed only its first and last acts, somehow remaining in the background. The curtain has come down, but you, the protagonist, still remain where the tragedy was played out.

I cannot find any peace until you, too, have become a mere spectator of those events and at least a small part of the compensation that should be yours will have eased the pain. Just know that the nightmare is over, and the future lies before us in brighter colors! With that in mind, I want to call out to you, Gerda: Be brave! I have full confidence in the fact that both of us will soon be very, very happy.

> In high spirits I embrace you and kiss you, your
> Kurt

Le Vesinet, September 17, 1945

My Dearest,

Three evenings lie between us now. How many seconds does that add up to, during which my thoughts were with you, Gerda? It's an oppressively hot summer night here in Paris, unusual for this time of the year. Or is it merely too long since I can remember a hot September like this?

We're staying in a suburb of Paris, in magnificent environs: splendid villas, surrounded by beautiful ponds, avenues, meadows, greenery as far as the eye can see. There's talk we'll most likely be here for six days, then on to a larger staging area somewhere in France or Belgium. Presumably we'll board ship at the beginning of October and a likely bet will be Le Havre or Antwerp, because they are the most logical ports.

First a few words about the trip so far. It lasted only thirty hours, in addition to which we got the "gift" of an hour due to a change of time. It turned out that the train was far more comfortable than we had expected. These were express train cars in good condition, even upholstered, and we settled in and made ourselves at home, though not without a big hassle with the luggage, which proved to be ten times too bulky, even after drastic reductions.

Of course, long periods of waiting ensue until the train gets underway, but by that time everybody is so fatigued that, thanks to our military training, we are able to fall asleep sitting up, or at least doze off inter-mittently.

When I wake up, to my surprise, we make a major stop in Karlsruhe. I say "surprise" because I know this city fairly well. After all, three of my uncles and their families once lived there, along with more distant relatives. Outside I spot a number of kids running across the tracks to beg for chewing gum. We expect to eat in the terminal proper, but are loaded onto huge trucks and transported to a large building somewhere in the city. Along the way I recognize details, among them the apartment once occupied by one of those Karlsruhe families. We pass along streets less familiar, now somewhat "modified," although I get the impression they are not as bombed out as those I saw in Munich.

We disembark and get into line for our chow break . . .

Love, Kurt

Munich, September 18, 1945

My most precious Kurt,
Another day has passed. Now the rest of your team is following you and came to say good-bye to us. And, again, I experience the pain of parting. For me, taking leave of anyone on whose sleeve the "A"* is displayed becomes difficult.

Now, first and foremost, I must thank you for your letter, which came so unexpectedly and brought me so much joy. I sought solitude, I wanted to be totally alone while reading it. Your photo stands in front of me—your flowers are still fragrant. The quiet, measured ticking of the little clock reminds me that each and every minute moves you farther and farther away from me.

Kurt, your letter touched me so much. Perhaps I should not say it because you don't want me to dwell on it, but I am so longing for you. I am glad that I can work, or I would fear the approach of madness. You write so movingly, so tenderly of our parting, of your thoughts at your departure. I, too, could not sleep and waited for the stirrings of the new day to drown out the droning of the motor that took you away from me—so far, so terribly far. Please don't be angry at the tone of this letter, but

*Third Army insignia.

I must write what I feel. You could sense it if I didn't. All my thoughts and emotions concerning you must be genuine.

Yes, for the third time in my life I am experiencing the excruciating pain that all that is dearest to me and to which I clung the most has been taken from me. First Artur, then my parents, and now you. Forgive me for not being as brave as I should have been when I said good-bye to you. But I promise you I shall be from now on.

You see, from the moment that I was permitted to think of you differently, to think of you as mine, the thought processes about my parents changed. My pain is losing its burning rage, the sharp edge of bitterness is softened by your love. The pain is deep but calmer now, and I have regained my aim in life once more: to live for someone I love, to pray for him, to make him happy.

The night before Yom Kippur, I went to the cantorial concert I had hoped you would also be able to attend. How differently I had visualized that evening!

Instead of with you, I went with the two boys from Berlin, and Mala. I completely buried myself in my seat. There is nothing more moving than music, the soothing, uplifting language without words that lets you dwell in a sphere detached from reality. It made it possible to be alone with you. And there, deep in my soul, stirred the haunting melody of Kol Nidre. It all came together, everything that was torn asunder was coming together, melding, forging something whole, something calming. I felt my father's hands on my head, reciting a benediction, and I whispered a prayer, the wish for him to bless you.

On Yom Kippur I could not go to a place where many people were gathered (maybe once there is a temple again, I will be able to go). The sanctuary I chose to commune with God was "our woods," where we often walked in silence, holding hands. And there, in the holiness, alone with nature, I retraced our steps and wordlessly prayed for our future.

I don't believe there is anything more exalted, more lofty than to feel a piercing shaft of light enveloping your being, uplifting and joyful. It is like looking into the mirror and seeing that you are still the same, yet knowing you are not. I am awed and grateful that that privilege was given to me.

So I think I have brought you up-to-date a bit, and hope you are assured that I am very strong. I only wish I could be certain that my letters will reach you, for I want to write every day, but don't know whether I dare to bother Captain Presser so often. I will be sending this letter through your companions, who will mail it to your sister's address. And I will continue to write regardless.

I just looked up at your picture, and you smiled. Are you laughing at me? How dare you. I am thinking how much work you have ahead of you now. How I wish that I could help you.

You write so to the point—how the curtain fell on the stage of our life's play, the action still thundering in our ears while others are oblivious to our drama. Fortunately the curtain fell on acts of pain and horror but did not rise again on that scene, because fate so kindly changed the sets, as we, the protagonists, listened to the prompter: our hearts. You were the first to exit, and I am eager to follow, to take our tale to a happy ending. Let us stretch our arms toward each other, until we can do it together. I love to echo your words that "We will be very, very happy together." Let that be the final applause that will erase the pain of the past. My thoughts of you are the core of my existence. They can conquer all obstacles.

> I embrace you with many kisses,
> Gerda

Paris, September 20, 1945

My dearest, dearest Gerda,
Our dark red roses are wilting, but I can't bear to leave them behind. They are a part of you, something you gave me, and, better than anything else, let me bridge time and space in order to be with you.

Meanwhile my impressions of Paris continue, but not without reporting them to you. Otherwise there's no fun to it. I had intended this time to catch up on everything I missed during my first visit here in March. Basically, of course, it is a rather futile endeavor, because you can't view Paris in the conventional sense. You have to live it. Since that is impossible in the time at my disposal, I can only convey superficial observations, like those of any ordinary tourist.

Quite aside from the opulence that it so abundantly displays, it's the small things that I like best so far, such as the elegant stores, despite their sky-high prices. They do give the impression of normality; no destroyed buildings here, no bombed-out sections of the city, no crowded streetcars, and, above all, no Germans! It feels like a touch of home, to have to dodge traffic while crossing the street, or to thunder along in the

Métro, almost like in New York. Only one thing is different: Missing is the odor of chewing gum, which, as I remember, permeates all the labyrinthine passages and platforms of the New York subway system.

During the entire course of my army career, I've never run around as much as I have during the past few days. That instills the hope that some of my civilian duds may still fit me on my return. Wherever I go here, I always come across the same military clubs, which are a welcome haven with their luxurious appointments. From there it's always best to plan your next step because all the necessary information is available. The meals are good in the hotels, and gradually you become human again after an especially hot afternoon in the cauldron of the city. Of course our dress code is far too warm: If fall is indeed around the corner, Paris is not aware of it.

The night before last I attended the Marigny Theater, near the Champs-Élysées, for a performance of an English comedy with an English cast. I have to admit that after all I had heard about it, I found it rather disappointing. English humor, at best, comes across as somewhat lame to American audiences, and these actors didn't exactly bring out the full effect either. It was about an American pilot who spends a few days in the home of an earl and shows his gratitude by nearly derailing the close and moving relationship between the earl and his fiancée (while jeopardizing a gain of nearly eight million dollars for the girl's father). The funniest part for me was the accent of the alleged "American lieutenant."

During the intermissions we went outside, and that proved to be by far the better part of the spectacle. Off in the distance, over the Champs-Élysées, two rows of lights led to the stunningly illuminated dome of Les Invalides, while a brilliant pillar of light, coming from the left side of the axis formed by the Champs, pointed to the Place de la Concorde. That was balanced on the right by the inimitable edifice that is the Arc de Triomphe, bathed in beams of searchlights. An entirely new and unforgettable view. Shortly thereafter, the Métro took me to the Gare St. Lazare, from where it was a half-hour train ride to the suburb in which I'm quartered.

How is everything with you, and how did you spend Sukkoth?* In general, what all happened?

Thinking of you constantly,
Your Kurt

*Jewish harvest festival.

What memories that letter evoked!

He is in Paris! How well I recall the day Paris fell to the Germans. The blaring of the loudspeakers at every street corner, the jubilant outcries of the victory-intoxicated crowds. The triumphant voices of the announcers, "Paris ist unser! Die Welt gehört uns," *their arrogant, self-satisfied proclamation that Paris was theirs and the prediction that the world would soon be theirs as well.*

My parents had huddled in their chairs, Papa paler than usual, his trembling hand spilling the Baldrian Tropfen* *he took for his ailing heart over his frayed shirt, desolately whispering, "Can no one stop them?" A day later, those imposing sights were splashed over every newspaper: prominent pictures of the Eiffel Tower, the Arc de Triomphe, serving to highlight the triumph of the* Wehrmacht, *its endless formations marching toward it, along the Champs-Élysées. All the same pictures I had seen in my French schoolbooks provided an ironic backdrop to the German conquest. "C'est Paris, la Ville Lumière," Madame Rose, our French teacher, had pointed out with pride. Now the spider claws of the swastika held those imposing sites in their grip.*

But Papa, Papa—Kurt is in Paris; he is there right now, walking along the boulevards in his American uniform! Papa, my poor Papa, if only you could know. Will I ever see Paris? Perhaps at some distant future date we might go there, so that Kurt can show me that luminous city. Quite likely though, once I leave I will never again return to Europe.

Paris, September 21, 1945

My dearest Gerda,

If only it were possible to get some mail from you; it's such a peculiarly empty feeling to be totally cut off from you.† I long so much for the day when I can at least receive a few lines from you, not to mention our reunion, which simply has to and *will* happen soon.

My sightseeing continues. I decided to take the bus to Versailles,

---

*Valerian drops.
†By being constantly in transit, without a temporary forwarding address.

although I usually shy away from arranged excursions. The monotonous litany recited by guides always puts me to sleep. Fortunately this truly splendid palace, with its colorful landscaping, requires few words, and if I stood there with my mouth open, it wasn't because I had an urge to yawn. It far surpassed all descriptions, especially from the outside. You can only wonder how much time, patience, artistic genius, and man-hours of labor went into such an excess of opulence. All this, surrounded by fantastic parks and pavilions, marble statues, swans floating in ponds, and thatched-roof summer retreats in rustic style. How I wish you could have been there with me.

Embracing and kissing you, and in the hope that all is well,
Your Kurt

Paris, September 21, 1945

Dear Gerda,

Today is the last day of our Paris stay. Once again we packed, filled out forms, stood roll call, and waited to take the train in the late afternoon. Our destination: Thionville, in the vicinity of Metz. Don't know exactly what awaits us in that town, but scuttlebutt has it that, contrary to our expectations, we're heading for Marseilles from there. We'll see—it actually makes little difference, as long as we're homeward bound, and soon!

I still took time to see what could be seen and halfway digested in a relatively brief period. All along I'm always conscious of how much your presence is missing in all this, my love. It simply wasn't what it could have been. My thoughts, in fact, alternated so much between Munich and New York that I had a hard time concentrating on Paris. I did get to attend the variety show performed by our troops, which really turned out well. Naturally everything was geared toward the impending demobilization, which provides grist for the mill, as far as that type of humor is concerned.

Last night absolutely nothing was going on in town, so we returned early after having "done the city" in a thorough fashion, from the Arc de Triomphe to the banks of the Seine, with their quaint bookstalls that offer all sorts of used books and artists' sketches. Once more we went up Montmartre, where I acquired some nice watercolors and etchings. I wish you could give me your opinion on them in person. After that we closed the chapter of Paris with a bottle of Burgundy, without much sentimentality. We had had our fill of Paris; our impatience appears to outweigh all the glitter of that much-sung-about city. To be honest it seemed somewhat superficial and dissipated to me, and I'm leaving without regret.

I'm curious about everything that has happened in your vicinity meanwhile. With never-ending, loving kisses,

Kurt

Munich, September 23, 1945

My dearest beloved Kurt,

It is Sunday, a long, long day. The first in many weeks that does not find us together. Until now I somehow retained the illusion that you are still here and that you will arrive at any moment. Yet the reality of this weekend dispelled that.

We had marvelous autumn weather all week, only blue skies and bright sunshine. And now, today, a relentless rain whips against the windowpanes. How strange that I can't recall such a sad, depressing weekend as this. So I am sitting all alone (no, I am not sad), your photograph in front of me, adorned with fresh roses, and lovely music wafting through the room.

Are ocean waves beating against the hull of the ship that is carrying you home, perhaps similar to the whipping rain against my windowpanes? Your small radio has given Mala and me so much pleasure; it transports me to another world and aids my flights of fancy.

I have not mentioned nor thanked you for the envelope I found after your departure. Your "Dimples" is angry at you, but only to a certain extent, for I am deeply touched by your concern to take care of me and all my needs. But didn't I tell you that along those lines there is nothing I require? My salary from the Civilian Censorship Division is adequate to pay for my keep. I shall bring the envelope with me when I come. I am sure there will be many things we will need to acquire. But thank you! Thank you!

I let my thoughts of the joy that lies ahead envelop me, but delving into the immediate past gives me chills. How strange and unbelievable life is. I can't fathom a life without you, you who are the very core of it. Thoughts of you fill my entire being, and yet five months ago I did not know of your existence. I can't even think of what dangers you faced before we met, what might have happened to you. And on my end, thousands upon thousands of incidents and twists of fate could have prevented us from ever meeting. I am in awe of that realization and thank our destiny and my lucky stars. Somehow, harking back now to my darkest hours and most difficult moments, I perceive, if only dimly, the force that impelled me to take the path I did. It all stems from the promise given to my brother, to go on for our parents' sake, to live for them. But was it something beyond that? Perhaps some feeling of a very personal, subconsciously perceived goal, a distant star of promise that made me keep a rendezvous with my own destiny, with happiness, with you!

What lies ahead in our lives to come? What mystery, what secrets does fate have in store for us? I am full of confidence that providence will deal kindly with us. Therefore I implore you, don't worry about me, don't let your concerns about my past or my present state spoil the joy and anticipation of your homecoming. Don't let *anything* obscure it. You see, my mind is over there, and I can experience it with my heart, which is always with you!

I am sorry if my letters lack form and style; they are random thoughts put down helter-skelter. At the office I read so many bad letters every day that even if I had a style, it would suffer through exposure to what crosses my desk daily. So please bear with me. I am chatting on about nothing and everything that I have the need to share with you. And I am eager to learn all there is to know about you. I do not want to pry, because my faith in you is limitless and was so from the moment I first laid eyes on you. But I do want to know what hurts you, what topics pain you, what areas you are sensitive about. Thus I will learn never to do or say anything that might hurt you or cause anguish. I want us to be joyful. Your love and caring has already unleashed my pent-up emotions. With you I have been able to laugh again as I never thought I could. I guess there is no pain or sorrow that love can't heal.

Thank you for your letter that expresses those same sentiments for our future. Your words fell on fertile ground; I feel so strong, so confident with the thought of your arms around me. I know that a desire will grow within me to be able to help you achieve your goals. It is wonderful that we both are so young, and in a few months spring will once again be here—this time our bright, new, fragrant spring. The rain still beats against the window without letup, but I can't think of it as tears that heaven sheds; rather as the balm that generates new growth.

I must close for now; my friends are coming.

Ten thousand kisses. Yours,
Gerda

Jarny [near Metz], September 25, 1945

Dearest Gerda,

I hope you weren't without news from me for more than a day. We only arrived here in Jarny last night, and at last I can take care of some personal matters. On one hand it wasn't to be expected that the army would put a "magic carpet" at our disposal to transport us from Paris to Metz; on the other we weren't quite prepared for the mule-like behavior of the French railroad system. The train turned out to be totally unpredictable, so that what is normally a six-hour ride, in this case projected to take fourteen hours, actually turned into twenty-three. By that time we were still far from the barracks that were our temporary destination.

Today was a fairly busy day, but we can already determine that the next ten days we'll presumably be spending here will run their uneventful course. As far as we know, we'll then be shipped to Marseilles by train, where it'll take a certain amount of time until we can embark and spend another two weeks on board the vessel. That confirms my previous estimate that it'll take till the end of October before we reach New York. You know, Gerda, it's not only the waiting, but I feel that every day still spent in Europe is a tremendous waste of time for both of us. By this time, if I were over there, I could be preparing so much to facilitate your coming. The sitting around inactively is driving me up the wall. At the same time I miss you so terribly, my love, and can't help wondering how everything is shaping up for you. No matter how smoothly everything may be going, new problems always surface, and at any rate how can I have peace of mind as long as you remain in Germany?

Regards to the Berliners, and you, my sweet, stay well!

Kisses from your ever-loving
Kurt

Dearest Gerda,

Today I can hardly claim to have earned my keep. It must mean something if I already consider this loafing too much because I'm not that easily intimidated by it. But, as mentioned, if it goes on this way the army will soon go bankrupt. It's even gotten to the point where I'm ready to watch a bad movie.

My dearest, how are you spending your spare time? Mainly at home, is my guess. A change now and then would be good; it would provide some diversion. If possible attend some concerts or whatever else is being offered. No sense in shutting yourself off from everything. While I don't expect it, I would be very glad to hear that you did something amusing or stimulating. In my opinion the Censorship Division can only *partly* contribute to your entertainment.

It just dawned on me that I didn't get to see your new dress after all. Well, just you wait! Don't ever complain that I didn't admire your new dress, hat, etc., because I'm simply not the type who notices those things. I must caution you, Gerdush, you'll throw up your hands because of all the flattery you won't hear! But you'll permit me to embrace you and do penance, won't you, my beloved?

Kurt

Jarny, September 27, 1945

Dear Gerda,

The days pass all too slowly; I feel like jumping out of my skin. It would almost be preferable to row the three thousand miles instead of having to wait for a ship. Now I sit here, a day's journey from you, feeling utterly helpless. The fact that I'm totally shut off from you for the time being doesn't improve my mood. My favorite pastime—and simultaneously the worst torture—is thinking of you, dearest! I can't imagine everything that took place in Munich since September 15. May I hope for your lines at the time of my arrival?

Our present location is quite familiar to me. As was the case with so much other territory, the Fifth Division liberated this place exactly one year ago. It's a strange feeling to drive through well-remembered sites that give an entirely different impression these days because of their peculiarly peaceful appearance. It's almost impossible to imagine that these same villages and fields exist normally today, while we harbor a vivid recollection of the thunder of big guns and the whistling of shells. That's how we knew it, and that's how it sticks in my memory.

Here and there some traces of the war are still visible, but by and large the wounds have healed and only scars remain. How odd to look over maps in the present, which we used to study for days until we were familiar with every terrain feature, right down to every brook and clump of woods, it seemed. It used to evoke the same questions a thousand times over: "How many troops are in those woods?" "Where are the machine-gun positions?" etc., ad nauseam.

Even the armory in which we are staying at the moment is not strange to us. I have a vague recollection of part of the division having been quartered here. I have to admit that I'm in a pretty vile mood after spending a few days in these desolate, dilapidated buildings. It's beyond belief how anybody could put up such inferior barracks—or what's even more difficult to fathom, how anybody can live in them. One thing is sure: Those French soldiers were certainly not pampered.

I'd best conclude this before a lot of the nonsense becomes too conspicuous.

> Good night, my sweet. A heartfelt kiss; with all my love, your
> Kurt

Jarny, September 29, 1945

Dearest little Gerda,

If it's really true that *"Faulheit stärkt die Glieder,"** then I fully expect to attain the reputation of a Samson. Last night, though, I had to make do with "only" eleven hours of sleep, but I made up for it in the afternoon, especially since I was left totally exhausted and had to plop down on my sleeping bag after a few sets of Ping-Pong.

Under the circumstances my transition to civilian life may be formidable. Just imagine, I might actually have to earn my daily bread through *work* one of these days! Impossible, after having tasted such things as breakfast in bed. To make matters worse, once we hit American soil after this period of *dolce far niente*,† we'll allegedly get a month's leave before being discharged.

---

*German proverb: "Work sweetens life, while laziness strengthens your limbs."
†Sweet idleness.

86

Joking aside, that happens to work out well for me, because it'll allow me to take my time about finding a position in New York and to take care of all my (or rather *our*) affairs. Aside from that I can remain in uniform until I claim my civilian duds in Buffalo. Of course I'll have to acquire a lot of new stuff, but some of the old will still come in handy, provided the moths haven't got to it. It's also possible that I'll remain in Buffalo altogether, although I have a few compelling reasons, well-known to you, that draw me toward New York. In general life in Buffalo is more relaxed, though at the same time less eventful. But wherever I wind up, as long as you are with me, I'll be happy!

I've become friendly with a captain, someone whom I couldn't stand in Freising, oddly enough. I still consider him a bit flippant and judgmental when it comes to others, but find that I can have the most stimulating conversations with him. I'm always fascinated to discover these unexpected sides of a personality, which often provoke nothing but perplexed headshaking among my friends and acquaintances, many of whom can't stand each other.

I haven't seen Walter since last week; he was sent to a different barracks. How are you spending this Saturday evening, my love? Could it be that you're also engaged in writing at the moment? It just turned 9 P.M. and it's too early to turn in, but I can dream of you at any time! Many kisses from your

Kurt

Munich, September 30, 1945

Dearest Kurt,

Just a little while ago, Henry* left—he came to say good-bye. I guess this is probably the last time I'll see the emblem of the Fifth Division on someone's sleeve. To take leave of a wearer of that symbol associated with you is difficult and sad. Hanka, Luba, and Mala are here, but my eyes were searching for your picture, trying to make you life-size and fitting you into the conversation.

I do have to share some nice news with you. I no longer work on the third floor but was promoted to be in the vicinity of Captain Presser and now work on diplomatic mail. It means being more on my toes for veiled clues, but thus far have not found much. Most of the letters are pretty

*A member of Kurt's team of intelligence specialists.

silly, and some are badly written and outright stupid. Well, maybe something will turn up. But I am glad about the promotion and it does seem glamorous for me to sit in the diplomatic section.

I was glad when everybody left—now I am again alone with you. What are you doing this very instant? Are your thoughts meeting mine? As long as you were here, I somehow found it easier to write to you—now that this is the only way of communicating, it seems difficult. And I long to tell you everything, despite the fact that my letters are not terribly interesting when compared with yours, telling of your adventures in such exciting, exotic places. You describe balmy nights in Paris, while here the weather has changed drastically. It's true: autumn, cold, rainy, and windy. The streetcar still stops at Sendlinger-Tor and tortuously snakes its way toward Töbenerplatz; by then darkness has fallen and I get off. I can barely make out the woods in which we walked, and the leaves* on my calendar are falling off, along with those on the trees—not rapidly enough, though.

Yesterday was a sort of historical first! Here in Munich, in the cradle of Nazism, the first Jewish wedding (presumably since 1939) took place! Everybody who is Jewish was invited. Unfortunately I couldn't go, because Hanka† told me that she would be arriving from Passau around the time I expected to be home from work. But Mala and Günther went, and of course I was very curious to hear all about it. Then, when I got home, I found a note from Hanka that she had been at the house but had been offered a ride back to Passau and therefore couldn't wait for me. So I missed the wedding and Hanka, but I hope they got married even without me, and will be very happy. Mala came home utterly disappointed. She too missed the wedding, but for a different reason: They couldn't find the house where it was taking place!

Keep well! I embrace you with much love and many kisses.
Gerda

---

*In German, *Blätter* means both "pages" and "leaves."
†Hanka and I had known each other since the Grünberg factory/camp, where both of us were slave laborers. Hanka was of immense help to me on the death march, giving me two potatoes when no food had been available for days. She also disobeyed an order by an SS guard to take my boots, thus probably saving my life.

Gerda, my dearest,

Being apart from you is a condition that is impossible to get used to. Parting from you has created a vacuum that will only be filled again once we are reunited. And there is no way of reconciling myself to that. After all, no substitute can fully simulate your proximity. For example, I consider letter writing at best an opiate that has all the symptoms of a stimulant. Perhaps it's possible to forget someone's absence for a few brief moments, but it's never a real substitute!

I wish you could let me know now everything that's happening. I assume this is about the time when that man* will be returning from Bielsko. And with what results? How happy it would make me to see the fulfillment of your hopes, which are also mine. I would so much like to be able to share everything with you personally, as always.

I just read something in the newspaper that brightens my day considerably: An American consulate is scheduled to open in Berlin in about six weeks. Thus far the absence of one was the foremost obstacle that I feared might unnecessarily delay your immigration. Now everything can be projected in a much clearer fashion; somehow you'll make it to Berlin, if that has to be. In former times there was also a consulate in Stuttgart, but I doubt that it will resume its function. There was no mention of that. I still believe that Turkey could serve as a way station for you, and I wrote to your uncle along those lines. To be exact, that letter has been committed to paper, but I purposely refrained from putting it in the mail on the assumption that the postal service will work better from the States.

And that brings me to my favorite speculation: When will I leave Europe behind? Let's hope that the first of the month will be the turning point. After all, October is allegedly the month that will take us home. According to a "reliable source," our departure from here for Marseilles is scheduled to take place on October 3, but nobody dares to predict when we'll get there, how long we'll stay, and how many days the crossing will take. We have a favorite saying in the army, which is also relevant to this case: "Hurry up and wait!" In other armies they sing a similar tune. . . .

Last night we had what can be considered a pleasant surprise. A few USO girls burst in here quite unexpectedly with their motorized kitchen, inclusive of built-in loudspeakers, and proceeded to serve totally fresh doughnuts, along with the usual coffee, of course. And that just at a time

*An acquaintance who went back to Bielsko to find out who had survived the war.

when we were discussing what to do about our rumbling stomachs. Some mathematical genius claims to have figured out that those same doughnuts, which can be bought for three cents apiece in the States, cost no less than fifty-three cents in Europe, if you count the cost of personnel training, the freight, etc. There is no end to our perverse pleasure in determining how much money the army is losing on us for every day they keep us here unnecessarily.

> But enough for today; to be continued tomorrow.
> Take my most ardent kisses,
> Your Kurt

Calas [Marseilles staging area], October 6, 1945

Gerda dearest,

Today is an especially sunny day in more than one respect. The reason? I came into possession of your marvelous lines. Do you know what it means to see that beloved, familiar handwriting after an interval that seemed like an eternity to me? It was as though the sun had come out after those dark clouds of uncertainty, anxiety, and longing.

My thanks and appreciation for confiding everything to me that is of concern to you. Our harmony would not be complete if it were any other way. I felt all the richer for having been allowed to share all your emotions. Yes, it wouldn't be the "you" of whom I gained a part and am closely tied to if I could only know one side of you. That's how it will always have to be between us, don't you agree? My spirits have now been so immeasurably lifted that it makes the waiting until your next message infinitely easier.

It was moving to hear how you spent Yom Kippur. As desirable as it might have been to attend a synagogue service, I find it equally meaningful that you gave expression to your faith in the midst of nature. At any rate I sense the existence of a supreme being and can be closest to Him, can best bridge the unknown gap in a setting of nature and music. That's how I perceive the meaning of life, of which you write in the most straightforward manner.

Many thanks for the program, which must have been excellent. I'm doubly sorry to have missed it, but as far as music is concerned, we'll manage to fill many gaps once we are reunited. The melodies that took shape and filled the room are constantly going through my mind, and that's one way of being with you.

As much as I look forward to your mail, I can only hope you didn't use my military address too much. I should have made that clearer to you, because as matters stand, my constant moving around will deprive me of your letters for quite a long while to come. Although they will reach me eventually, the fastest way is still via my sister. On the other hand, I've had second thoughts about your availing yourself of Captain Presser's office. She probably has enough points by now to qualify for discharge. In case that happens, I can only hope you'll find a substitute soon. And by all means, do let me know about it right away. The prospect of my mail to you floating around somewhere between two continents is not exactly encouraging, especially when I imagine how long you might be without news from me.

I'll report later about the trip itself and the new camp; for the moment just a few words about what we can expect here: The prospects for embarkation within three to four days look good. Presumably we'll leave soon thereafter. Because nobody's informed us yet as to the type of ship we'll be taking, it's hard to estimate the date of arrival in the States. The crossing can take anywhere from eight to seventeen days, so we wouldn't be very disappointed to get there within two weeks.

> Without further ado, my most ardent kisses and the
> promise to write more, soon.
> Your Kurt

In June 1940, nine months after World War II had begun, we in the United States were still reeling from the unexpectedly rapid fall of France. Once again the Wehrmacht *had carried out its lightning strikes to perfection, and no military power seemed capable of stopping its advance.*

By October of that year, my sister, my brother, and I took a bitter personal blow in addition to the dismaying military news. Although the prospects looked dismal, we were nevertheless trying to find an escape route for our parents who, by now completely isolated, were still living in my hometown of Walldorf.

It was then that we received a letter from a relative residing in Switzerland, apprising us of the most recent catastrophy that had overtaken our parents. On October 22 they, along with all the Jews still living in the two German provinces of Baden and the Palatinate, had been deported on an hour's notice to the then unoccupied zone in southern France. There they had been left in the Camp de Gurs, under the most extreme conditions of hardship. Their fate was now in the hands of the Vichy government, which was collaborating with the German occupiers of France.

For almost two years following my parents' internment, we were to go through an endless exercise in futility that brought us tantalizingly close to rescuing them on several occasions, only to be overtaken each time by events and human-made obstacles beyond our control. In anticipation of obtaining an American visa, Father had been transferred to the Camp des Milles, outside Marseilles, where the American consular offices were located. Mother had followed later, being accommodated at the Hotel Levante, quarters that could bear the appellation "hotel" by only the farthest stretch of the imagination. It was from those two addresses that our letters to them were returned in the fall of 1942, stamped: "Addressee moved—left no forwarding address." The supreme irony was to come subsequently in the form of a letter from the State Department, granting approval of their visas, two-and-a-half months after they had been deported to Auschwitz, as we were to find out after the war.

Marseilles, October 7, 1945

My beloved Gerda,
There is a letter for you—incomplete—back at the camp. Meanwhile I had occasion to visit the city proper, about sixteen miles from our quarters. So I'll report about my day in town instead.

At the moment I'm sitting at the Red Cross Club, an ultimate haven for any GI in a strange town. It's always a way to freshen up, get information, or write letters. From where I'm sitting I can get a glimpse of the harbor I'll be leaving either tomorrow or the day after. The sounds of music from a trio are putting me in the right frame of mind to share my impressions with you.

Today is a somber day for me, because it was here in Marseilles that my beloved mother bore the heavy burden of those last difficult months that led to her being torn away and consigned to the black abyss of the unknown. For me this city will always be connected with those unfulfilled expectations, the desperation, and the last contacts with my precious parents. I *had* to see the site that witnessed the sweeping tide of that cruel, horrendous time: a shabby, insipid, third-class hotel that had housed a number of elderly women in its tiny rooms some three years ago. Gerda, can you imagine how I felt when I saw the address—so familiar to me—standing before me in reality? With what hope and trepidation had I clung to that loathsome location during those days! Somehow it struck me as particularly painful to see the American flag waving over the entrance, a sign that American troops had recently occupied this now-vacant building. Too late, too late! Why was Mother never privileged to take in that view?

How can I tell you what thoughts assailed me when I entered the hotel? Was this the room where Mother spent those dark nights in anguish? Are these the corridors that echoed her hopes, her doubts, her prayers? And are these the walls that reverberated the endless discussions with her companions in agony, and whose focal point always came back to the one topic that was left to hope for: "When will we be reunited with our children?"

At that time it was Father's lot to be confined in a nearby camp [des Milles], getting permission from time to time to pay a visit, until that, too, ceased and the great silence set in. What really passed during those visits, each one of which could be the last, each farewell that could be final and laden with ominous premonitions?

All the same I am so grateful that I could be here, that I was able to follow in the footsteps left by my beloved parents. All this after a span of time that, depending on how you look at it, can be regarded as either the blink of an eye or eternity. Following their tracks, my thoughts united me with them.

I had an urge to find a house of prayer and came across a temple, magnificent and untouched, where in solitude and without disruption I found some release. It was liberating to include you in my thoughts and to realize what happy approval and warm welcome you would have been assured of from my parents. You give me so much, Gerda, my dearest!

Tomorrow I'll finish the other letter; meanwhile I send special greetings and embrace you, your

Kurt

Calas, October 7, 1945

My dearest Gerdush,
Now my report continues, although I will probably not have enough time this morning to finish what I started here. There are constant interruptions because this or that still needs to be attended to, despite the hope

of finally being done with all preparations. Going to Europe was so much easier than doing the reverse now. This may well be peace, but the paper war continues unabated. Wherever we go we need to fill out dozens of forms with three, four, or five copies, only to have to tear them up at the next point and start from scratch. I sign everything automatically and expect to have writer's cramp at any moment. So far everything seems to move along smoothly, though, and it's almost certain that we'll board ship on the ninth. That's the main thing, after all.

Now my nerves will only act up again once I take the subway from the railroad station to my sister's home. It's possible that we won't land in New York, rather in some port in Virginia. In that case we'd have another train trip that would take us to New York in one to two days. But that's only one of the countless rumors that are currently circulating. Somebody claims to have seen our ship and reports that, contrary to our expectations, it's not one of those freighters that were built in a hurry and in which most of the troops are returning, although those buckets were never meant as troop transports. To much general relief it's supposed to be a regular navy ship. However that may be, it doesn't really matter if you consider that the boys would just as soon *swim* home if that would turn out to be faster. It's allegedly going to take only eleven days to get there. That's how the rumor mill operates incessantly. But you learn to take everything with a grain of salt. Aside from that everybody is in high spirits, and if there are a few who are anxious, it's about their reaction to the jocular play of wind and waves. Seasickness for me? That's out of the question! That's all in your mind, isn't it? Even as a young boy, I could never understand how it's possible to get seasick. I was always an admirer of even the steepest roller coasters and could never get enough of them. Oh, well, I suppose I'll soon find out how the years can change you. In the end I should be able to rely on the usual pills, because it would hardly do for the conquering hero to arrive in dismal condition. Can't disappoint the cheering throngs, after all.

Enough of this nonsense; what I really wanted to describe was the train ride from Metz to Marseilles. Despite its duration of fifty-three hours, it turned out to be more pleasant than the one from Paris to Metz. At our disposal were second-class wagons that allowed us to settle in comfortably. You could call these compartments minimodels of the democratic process. Everybody in them shows concern for the others, and if there are any suggestions by anybody, it's only by unanimous consent that they can be carried out. All occupants try to be helpful and in general do everything to make life as easy as possible.

Some favorite pastimes were reading and card playing (hundreds of dollars changed hands). Everybody contributed some snacks to the general pool of chocolate, fruit, tomatoes, etc., and a young Negro lieutenant had managed to bring along a whole crate of provisions. Thanks to the carefully planned "fuel" stops along the way the crate remained untouched. Because of the inevitable delays, our meals were served at the craziest hours. For example, during the first night about one thousand of us got off at a stop at 3 A.M., then proceeded to a brightly lit tentlike "dining area" where German POWs served the *evening* meal. I would have much preferred to keep on sleeping, but forced myself to try a little of the meat and potatoes. I couldn't swallow more than a few bites, so I saved the rest for a more reasonable hour. By the time the whole herd had been fed, it hardly paid to go to bed anymore, so we dozed for a few hours until sunrise.

By the time we woke up, the landscape had turned noticeably more southern. During the night we had passed Lyons and were headed for Valence. The vegetation was totally different, and during one of our frequent waits on a siding, I got to see my first olive grove. In general the houses, with their red tile roofs, actually looked more like those in Italy—in part quite different from those I observed during my Riviera visit. At every stop there was this incredible barter going on between boys and women loaded down with baskets filled to overflowing. Most of it was a trade of bread and fruit for cigarettes and chocolate, but there were also cases in which the exchange was handled from train window to train window. We had the good fortune to catch the dining car of a train headed in the opposite direction, so we managed to have hot coffee even between meal stops.

Once we made our way along the Rhône Valley, past Avignon, the temperature and weather improved markedly. Along both sides you could see the French Alps in the distance, actually the foothills, but it imparted a wild, southern character to the landscape.

Finally, around 11 P.M., we arrived at our destination, Pas de Lanciers, and in no time at all were loaded onto trucks. The trip continued under a magnificent starry sky, over terrain that looked as though it had been borrowed from the second act of *Carmen.*

Suddenly we climbed a tremendously steep incline, which afforded us a sweeping view back over a sea of lights, presumably another camp. We labored up the serpentine road until we reached the summit. Before us stretched an immense, far-flung camp, bigger than any we've ever been to. It extends more than seven kilometers and is capable of housing, in barrack after barrack, tent after tent, more than one hundred thousand men. As I determined later, at daylight, the whole thing is built on a vast plateau, nothing but desert landscape, which now has been transformed into a bustling city of streets, houses, canteens, stores, banks, etc. I never expected the environs of Marseilles to look like that. Rather I think the terrain near the Sierra Nevada in California must have the same character.

The nights are extremely cold, but during the day the sun is always shining, and toward noon it can get burning hot. I use the opportunity to take a few more late-season sunbaths. Toward the horizon, though in a haze, you can make out the silhouette of a mountain range. You get the feeling that you're in the mountains yourself, and if you do a 180-degree turn, you see more mountains, or cliffs and valleys that reflect a reddish glow.

We live in lightly attached buildings, sleep on folding bunks, and make our final preparations. We can still acquire this and that in the "stores." We attend countless briefing sessions, which are always announced via an effective sound system. The evenings are spent, according to your preference, in overcrowded USO clubs or in an open-air cinema, conceived in grandiose Hollywood style, along the lines of an amphitheater. The camp is fantastically well organized, everybody knows his exact place in this ant heap and what he is expected to do; in short, everything has been meticulously planned.

Because I don't know how much time will be at my disposal tomorrow, I've put down all these facts. You'll hear from me once more, barring unforeseen events. Let this suffice for now, dearest Gerda.

With many most ardent kisses, I am your ever-loving
Kurt

Calas, October 9, 1945

My beloved Gerda,

The suspense persists to the last moment. We were actually supposed to be taken to the port this evening. Now it may happen tomorrow. That is still subject to change from minute to minute, but I suspect we'll get the go-ahead tomorrow. The other group hasn't left yet either, which means I constantly run into people I believed to be still in Freising, or at least somewhere in Germany. Aside from that there are acquaintances

I haven't seen since my training camp in the States. This is a veritable reunion of the class of '43, without the usual attendant festivities. Naturally it leads to a big "hello" each time you discover yet another old "classmate." But the real celebration will only come at home and in an individual manner. And our day will come, too, Gerda!

I do admit that your physical absence is being felt with ever-increasing intensity, but I'm glad to find you at least on the path my thoughts are taking.

Last night I wished so very much that you had been here. The scene that I saw will remain with me for a long time to come; unfortunately I will not be able to do it much justice. It only lasted for a few minutes, but the view was so enchantingly beautiful that it took my breath away. Let me describe the setting. I had just watched a movie in the amphitheater, from whose celestial dome hung the thin sliver of a flame-red crescent moon. It was a color such as I had never seen anywhere else before. The audience sat at the deepest hollow of the amphitheater, as well as on the terraced "stairs," which provided a perfect "balcony" for outdoor viewing. Behind the center at the back of this horseshoe rose a steep mountainside, sandy and full of low-growth vegetation. From those natural steps, perhaps carved out millions of years ago by a river, now illuminated by shafts of light, flames shot up high into the night sky. The two ends of the horseshoe tapered off to a more gentle incline, and it was here that the mass of people left the "auditorium" at the end of the performance. Was it this view of the countless flashlights that were floating around in the dark or the impressions in the sand that indicated the slow, laborious ascent of the men that held me in such thrall? Viewed from below, the torchlight parade, a festive procession, slowly moved higher and higher until it gradually disappeared over the crest, where the outline of the mountain melded into the star-studded firmament. It is at such moments that I miss you terribly, Gerda!

There is so much I'd like to know about your daily routine. I am aware of how futile it is to pose the same questions over and over. After all, the answers can only reach me in a few weeks, so I have to be patient. You, too, have to be brave, because the mail will presumably come to a halt for three weeks or more. I suspect that I'll be able to write once more; if, however, matters should run a rapid course, then I want to call out to you now:

Farewell, Gerda dearest, and do think of an early reunion with your
Kurt

Gerda dearest,

As far as the army is concerned, it's always the exception that seems to apply rather than the rule. I find it's best to assume that everything will take at least two to three days longer than has been officially announced before. So it will probably be tomorrow, rather than last night, as originally scheduled, that we'll start off on our "tour" to the harbor.

Walter, Max, and Werner went on ahead at 7 A.M. today, and are presumably aboard by this time. All we can do is loaf around here and feel useless. So far, our stay here was quite pleasant and we convinced ourselves that a day more or less doesn't really matter, as long as we got this far.

I'm taking this opportunity to get to a few books that have been on my agenda for some time. After all, I have plenty of time to read. Once you get into the swing of things, boning up on English, I'd like to recommend a reading list to you. I'm quite certain I still have a few books among my belongings in Buffalo that I used to study English before going to the States. If you believe they might be of some help to you, considering your current degree of perfection, I'll send them to you when I get back.

I want to convey a few more random impressions about Marseilles, just as I took them in through the eyes of a tourist:

The Canebière, Marseilles' famed main street, immediately transformed by GI lingo into "can o' beer." You can't help noticing the tricolored traffic signals, as compared to the red-and-green ones we have at home, and the big-city street noises are intensely amplified by their incessant ringing* as the lights change. . . . the ancient churches, among which one is especially noteworthy: Nôtre-Dame de la Garde, situated on the top of a hill, overlooking the entire city and harbor. From what I hear it's usually the last landmark visible to a departing seafarer . . . the large crowd assembled in front of a flag-decked podium, from which a woman, reinforced by a battery of loudspeakers, delivers some sort of political harangue. As far as I can make out in my *français manqué*, it includes a list of her party's achievements since the end of the war . . . a gang of unscrubbed street urchins who are apparently engaged in a booming shoeshine business . . . the only

---

*Traffic signals that were "audiovisual" lent a truly novel touch to the Marseilles street scene.

park benches known to me that carry advertising on their backrests . . . and the multitude of American troops, including hangers-on who take advantage of them. The incessant offers by shady characters to turn a quick profit on the black market with cigarettes and chocolate, which any perambulating American has to fend off . . . the miracle of once again seeing a big city illuminated at night in a sea of lights, and, finally, the best-dressed sailors in the world, that is, the French, recognizable from afar because of the white caps with fiery red pompons, the blue-and-white striped knit shirts and navy blue jackets and trousers. All that makes up a small part of the character of France's second-largest city, as seen by your correspondent, who wanted nothing as much as to have you by his side. By the look of it you'll hear from me once more before our departure. Do while away your time with thousands of my kisses, so that it won't seem so long.

Your Kurt

Calas, October 11, 1945

Gerda dearest,

I claim every day that it'll be the last one here in Calas, and each time the matter is promptly delayed. Now it's supposed to be October 12, but if that should by chance not materialize, then I'll desist from any further guesswork about our embarkation date.

The ship is now allegedly ready, and we should be on our way to-morrow morning. I believe if Columbus had encountered such obstacles, America wouldn't be discovered yet. I have an itchiness in my bones. I've never done so little in my life!

I sent a small parcel to you yesterday, which I hope will arrive in good condition. I trust that the chocolate doesn't taste of soap and vice versa. In the worst case, you might eat the soap and wash your face with chocolate—yes? Should Mala get hold of this letter, I urgently implore her to let me know what things you lack most, except if you should come to your senses and write me about it yourself, my darling!

How are you managing at all as far as food is concerned? According to the papers, there is a noticeable difference in the rations, or doesn't that apply to you? President Truman is supposed to have taken up the question of better living conditions for all Jews with General Eisenhower. It's mostly a matter of people who until now were still in camps, but if the rations should improve, you ought to be included in that as well. I take it as a good sign that Eisenhower got somebody directly from America as an adviser. Despite so much negligence, the matter wasn't entirely forgotten. Apparently completely new guidelines are being issued as far as Jews are concerned, and the hope is that there will be an early concrete solution to the problem, or at least the beginning of one.

A great amount of pressure is being brought to bear to make a more generous immigration to Palestine possible. But it remains to be seen whether the British Parliament can get over its petty ideas. As you may know President Truman openly came out in favor of it, and England's new prime minister, Attlee, also made some favorable remarks in that regard. Nevertheless, nothing has been decided either way.

You might say I'm curious about what, if anything, will be done on the American side with respect to a possible immigration of the majority of the remaining Jews. After all, a plan like that could be implemented without violating existing immigration laws. What, in fact, will become of all the quotas that weren't filled at all in the course of the war? Truly, there is room for most of the people!

I'm looking forward to an early reunion.
Your Kurt

Homeward bound [aboard Victory ship*], October 12, 1945

Gerda dearest,

Are you in the habit of starting a book from the end? If not, then you won't have to peek in this case either, because I can relieve the suspense by assuring you that I arrived very well indeed.

October 12. We're jolted from our slumber at 5 A.M. by a combination of travel fever and the merciless wailing of a few habitual early risers. So is it really true what they told us—or will some last-minute hitch come up? First off, a hearty breakfast, then back to the barracks in order to finish packing. Meanwhile I notice that in this part of the world dawn turns into day as fast as night comes upon you, almost without twilight.

This particular morning chooses to don a garment of fog, however,

---

*Used of the ships bringing home the victorious U.S. troops. They were a category of ships designed mostly, but not exclusively, as troop carriers. Five hundred were built toward the end of the war.

which is nearly impenetrable, and it takes many tries by the sun to succeed in cutting through that cover. The sun is merely a dull disk, not much bigger than a full moon, by the time we mount the trucks with unnecessarily heavy loads. We're off (apparently by detour) along a smooth highway in the direction of the harbor. To our left and right appear phantomlike exotic trees and plants, only to disappear again immediately. Actually the landscape strikes me as somewhat desolate. Here and there is a large rock, a few shrubs, and everything covered by the red dust that we got to know so well. Before we know it, though, the pier is in sight—the sun is strong now—and before us lies *mare nostrum* in deepest azure.

The USO has already anticipated that our breakfast won't hold us for too long. Presto, a table is improvised, and what do they serve? Coffee and doughnuts, of course! We fuel up some extra energy, because we're about to stagger along the endless gangplank, loaded down with all our earthly possessions. Some just barely manage to do it while others accomplish it with ease, but all gladly take the outstretched hand of a helpful navy officer at the far end. Technically speaking then, we've left the Continent and are stepping on American "soil." Even if that isn't quite correct, it's great to luxuriate in that feeling.

The exterior of this so-called Victory ship is not much different from the uncomfortable crate that took us to Normandy. Once we are swallowed up by the interior, we are in for a pleasant surprise: There are actually certain conveniences. Well, it's hardly a luxury steamer, but who expects such a thing? We're shown to a room with triple-decker bunks, and I choose the upper one because, first of all, it's more roomy and second, you can definitely reap the benefits of the ventilation system up there. (It's almost too cool right now.) What really slays us is that all this comes with sheets, pillows, and sparkling white towels! Well, this has all the earmarks of a pleasure cruise.

Right on the heels of that, the squawk box announces that our money is ready to be claimed. Up to now they merely gave us a receipt for our French currency, most likely because all sorts of black marketeers would have been interested in American dollars in Marseilles. To us the dollars still seem a bit peculiar and unaccustomed, after years of changing from one currency to another, each of which looked as if it came from a child's game.

Shutters are clicking all around, and we watch a few USO girls down on the dock engaged in lighthearted banter with some high-spirited GIs up here. Wherever you look, there are smiling, animated faces. Music blares from the speakers, adding to the euphoria, and before we know it, it's time for lunch. Mealtimes in the dining room are split into three shifts. We no longer need our aluminum utensils. Everything is provided, and the food is good.

Before casting off we're already one hour closer to the United States, which requires us to set our watches back. Now we have a chance to explore the various decks, scrutinize the vicinity all around with field glasses, and discuss for the umpteenth time what we can't quite grasp yet: In ten days we'll be over there!

October 13. Today you and I celebrate our first "anniversary." One month has passed since our engagement, a whole month without you— incredible! I would so much like to propose a toast to our relationship, but I lack the requisite anisette.

October 14. Getting up is a lot harder than it was yesterday, although I can't immediately determine the reason. But the first truly "American" breakfast in years reconciles me to putting up with the world, which usually doesn't exist for me before 10 A.M. We can hardly believe that we're getting grapefruit, along with the best dry cereal I can imagine, and its packaging is the same as when I used to buy it in the stores. It's prepared with genuine "fresh" milk in cartons, pasteurized exactly as at home. Although I am no milk drinker, I feel I never knew how good and different American milk tastes. I even guzzle an ice-cold glass of it. In addition there is a choice of fried eggs, and coffee and bread. That even surpasses our daily dessert, real ice cream, so far the sensation of each meal.

Now we're ready for the main event of the day, cameras at hand. We're about to pass the Strait of Gibraltar, and the first signs become noticeable. We'd like to do a little tanning in the warm sunshine, but there is a cloud cover, from which the sun peeks out only occasionally. The sea is no longer as smooth as a pond on a summer's day; rather it's adorned by whitecaps as far as you can see. But it's very attractive and doesn't affect the ship's stable course in the least. Gradually the azure color fades and changes to one of gray-green, proof that we're getting close to the Atlantic.

Off in the distance, we sight the coast, at first still rather hazy. Then the outline comes into sharper focus. A mountain chain is silhouetted against the horizon: Morocco. That makes me curious to see what's on the starboard side of the ship. An immense rock lies before me, still somewhat pale, but I am able to bring it closer with the help of field glasses. Yes, the shape is familiar, if only from photos. As we approach, individual houses, installations, etc., become visible. What perplexes us is a smooth, square, apparently human-made area which covers nearly the entire side of the rock. Presently the loudspeaker enlightens us; it's a sort of "rain roof," meant to catch precipitation, providing the population with sufficient drinking water. Here and there we can spot a white house, glued to the wildly dramatic rock. You can only wonder what prompted somebody to pick such a monotonous piece of real estate, then to erect an impressive building right in the midst of this desolate site, devoid of vegetation.

The coast of Africa doesn't show much evidence of life. If there is such a thing, it's well hidden behind a row of mountains. We look alternately toward the Spanish side, and then Tangiers, until the coast is nothing more than a thin line that melts into the gray of the horizon. Now, finally, Europe lies behind us. It had the power to attract us during those turbulent times, proving the fallacy of the madness that distance alone spells security. Well, the work is done, and may Europe never again have the power to exercise such magnetism!

October 15. Today's report should be entitled: "Closed due to 'imagination.' "* Some of the world's greatest masterpieces were often created out of indescribable suffering. Right from the start, in my bunk, at a time when all is still darkness, I notice that something is awry. It's no longer a bunk, it's a damned cradle, only I'm in no mood to go through a second childhood. I turn to the other side, but the rocking motion is exactly the same. I try to tell myself that the whole thing is a bad dream, but nothing helps: The queasy feeling in my stomach is undeniable.

After the lights are turned on, Harf, who sleeps in a bunk across from me, drops a remark about the weather. I dismiss it with a hoarse laugh, "Nonsense, that's nothing at all." As soon as I plant myself on the floor though, I pay for my recklessness. Gone is my entire equilibrium. You feel alternately as if you had sprouted wings and then again as if your feet were chained to a ball of lead.

There are only a few hardy souls at breakfast, and they can be divided into roughly three categories: those who came with the best of intentions but disappear from the scene after the first bite; those who, by hook or

*Refers to a previous jesting remark that seasickness is merely a figment of the imagination.

by crook, manage to gulp down a tenth of their usual intake, then push the plate away with a casual "Oh, well I wasn't hungry anyway" gesture, then beat an "honorable" retreat; and finally the third group, far in the minority, who give signs of being endlessly amused by the other two. Actually nobody dares to gloat too much, because nobody knows from meal to meal in which category he is going to be.

There is only a skeleton crew of kitchen personnel on hand, because they are of course not spared either. Among the tables I spot one lone "waiter," staggering about as if intoxicated, and my heart goes out to him. I'm determined to find out what's causing this infernal state of affairs. Once I get up on deck, it's pouring buckets. The sky is covered with low-flying clouds; the waves are high, but not as bad as you might surmise from the heaving motion of the ship. The wind drives the white-caps around until thin sheets of spray hit you in the face. Instead of being unpleasant this actually refreshes me, and I prefer to remain on deck, even when we get into a real torrent of rain, in which you can't see more than three hundred feet.

Wherever you look pathetic figures are hunched in various stages of sickness, or are leaning over the railing. It would be humorous if it weren't so contagious. And by now, Gerda, you must be wondering how I am faring throughout this. Very simple: In any situation there are always people whose complexion, as before, glows in rosy hues of pink. Well, mine is the same in green!

October 16. The sea is calmer, the sun is out again, but the bouncing up and down persists, although somewhat diminished. Now I know how this ship got the name *Sea Fiddler.* But why can't it restrict itself to playing more tranquil airs instead of these relentless staccato passages?

I must confess that for purely egotistical reasons I need someone who feels sorry for me and who spoils me under these circumstances. Besides, you'd probably get a big kick out of seeing me in my present disheveled condition, caused by the wind and the absence of a barber.

Tonight at eleven, we'll allegedly be able to sight the Azores to our right; that is, they promise us a lighthouse, assuming the right visibility exists. Very nice, but I have a peculiar idea that one lighthouse looks like another, whether on the Azores or in Buffalo's inland harbor. Who could expect that I'd still be on my two legs at such an ungodly hour?

Now, good night, Gerda, my dear. I constantly think of you, have your picture right next to me, so as to dream better. What might you be doing at this hour? How long is it since I heard from you? An eternity! Another two weeks yet before my impatience will diminish somewhat. Is everything moving along routinely for you? If only I could have an occasional dialogue with you!

October 17. Once it's your turn to cross the "big pond," you are in for such a varied and enchanting face of nature as I can hardly describe. One sunset leaves you more breathless than the next. In the Mediterranean it was a red-hot fireball that submerged within minutes in the mirror-smooth sea until twilight totally enveloped the horizon. And what I witnessed just now was no less impressive but in an entirely different way. The yellow disk descended slowly toward the water, soon distorted by the fantastically bold brushstrokes that cover the sky in multicolored splendor. They transform the entire vastness of the low-flying clouds in the foreground into mountains of gold. Truly Apollo's fiery chariot and Poseidon's deep blue waves appear to be in passionate competition to pit the beauty of their respective elements against each other. Who can possibly judge the outcome of such a contest? What makes the decision even more difficult is the fact that the Queen of the Night is about to unfold her bewitching charms.

From my vantage point on the highest deck I watch how the waxing moon, directly in line with the ship's bow, opens up an infinitely long, broad, silver avenue. Millions of diamonds glitter over everything in the velvety night sky. A peculiar illusion can be achieved by letting your gaze wander vertically, along the ship's mast, toward the night sky. At each turn of the vessel, this immense planetarium revolves like a roulette wheel. You feel motionless while the star-studded sky spins around the mast at breakneck speed. How can I witness all that without wanting to share it with you? A thought runs through my mind ceaselessly: If only Gerda were here!

October 18. Until now the weather, though at times stormy, was always warm, but gradually it is turning more inclement. And so we prefer to spend more time in our cabins. Oddly enough, the rolling motion has almost entirely subsided, and even those who were most prone to seasickness are up and around. But everybody follows the course of the ship, posted on a huge map, with great interest and considerable impatience. One of the navy officers tells us that we are not due to land before Tuesday the twenty-third. Obviously the weather has slowed us down somewhat. It makes me think of the eighteen hours it took to go in the opposite direction, and I get very fidgety.

Under those circumstances the library becomes a favorite hangout for all. Everyone exchanges books and magazines and is up to his ears in reading matter. And there are other pastimes for those who don't take naturally to books. On the deck, money flies around like leaves carried by autumn winds. This is caused by a fanatical breed of dice players who, within a span of minutes, might win or lose hundreds. There also are card games of every description going on, to such an extent that this ship could be likened more to a giant floating casino than to a troop transport.

October 19. Today I attended a religious service of an extraordinary nature. It was not the reason for the occasion—Friday evening prayers—but rather the circumstances that introduced a novel note. Among other things we've learned to preserve notes and sounds that can be reproduced at will. And we've given the matter a name: records. Perhaps one use of this wax disk has eluded you thus far—it did me. What do you do, for example, if you're on the high seas, at least two thousand miles from the nearest rabbi or synagogue? All you need is a Catholic chaplain, a record player, and a loudspeaker with accessories. The chaplain, by the way, is not absolutely necessary but appears to be the most logical person under the circumstances. He can find storage for the necessary records with accompanying prayer books. This method has certain advantages: You see, the reciter chosen for these records was in exceptionally good voice and had a modest choir to back him up. Basically there is no substitute for a prayer that emanates from a live mouth, forming an individual event, different from any preceeding one. You might look at this as an example in which modern technology came to the rescue of an ancient culture under exceptional circumstances.

You are ahead of me now because of the time difference, which means you must be sleeping by this hour, Gerda dearest. Well, take this good-night kiss!

October 20. Once I'm back, perhaps I can publish a work entitled, *How to Avoid Seasickness,* a condition for which I have found a foolproof cure: Be sure to travel only on land.

We were just sitting around on deck, watching a full moon, when an important announcement came over the speaker in the most dramatic fashion. Our destination has been changed. We will not land in Newport News, Virginia, but rather in New York. That was immediately greeted with loud cheers by all those from that area. I much prefer that myself, because it ought to avoid the hassle of long waits for trains and the ensuing long ride. Besides, I really would have missed the welcome from the Statue of Liberty and the skyline of New York. It belongs to a home-coming!

October 21. I shouldn't have boasted so much about the weather yesterday. From the moment we entered the dining area, we were greeted by wild chaos. In every corner there was a jumble of tables, benches, remnants of food. Each motion made cups roll across the floor, and the sound of breaking crockery was everywhere.

By lunchtime the tables were secured by ropes, but that didn't stop the raging of the elements. A major storm was whipping the rain across the decks, and anything that wasn't nailed down was swept overboard. Oddly enough it was still sufficiently warm to remain outdoors without a jacket, as long as you could find a halfway protected corner. We were tossed about all day long, to the point where I now know how it feels to go over Niagara Falls in a barrel. In time one does become more "sea-worthy," and time is one commodity we have lots of. As a matter of fact, it seems so long since we embarked that I wonder sometimes whether I boarded the "Flying Dutchman" by mistake. And the prospects are getting ever more elastic. First we were supposed to dock tomorrow, then the day after, and now, by the look of it, it'll be Wednesday. We're "racing" at a speed of twenty knots, ten knots forward and ten knots sideways. Bet Columbus wasn't any happier to sight land than we will be. Until tomorrow . . .

October 22. One medium that lets us shorten the long hours has gone unreported thus far: the movies. Wherever the troops have gone, whether to the jungle, to the desert, or on the high seas, they've always taken the movies along. Aside from the fact that it is a part of American life, as perhaps in no other country, it has an additional peculiarity of which there is little awareness in the United States. It has the ability to conjure up illusions of home for the GI who has been away from his roots in far-flung places for a long time, thereby lifting his mood and morale, often when it is needed most. While the war may be over, America's general love of movies persists.

But now for the news of the day. Everybody is animated, delighted, in a state of suspenseful anticipation. Tomorrow morning, when we get up, land will be in sight, the view we have waited for for so long. Allegedly we'll dock as early as 7:30 A.M., but it's doubtful whether we'll leave the ship before evening. The worst time will come after that, though, because we may have to stay several days in the vicinity of New York without being able to go home.

Much as I can understand that those formalities are necessary for such masses of people, I don't know how much patience I'll be able to muster, knowing that only a ridiculously short distance separates me from my dearest ones. A thousand questions run through my mind: How will my sister, Gerdi, have changed? Wonder how big Barbara is by now? How does Lawrence Michael look? Has my brother, Max, gotten back* from Europe yet—and how are all the others? What impression will I make? (I don't believe that I'm the same person who left New York two years ago.) Oh, and I can hardly wait until I can tell everybody about you! I can only hope your letters got there ahead of me, Gerda, my beloved!

How will America seem to me? Will I have to discover it anew and get used to civilian life? But we will soon explore it together, and believe me, there will be much that I can enjoy only if I live through it with you. We'll have fun and appreciate even the smallest things, won't we, Gerdush?

The new life that is in store for me is full of promise, rife with wonderful, undreamed-of possibilities. But it will only be complete once you are with me. With that wish I am going to close this diary and await the dawn of a new day.

Munich, October 16, 1945

Kurt, my beloved, my dearest,
How beautiful is this hour, to which I joyfully look forward all day long, when my thoughts center on you alone and words flow onto paper that your hands will hold and your eyes will see.

I hope finally to be able to send the letters to your sister and imagine you in that environment when you receive them. To send them to your army address will only delay them, as I was told, and knowing you, knowing that you want to surprise your family, I am holding them, as Captain Presser calculated, and will send them off to coincide with your arrival home. I have been writing every day as you have, and am so happy to confirm your nine letters ranging from September 16 to October 6. For each and every one of them, my thanks! Needless to say, your letters make me very happy. When your mail arrives, it is as if the sun breaks through on a dark day—my entire self becomes in-

---

*From an army post in the American sector of Berlin.

fused with light and joy. A feeling of well-being envelops me such as I have never known before.

But I guess I must now get down to answering some of your thoughts and questions. First of all your suggestion to come back to Europe: No! There is absolutely no question. I put a strong and final veto to that idea. Naturally I am deeply touched that you would be willing to make this supreme sacrifice for me. At the moment it is quite calm here. There is a lot of preferential treatment for foreigners. I had to get a new ID card and so needed to go to the police. It was a very, very strange moment. I was interrogated, and with a name like Gerda and my fluent German, he looked up when it came to the question of my place of birth and citizenship, hesitated, and before I could answer said, "I will leave it blank, and you can make up your mind later." What a strange thought, after all that has transpired.

So please, dearest Kurt, don't worry so much about me. How can you even suggest coming back? You say there might be a possibility for me to go to the States while you would stay in Germany. Me—go without you? That's unimaginable. And it would mean you'd be coming back to this hateful, despised Germany. A thousand times no. I can be pretty brave if I must be.

I hope that all will go well for us, so don't worry so much. The only thing is that the hours are so long, but they do add up. Amazingly it is almost five weeks since we were together. In all the five months since we met, that has been the longest stretch during which we haven't seen each other. I can't believe it, nor can I comprehend how I managed to live for twenty-one years (minus one day) without you. I know it's not good manners so shamelessly to reveal one's feelings. What would Papa, Mama, and Artur think? I guess they would agree that I should tell the truth, and the truth is that you mean everything on earth to me.

I have had occasion to visit the German Museum* almost daily. It has been transformed and hardly seems to be the place where people feared the news they would receive, praying for information about family and friends. It boasts an orchestra now, with lively music, and there is much activity and crowds of people, only foreigners. The nice part is

---

*A museum of science and technology, then serving as a clearinghouse for survivors, mainly Jewish. Lists of names were posted daily to facilitate searches for kin, along with all pertinent information regarding their respective camps, as well as news about their hometowns.

that one does not hear much, if any, German being spoken. Polish is much in evidence, as is English, because of all the U.S. Army personnel.

Tomorrow I'll go to the German Museum to hear a performance of *Halka*. I am most interested in seeing and hearing it because it's the most popular, and probably the best, Polish opera.

I try to imagine your sister's eyes when she sees you again. I do hope that she is all well again. Is little Barbara afraid of you? I wouldn't be surprised if she were. Are you allowed to hold little Larry? If I were your sister, I wouldn't let you. I know I am being terribly mean, but it's my envy showing. I envy you so terribly that you can play with a baby. Please do tell me everything, everything. Does the baby smile? What color eyes and hair does he have? Please take some photos soon, *very* soon, and then send them to me! Now I really must go to sleep. Until tomorrow, a thousand kisses and much love. Good night!

Gerda

Munich, October 18, 1945

Dearest Kurt,

I thought for quite some time before I started this letter, deliberating what tone and character it should have. But since you always emphasize that you want me to write exactly what I feel, and you would soon discern if I were not honest, I will inflict my sorrow on you.

Tomorrow morning will be six years since I saw Artur for the last time. Tonight, at just about this hour, the four of us sat together for the last time. Six years ago tomorrow. Was I really only fifteen when I came face-to-face with the cruel realities of life for the first time? Where is Artur? Will I see him again?

My beloved, perhaps I would not have written the above in such blunt words, had fate not put your letter into my hands this morning, with its description of your feelings as you stood in front of the building that housed your dear mother before her last journey.

How much the waves of memory, of pain and loss, beat against each of our hearts. Your letter left you in precisely the same mood as it found me. Thank you, my love, for a glimpse into your soul. I understood you so well. Comfort you? I know there is no comfort for what has happened, but let me say this: Even though you are torn by this overwhelming anguish, you must find comfort in the reassuring conclusions your parents must have arrived at when thinking of you.

Let me explain: Our parents belong to both of us; please permit me to think of yours as mine. Unfortunately, or fortunately, I was with my parents when Artur was taken away. I saw what it did to them. My father, crying like a child (the first time in my life that I saw him cry), and my mother mute, like a petrified tree. I threw myself weeping into Artur's embrace, and still hear his words in my ears: "Don't cry, silly little sister. You have to be brave—promise me."

And when I ran after him to embrace him once more, he broke the tension. "It will be a relief not to have you trotting after me all the time." His lips were smiling, but his eyes were bright with unshed tears.

But what I really want to tell you is not my parents' unbearable pain during the long months of uncertainty, but of their joy and relief when we knew him to be in Russia. He was not under the Nazis; he was free! They seemed to have shed years. They smiled, talked to each other as they had in happier times, and their unspoken fear, cloaked in silence, was lifted.

Your parents, thank God, knew you to be in America! You were far away from hateful Germany. You were safe! Your parents gladly endured everything, knowing their son was safe. Even though your heart may break now, take comfort, my love, in their love for you. I always prayed and pray still: Oh, God, let my parents know, let them feel that I am alive. Your parents knew and also knew that their love and hopes were embedded in you. That gave them comfort, solace, and peace. You have built a perpetual memorial of love and remembrance in your heart for them. Let me be a part of honoring them as well.

I pray that we will have children and that we shall give them what is best, most beautiful, and noble in us, and through that we will find our parents again and be bound to them forever.

I can feel how sad you are, how heavy is your load of pain. I just want to help you carry it. You know that I will always be at your side, especially when the going is rough.

I love you so much.
Gerda

Munich, October 23, 1945

Kurt dearest,
It was truly wonderful this morning as I found mail from you, even though the date seems almost prehistoric. It is from you, and that is all that

matters. Naturally I plunged into your letter right away, ignoring the bundle of official mail I had to read. I was deeply involved in your words and didn't initially hear my supervisor's comment, "Must be an interesting letter."

"Oh, yes, fascinating!"

"Will you let me know your opinion on it as soon as you finish?"

"Oh, I can tell you that right now." The entire unit broke into laughter.

"Really?" he continued. "You don't usually give your opinion so soon."

"No, but in some cases without even reading the salutation, I know what to do with it."

Finally he caught on. "I gather, then, that you won't release it."

"Right!"

Now to Uncle Leo's letter. Please do write him everything regarding us. You know, it is so strange: until a few weeks ago, to see him was the dearest wish of my life, and I do so much want to see him. But now there is someone I want to see even more. Can you guess who? It will be so incredibly wonderful for us to see my uncle together, and I am so eager to show you off. You know, at times I can't believe that what is happening in my life is true. Sometimes I think that all this is a beautiful dream and that I'll wake up and be in . . . But I keep your picture placed so that every time I open my eyes, I'll see you!

Oh, yes, there is a rumor that the American consul will be here in January. I hope so. Perhaps then the opening of the consulate is not too far away. You ask if I can decipher your writing. Have you forgotten what my profession is? I love to censor your letters; no, not to censor but to scrutinize them.

I picked up a newsletter at the Deutsches Museum listing names of survivors. It's published in English, French, Polish, and German, and I devour it, of course, in the hope that one day—oh, God, how I pray for it—Artur's name will be in it.

With love and kisses,
Gerda

At the end of the war tons of civilian and service mail were confiscated by the Americans at German post offices, and it fell to the staff of the American-run Civilian Censorship Division to screen those letters for incriminating evidence of former, or perhaps current, Nazi activity. Frequently we found that no attempt would be made to veil directions given to the writers' kin as to how to dispose of just such evidence. Those were the letters that would be relegated to the "condemned" pile, to be turned over to the American authorities.

Polish civilian mail, on the other hand, contained many coded messages that attested to the abominable treatment the writers and their families had received at the hands of the German administrators of the "protectorate," as annexed Poland was called by the German authorities. Reference would be made to some of the German officials, usually SS personnel, likening them to some character from Polish fiction, understood to be villainous. Generally speaking, in the course of my duties, handwriting in either German or Polish was often extremely difficult to decipher.

New York City, October 24, 1945

Gerda dearest,

Only a brief postscript, because my head is swimming after today's events. A short detour into New York City afforded the long-awaited reunion with my family. Immediately on my announcement of our engagement, they plied me with thousands of questions about you. Everybody is beaming; they can't hear enough about it.

By tomorrow morning I have to return to the army. It may take another few days, or perhaps even somewhat longer, until I'm discharged, but this one day was better than nothing. Unfortunately nothing by way of mail from you was at my sister's. That means it's been forwarded to the same old address. I'm going to cable you my safe arrival. Excuse the brevity, but I'll make up for it.

With countless kisses, your
Kurt

Fort Dix, N.J., October 25, 1945

My dearest Gerda,

First I'll have to collect my thoughts to be able to report the most important happenings in a coherent manner. You see, since I've set foot on American soil, the events and impressions have unfolded with lightning speed. That means that during the forty-eight hours since then, I've spoken to countless people; received letters (only not yours), telegrams, and invitations; have been welcomed; and told stories, told stories, told stories. At the moment I'm waiting my turn to be able to call Buffalo—my relatives and friends—and am utilizing this time to dash off a few lines. I can't imagine how you'll ever make heads or tails out of this mishmash, so I'd best stick to the right sequence.

As you know we docked in New York Harbor on the twenty-third, saw nothing but fog early in the day, then had to wait a considerable period of time until we could enter. Finally, at 1400 hours, we spotted the sight we had been dreaming about for so long: the Statue of Liberty, with the skyscrapers forming the backdrop. Boats carrying brass bands stood in readiness to give us a big welcome. There was a forest of waving arms, screaming, and general pandemonium. In passing each boat gave a blast of its siren by way of greeting. It all was a hellish noise, considering the multitude of ships in the harbor. Wherever you looked, from the pier, from buildings, from steamships, there were these huge Welcome! signs. All along the shore and from many windows people were waving. Truly a magnificent homecoming. We continued up the Hudson River, along all the familiar building outlines and landmarks, then farther upriver for about twenty miles. We couldn't get our fill, noticing the most insignificant details, added to which was the colorful blaze of nature's canvas amid the sweet scent of autumn in America. You have to take some deep breaths of air, and while savoring it, the thought slowly penetrates: I am home again! You see, New York will always symbolize America, although—or because—it stands unique among American cities.

We docked toward evening, having gone through countless other manifestations of welcome, then consumed an enormous "reception meal." By that time it was pretty late, and we were thoroughly tired, but despite that much too excited to turn in. We were promised a twelve-hour leave to see our next of kin, starting the following morning, which meant we could go to the New York City area for that relatively brief period, but as it turned out we all overstayed our leave and returned the next morning without dire consequences.

Well, I can tell you, Gerda, it was thrilling. Although Gerdi was expecting me, she didn't know it was going to be on that exact day, so that it did turn into a nice surprise. As you know I had not gotten any mail from her except the letter announcing baby Larry's arrival. But everything had gone all right for both mother and son, and she feels quite normal again. I found her slightly older looking, but nearly unchanged. The baby is a lovable guy. They say he looks a little like my brother, which I can't see.

My niece, Barbara, and I became fast friends. She didn't want to let go at all: a tremendous honor, I was told. She has turned into a pretty little thing and has grown immensely! But then, we all grow old! My brother-in-law, Gunther, got home rather late; meanwhile, my sister-in-law, Sue, also joined us for dinner, and we chatted and chatted. She doesn't know yet when Max will get back. Wish you could have seen what a pleasant surprise our engagement triggered all around. They simply overwhelmed me with so many questions that it became impossible to answer everything in detail right then and there. They all expect to see you here soon, and countless welcomes and greetings were extended to you.

Now to the main issue. Unfortunately no letters from you have arrived yet. I hope there's no reason for it other than that you've continued to use my army address. What did reach me were two cables from your uncle, who acknowledged my letter that went via the States. He inquired how much money your emigration would require, because he could send it by way of Switzerland. The answer was prepaid, and the second cable was merely an inquiry as to whether the first one had reached me. I'll wire the reason for the silence and will answer the financial question negatively. But do tell me what else you'd like your relatives to know, or enclose a letter, whichever you prefer.

I just read that there is about to be a consul general in Munich, which comes as a big relief and should facilitate matters considerably. To get back to your uncle, I'm going to mail a letter to him tomorrow that will fully explain everything and will enclose yours.

It looks as though I may have to sit around here for a while, although there's a chance I'll be discharged in a few days. Then I'll be able to devote myself to the matter of your coming. I've made a few inquiries through my sister, and now we'll have to see what else can be found out.

Good night, darling—I love you!
Kurt

My beloved Gerda,

The camp in which I'm staying for the purpose of separation from the service is much like a mill through which thousands of GIs of every description are being ground. This torrent has gotten hold of me as well and is irresistibly sweeping me along. Tonight the fun begins in earnest, after which it may go relatively fast. I feel terrible that I'll have to neglect you a bit because of that, but I'm hoping you'll close an eye to my omissions. The upcoming weeks should be tremendously busy ones, and whether I'll get to write daily is in question. Can I count on you to not be angry, so that I'll be able to sleep in peace?

A cable, as well as your letter and mine, went out to your uncle. I wired him all about our engagement, and I'm told that the cable should get there within one to two days. It looks to me as if the exchange of correspondence will go a lot faster from now on.

I did call Gerdi yesterday. She still had no mail from you. If only I had explained that to you more fully at the time. I don't want to be unduly worried about you, but something should have reached me by now, unless you kept writing to the old address.

How are things with you, my love? Is work still tolerable? If not, you ought to leave it without any worry whatsoever. After all, you don't have to work. Do you have any fun at all from time to time? Do you still have visitors once in a while?

A parcel, containing chocolate, a few cans, and other comestibles was dispatched to you, and I hope it'll get there soon. Unfortunately we can't send more than five pounds at one time, but I believe that will change soon.

America is wonderful! I've come to appreciate it as never before, if that's possible. You'll be totally enthusiastic about it and I'm having a tremendous amount of fun speculating that I'll soon be able to show you everything myself. Some of it seems like a new discovery to me as well. You sort of forget that certain things exist at all. It'll be wonderful, Gerdush!

> With a thousand love-saturated kisses, I'm always your
> Kurt

My beloved Kurt,

It's Sunday, and I'm all alone during the hours we used to spend together, but I welcome the solitude. There are no intrusions on my thoughts, and I can communicate with you much better because of the quiet around me. How divine it would be if you were here.

I was supposed to go to the theater tonight, but something went wrong about the tickets so I didn't go. All the same I'm not in the least sorry. I would rather be with you anytime. I realize it may be unbecoming to be so open with my feelings; you might consider it gushing. Yet, in normal life most of us are with those we love. They are the people we trust, so there is no need constantly to remind them of our feelings.

In our case our feelings toward each other remained unexpressed until the last two days, when you asked me to marry you and expressed your love and all that you felt for me. From that moment my life changed completely; the void and the loneliness were gone. You filled that emptiness and now I have you, one who cares, understands, and loves me as I love you and always will.

There is something else that triggered this outburst that I should tell you about. I am very sad and upset, after seeing several girls who were with me in the camps. Their situation is abominable; they have no one. Some have found love, while others have plunged into marriages out of sheer loneliness and desperation. Often the fact that someone comes from the same town and knew part of your family provides the flimsiest of reasons to rush into a union, even on very short acquaintance. As one of them told me, "Of course I don't love him; what is love, after all? Love was killed along with my parents. It's better than being alone." What will become of them? What can I say to them? Some are sick in mind as well as in body. It is so sad, but what can I do? Why am I so lucky? I know I was fortunate in loving my family, and in turn being loved by them; nothing can detract from that. But I love you with a joyful intensity, a feeling that I never knew existed and that blots out so much pain. Thank you for being you.

I love you,
Gerda

The perspective of the years has given me another view of what I once considered hasty marriages. I am embarrassed now by my impertinent,

*conceited, youthful view from my lofty, "all-knowing" perch—sitting in
judgment of others, who I believed were entering "rash" marriages. I
wonder whether others regarded me as having thrown myself into the arms
of the first American who came along, but in my mind I felt that, naturally, Kurt and I were "different."*

*It gives me great pleasure to report that among the cases I know of, my
friends' marriages have well withstood the test of time—not one divorce
among them. The return to normality for all of us was finding an anchor
that would let us forge a future. For many, just meeting someone from
their hometown who had known their families or could share some other
common memory provided a base for beginning a new life. Above all there
was a quest for companionship and for once again having a family. It
seems that what we experienced let us gain a deeper appreciation for basic
values in life.*

෧   ෧   ෧   ෧   ෧   ෧   ෧   ෧   ෧   ෧   ෧   ෧

Fort Dix, N.J., October 28, 1945

Gerda dearest,

Today it's three years since I've been in the army, and it was almost the
day of my discharge. It's going to take a little while longer, though, and
so I went to New York for twenty-four hours, instead of squandering the
time uselessly right here. That afforded the opportunity to discuss matters at greater length with Gerdi and Gunther.

An article I read in the *New York Times* suggests that the opening of
the American consulate in Munich can be expected soon. Meanwhile I
was able to make inquiries in camp, which netted the following:

As the fiancée of an American, you will be subject to the quota regulations. On the other hand, you will receive preferential treatment, as
long as I declare that I'm going to marry you soon after your arrival.
Marriage in absentia is not being recognized. It can be done, but it yields
no advantages whatsoever in regard to immigration. The Polish quota
will hardly be filled under the present conditions. I still want to explore
that further with better-informed sources. At any rate I will issue the
required affidavit, but it would be best if I could list having a job. Aside
from that I was advised to have a relative issue an affidavit, which I will
take care of once I get to Buffalo. No doubt it will take at least another
two to three months until the consulate is fully operational. I plan to go
to Buffalo during the next few weeks. Meanwhile I'll inquire about a

ship reservation. Perhaps they will accept applications, although I would guess civilian passage will not get underway before spring.

Once the affidavits are verified, you'll be able to apply for a quota number. But the simplest thing would be if you'd go to the consulate in person as soon as you hear that the affidavits have been approved. To avoid disappointments, I don't want to get overly optimistic, but my guess is that we'll have an exchange of correspondence with the consulate that will stretch well into the summer. I hope it won't take that long; my main question is when can we count on halfway normal civilian ship crossings?

At any rate that's far too long, and I have a faint idea how you must feel about that. Every day without you by my side, Gerda, seems only half lived. We talked a great deal about you this evening, Gerdush, and I fashioned all sorts of plans regarding the type of position I'm going to look for, what sort of apartment would be right for us, etc. Gerdi and Gunther are getting to know you better each time I see them and are very happy with my choice. It's a fact: The greatest dunces are usually blessed with most of the good luck!

Regarding my separation from the service, everything has been fabulously well organized. We spend hour after hour filling out documents, often until well into the night. Nothing is as simple as it looks, because there are hundreds of different cases, and for each one a special regulation applies. As complicated as it is, everything is moving along pretty smoothly.

Since I probably won't get to any correspondence soon, take a double ration of my regards and kisses to last for two days. Regards also to all and do write soon.

Kurt

Fort Dix, N.J., October 30, 1945

My dearest Gerda,

Days go by without any news from you, and there are dozens of reasons why that should be so; yet I cannot fend off a slight concern. Well, the next time I'll go see Gerdi something will be there for sure!

This was the second time, then, that I had twenty-four hours in New York; now I'm back in camp to await my definite separation from service. I'm sitting in a rocking chair, taking in the surprisingly hot late-October sun. Meanwhile, I've made use of my free time to explore the matter of your immigration in greater detail. According to all I could find out so far, I've come to the conclusion that it would be best for you to remain in Munich to await the opening of the American consulate. I believe that, under the circumstances, going to Turkey will not be as simple as your continued stay in Germany. I know that won't be very pleasant for you, to put it mildly, but it is the fastest way. Immediately after my discharge, I'll go to Washington to find out more details. Then I'll determine what papers will have to be sent to the State Department. I need to get more information on that. In the meantime I can also sound out the various steamship companies about whether tickets are already available. I assume that once you get that far, you'll be leaving by way of Bremerhaven.

Out of sheer curiosity, I conducted an experiment yesterday. I looked at the "Help Wanted" columns in the *New York Times*, just to find out what I can expect in the field of printing. The second company I spoke to was willing to hire me at fifty dollars a week. I can't judge yet whether that would be a decent salary to begin with, because prices have changed so much since I left. The end of the war has not brought a reduction in the cost of living thus far; quite the contrary, you read about one strike after another because, no matter what their position, they all want to use the opportunity to maintain their level of salaries, which have shrunk considerably since the discontinuance of overtime.

Quite aside from that, it's no longer considered unpatriotic to go on strike, and so everybody is trying to make up for lost time. This, then, is the situation: On one hand, there are all these strikes because of the high cost of living. On the other, those prices will be with us for quite some time, because a great number of people really earned a lot of money during the war, and many items are still scarce and much in demand.

Because I covered so much ground in the city, I was able to see again so many things that I appreciate about New York. When you go downtown, all you have to do is let yourself be swept along by the crowd, knowing that at every turn something new and interesting will greet you.

Not far from where I was walking, a large crowd was gathering to listen to none other than Mrs. Roosevelt, or "Eleanor," as she is known colloquially. And that's a moniker that's meant good-naturedly, affectionately, and not at all lacking in respect, as it may sound to you. She was touting the new "Victory Bonds," and talked about the responsibilities inherent in peace. She spoke from a podium, behind which stood a replica of the Statue of Liberty. She is such a marvelous woman and keeps amazingly active. I was able to see and admire her from up close.

I got a glimpse of the late president only once, for a brief moment, as he sped by in a car with Prime Minister Churchill.

So much for today. Please do let me hear from you soon to reassure me that all is well with you.

Regards to all acquaintances,
Kurt

Munich, October 31, 1945

My dearest Kurt,

At work today I couldn't shake off a strange yet compelling thought. The entire building seems like a huge arena where a play is being performed on a continuous basis. It's called "Letters That Never Arrive." Seven hundred letters were brought to my section today, and I saw some of my coworkers glance at them in the most casual, superficial way, then toss them into bins marked "Release" or "Condemn."

I always think of who might be waiting for a particular letter. What hope and anticipation go into their expectations? I know that some of these letters will never reach their destination. I'm having a hard time with that, but then I concentrate on those that contain joyous messages, think of the recipients, and that somehow eases my agonizing.

My poor Kurt, I hope I'm not boring you with my endless tales. Sleep well. When you wake up tomorrow morning, I will have been thinking of you for more than six hours. Maybe I will have something more interesting to report by then.

For me, another day has gone by, one day closer to being with you.

I embrace you with much love,
Gerda

Munich, November 1, 1945

Kurt, my beloved,

I am so happy! Can you imagine the grin I broke into when your cable arrived? I flew from the first to the fifth floor, two steps at a time, to share the news with Mala!

Kurt, I knew that today would be a very special day, that something extraordinary would happen. When I awoke and went to the window, I beheld an incredible sight. The sky was still quite dark, but a deep red horizontal line was trying to crack through the darkness. The band was widening, forcing the light upward over the pine trees, which stood like sentinels guarding some enchanted gate. Soon golden rays touched the pine tops, giving them an illusion of coronets. Then the darkness rolled back, the sun rose, bathing everything in a fresh pink-golden hue. A breathtaking dawn of a new day. I knew it was special, but could not imagine how special it would turn out to be and how symbolic. That new bright day brought the first greeting from you after you stepped onto the shore of America. Can you possibly comprehend how happy I am? How delighted that you are well, that you have escaped all the dangers of that horrible war, that bloody devastation and destruction, and that you have safely returned home! I wish I could embrace the entire world with joy and gratitude but, above all, put my arms around you.

Everything I touched today had a new significance. The stamp with which I stamp the letters to either "Release" or "Condemn" documents bears the legend "Made in the U.S.A." and to know that you are there links me to you. The slips on which I write comments bear a tiny inscription, "U.S.A.—printed in New York," and this becomes my bridge to you. It is like another greeting from you. I love each slip of paper that comes from America, made there and not in Germany.

Oh, yes, let me tell you of my adventure today. On the streetcar I encountered a man who works in my section. I asked him whether he was taking this holiday off. "All Souls' Day is not my holiday," he said. "I am a Muslim. You see, I am a Turk." I remembered a Turkish greeting that Uncle Leo taught Artur and me, and spouted it out. You should have seen the reaction! Tears welled in his eyes. He said he had not heard his mother tongue for years!

Your picture got a fresh flower today. I change flowers every few days. Today I feel it should be special, in honor of your homecoming, and I am sending one on to you as well. The last rose of this summer.

The dream has become reality now. You are home, far away from here—far from loathsome Germany, away forever! May your homecoming be blessed with the fulfillment of all your wishes.

I embrace you happily with love and many kisses.

Yours,
Gerda

Gerda dearest,

My life is made up of waiting for your letters, as well as for discharge. I picture it all the more wonderful, though, to receive a whole bundle at once. At least that's how they usually arrive. Are you quite well and is everything all right?

I read something again in the newspaper that applies to us. Plans are underway to make it possible soon for Jews in Germany to maintain direct exchange of correspondence with foreign countries. It will, however, be routed indirectly by way of Paris. So we'll have to wait and see how much time will be lost in that manner.

While sitting around, I devote a lot of my time to reading and avail myself of the extensive record collection here. Last night there was a recital given by a baritone, accompanied by a pianist—and it was actually better than could have been expected. Then there's always a visit to the movies or possibly to the "clubhouse." What's being offered in Munich along those lines? Have you seen anything decent? Also, were there any more concerts, and do you get a chance to attend them once in a while? Is my little radio still functioning, and do you still use the gramophone to play our song, "Unkissed . . . [is no way to go to sleep]"?*

Fall here is magnificent. I wish I could take you into the countryside for us to admire the blaze of color, to walk over marvelously fragrant leaves and twigs, to inhale the bracing fall air and share a feeling of tranquillity, freedom, and inner composure. Everything looks so clean here and untouched. Houses, trees, streets have such a bandbox appearance, and the people are of course so friendly. Animated by the sight of the uniform, strangers will inquire after my well-being and will want to hear all about Europe. What I've always liked about America is the fact that, even without uniform, total strangers chat with you, completely uninhibited.

There are also the brightly illuminated stores, full of merchandise. I still can't get it into my head that all I have to do is ask for an item and pay for it. I occasionally lapse into questions such as, "How much chocolate can you sell me?" or words to that effect. I'm not writing this to make your mouth water, rather to show what's in store for you.

So far, I can't ascertain my brother Max's exact arrival date, but I keep watching the notices in the papers. They're projecting arrivals,

*German hit of that era.

including this coming Sunday, but Max's ship is not among them. Quite likely it'll arrive by next week.

Soon I'll be able to enclose a few photos. I can't wait to see how your picture turned out, my love! I should have taken a lot more snapshots of you, despite your protests and general camera phobia. Somehow, you always knew how to evade it. Perhaps a few kisses would induce you to be in a more tolerant mood?! And may I add to that that none other loves you as much as

Your Kurt

Munich, November 3, 1945

Kurt, my dearly beloved,

All day long I wait for the hour when I can be alone with you. Sitting in front of your picture and writing to you, I feel closest to you, connected by my thoughts and putting them on paper, the paper that you will hold in your hands, the words that you will read: my thoughts meeting yours!

It was a strange day. As I have told you, I was given the identity card of a "privileged person" because I work for an American agency. This entitles me to go to the *Insel*, a private club for just such privileged people, in Munich of all places. What irony! I really had no desire to go, but Mala and Günther were after me, as was Gretel, whose real name is Margaret, you know. She is one of my English coworkers. Afterward we were to go to her home. I finally gave in, more out of curiosity, because I have never been to a club before. At first, I felt somewhat ill-at-ease and furtive, much like those times during my adolescence when I would look at "forbidden" books, and it was understood they were "for grown-ups only." I must remind myself every so often that I *am* adult and twenty-one years old. But it takes some getting used to, for I have never lived in freedom as a grown-up. Well, anyway, I always wondered what nightclubs were like. It looked very beautiful and opulent. Everything was new to me: the upholstered chairs in hues of purple and black, the dim lights, and best of all, the food they served required no ration coupons! You should have seen the drinks that were available! I have never had an alcoholic drink, except with you when Japan capitulated. There is a six-member band there and they played German song hits. Their dance music is said to be the best in Germany.

All kinds of creeps asked me to dance. Needless to say, I refused;

some of them were probably SS men not so long ago. I didn't like the entire experience *here*, but I would love to go dancing with you—over there!

When we went to Margaret's home afterward, her parents and brother were all extremely nice and friendly. They played English songs on the record player, which I enjoyed. That gave me much to think about on my way back. Margaret had walked into her house very matter-of-factly, introducing me to her family—a commonplace enough gesture—oblivious to the fact that, by doing so, she was acting out my keenest dreams.

But then I think: You *are* at home. I am so lonely for you, I long for a home, to belong somewhere. I take refuge in writing to you, in belonging to you, in loving you; my thoughts are with you. What is happiness? A word, a state forged of many feelings: love, contentment, friendship, understanding, trust, joy, and sharing! I do believe that is happiness. I feel that for you, my love.

I am listening to the radio and they just announced: "We now bring you the voices of America—this is New York!" The voices of New York! Hearing that, I don't feel that you are so far away. The sounds of America fill the room and with them the sound of you. Soon you will let me know how your homecoming was. I'm so very eager to hear all about it. Meanwhile I will listen to the voices of America and dream of you. Good night, my love.

Gerda

The normality of Margaret's life hit me with painful force. Her everyday life was the fulfillment of the dream that had nurtured me during the years of darkness. The crutch to my survival was always the image of an evening with my family in the living room of my childhood, all of us engaged in simple pursuits, something I had regarded as "a boring evening at home." Whenever the going was rough, I would take out that memory like a precious jewel. Now Margaret was taking for granted precisely what I had so heedlessly taken for granted during my childhood.

New York City, November 4, 1945

My dearest Gerda,

I'm spending the weekend in New York again, to see what if anything has happened. My patience is being tested to the limit. Unfortunately there is nothing from you as yet. The uncertainty is mounting, despite all attempts to explain the long silence rationally.* Nothing is easy where emotions such as these are concerned. But I won't spoil your day with these idiotic complaints, because: (1) it doesn't change anything, and (2) by the time these lines reach you, news from you will long have arrived, and then it would be groundless and egotistical of me to throw cold water on your good mood.

A letter from your uncle arrived, dated July 29, 1945. It truly reflected the relief, the joy, and the gratitude for the still inconceivable miracle of your rescue.

Your Uncle Leo suggested rendering financial help via France or Switzerland. He was concerned whether you'll be able to continue to remain in the American zone, and he hoped for an opportunity to be in direct contact with you by mail. He mentioned that immigration to Turkey can only be accomplished by way of Palestine so far. That confirms what I wrote you recently, that is, that I no longer believe in emigration via Turkey, inasmuch as more direct ways appear to be opening up.

There's so much more I'd like to tell you. Not so much regarding matters of importance, rather of a reportorial nature. So, next time. My sister will definitely write to you any day; please excuse her, she's not quite used to taking care of *two* children yet and has her hands full.

A thousand kisses, from your
Kurt

Fort Dix, N.J., November 5, 1945

My dearest Gerdush,

My weekend in New York is over, and this will be the last time I'll report back to the army. And now that everything is done, I can tell you what held me here. Actually I would have been separated from the service a

*Gerda kept mailing her letters to my most recent APO address, and it took the Army Post Office some time to catch up with the records as they existed at the Fort Dix separation center.

week ago, only I spent a brief period of time in the hospital due to an insignificant intestinal disorder. There is absolutely nothing the matter with me. It was more like a week's vacation, during which I was able to spend four out of seven days in New York. In typical army fashion, it took much longer than necessary before I could be pronounced "in good health."

I believe that even you can hardly hate hospitals more than I do, but I have to admit that the army left nothing undone to disguise the fact that this is supposed to be a hospital. "R & R home" would be a better expression for it. I couldn't help but wish that it could have been like that for you; I know that all the girls would have recovered a lot faster.

This hospital, then, is an enormous one-story complex with a mile-long series of individual wards. It's quite simple, bright, warm, friendly. Each ward is a self-contained unit with a veranda, rocking chairs, facing well-tended lawns. Each bed is equipped with a mini-loudspeaker that can be tuned to different stations by pulling a string. The volume is controlled so as not to disturb the person next to you. A phone can be plugged in behind each bed, and once you've completed your call, a "meter maid" promptly arrives, presents the charges, and, if necessary, provides the right change. There are also facilities to play movies in wards where patients are confined to bed. Others can visit a real movie theater on the premises.

Needless to say there is an interdenominational chapel, an extensive record collection, and every conceivable newspaper and magazine is available. Among the many facilities you can find a canteen, a PX, a barbershop, a tailor, along with dining rooms, a clubhouse, and an entertainment lounge. Further, there is a room for arts and crafts, and some of the patients are quite adept at that. But the most amazing thing is the TV set we have in our ward, one of many, which allows us to view programs, mostly in the evening, from stations in New York and Philadelphia. No question about it, a new era has begun.

New York was wonderful. Saturday night I spent with my sister-in-law, Sue, taking in Broadway, bathed in the brightest of lights. We had a leisurely meal in a French restaurant, such as you couldn't get these days in France, and, following that, went to the Paramount Theater, a large movie house that offers both films and a variety show. Last night I went to the movies again, this time with Gerdi, who can't usually get away from home, because of the baby.

I talked myself blue in the face over the weekend, and who do you suppose I was talking about all this time? Were your ears ringing?

Kisses,
Kurt

Washington, D.C., November 7, 1945

My very dearest Gerda,

I do want to report on the results of today's inquiries and explain the steps necessary that we'll have to take.

Seeing the Visa Division of the State Department netted the following information: Although it is true that a consul will "soon" resume activities in Munich, he does not intend to concern himself with matters of emigration for a considerable time to come. Those cases will only be considered once the United States decides to admit Germans to this country as well, and that can take years. Naturally that was a big disappointment; however, I was subsequently able to find out something more favorable. What emerged from it is the fact that you *have* to get out of Germany by hook or crook, because the Polish quota is open and is little-used at the moment.

The Turkish embassy suggested that your uncle pursue the matter from there, only it wasn't clear to them how you would be able to get to Turkey. Inasmuch as that would presumably be achieved via Switzerland or France, it would of course be much simpler to obtain an American visa in either one of those countries. The question of food availability has to be considered and is a serious one in France, worse than it is for you in Germany at the moment. I know of a family in Switzerland, distant relatives of mine, to whom we might turn for assistance. Even if they themselves couldn't accommodate you, they could at the very least find you a place to stay. Your uncle writes that he can put funds at your disposal in Switzerland. I, myself, will send you whatever you need and take the matter up with my relatives.

We might consider France if none of this should jell, but Switzerland looks much more promising. My suggestion is the following:

Go to the Swiss consulate in Munich and explain your case and find out what their requirements are. Do the same thing at the French consulate, perhaps a temporary stay in France is now permitted. Something else—the American consul will require proof of your citizenship, pre-

128

sumably a Polish passport. Therefore go to or write to the nearest Polish consulate, committee, or whatever the case may be and apply for a passport or any other adequate identification. I realize that all this may not be as simple as it sounds, but that's what I found out, and that will be the fastest way of getting you here.

Don't for a moment be plagued by doubts. This matter may well shape up to be somewhat more complicated than we initially thought, but we're going to do it! You always had a lot of optimism—as you say yourself—and have overcome much that was incredibly more difficult, always retaining hope, and this, too, we will overcome.

If I didn't think that you'd understand me correctly, I wouldn't be saying this to you from my "secure" perch, but do know that I will assist you wherever I can. More tomorrow from Washington.

Regards and thousands of kisses,
Kurt

Washington, D.C., November 8, 1945

My dearest Gerda,

A few quick lines before leaving Washington. I tried to get some additional information, went to several organizations, and then was referred to the "Joint"* in New York. They might be of help to you and are represented at the German Museum in Munich, and in Switzerland as well. I am curious what the people in New York will advise. Most important, you should go to the Swiss legation and apply for a temporary stay in Switzerland. For my part I'll take the necessary steps here.

I'm enclosing a really nice photo of you. You and the flowers blend so well, and it's impossible to say which underscores which beauty. Don't ask me for a picture of myself; I have only one, and it's just too stupid. I can well imagine how Gary's picture of me must have turned out. Am I really that idiotic looking in reality? Don't answer that one. Soon I'll have civilian clothes, perhaps then.

There is a package on the way to you containing shoes. Unfortunately I had to select them at random, so do write what your actual size is, and

*Joint Distribution Committee, an organization dedicated to helping Jews in need overseas.

please give me all your measurements. Above all, you *must* tell me what things you are lacking. After all, it's so easy here!

> So, for now, regards to all the girls, Gerdush,
> and ardent kisses from your
> Kurt

Munich, November 10, 1945

My dearest Kurt,

There is much I have to tell you today. A girl I know just returned from Bielsko, where she saw my former nanny. The latter said that she had heard I was alive and suggested that I should come back immediately. She has saved some items from our home.

That feeling brought forth twofold emotion: joy, to hear from my beloved Niania, Frau Bremza, who knew me from the day I was born and lived in our house for thirteen years! But, more so, disappointment and unbearable pain, because there was no news from Artur. If he were in Bielsko, Niania certainly would know. What should I think? What should I do? I said I could never go home, but now with Niania's words a feeling of home creeps into my heart, a longing. How can I see my childhood home without my family there? But I must look for Artur; thoughts of him are constantly with me. Where is he? Where? He must be alive, he must; any other thought is unthinkable. After all, there are miracles; just look at us.

I read an article today in a south German paper that details what happened to Jews in the Volga-Vistula region. But that can't be what happened to Artur, it can't. I will never give up hope, never!

With you at my side, I must believe in good things only.

I will be changing jobs; I can get something better and more interesting. Will write about that tomorrow.

> For now, with all my love,
> Gerda

Munich, November 11, 1945

Kurt dearest,

It is Sunday night, and I'm glad that I will be working again tomorrow. Sundays are hard to take.

Please, Kurt, forgive the tone of yesterday's letter. I have earnestly resolved, and hope to stick to it, not to write about fear and loneliness and such emotions. My moods will darken your day when my letters reach you, weeks later, while I will have coped with it and the pain will have passed. But you see, when loneliness and longing for you overwhelm me, it's hard not to share it with you. Since my thoughts are always with and about you. I can't control my pen, or perhaps don't want to, for I share *all* thoughts with you. So please forgive me, and don't take it too seriously.

This morning when I woke up, there was an eerie brightness. I jumped out of bed and saw a white blanket of snow covering the earth. To me, it is soothing, covering the ground that in former days has seen such gruesome sights. I like to think of this winter as being different, not of the horror the last one imparted, rather as the wonderland it was during my childhood.

An uncontrollable desire came over me to run out into the snow and build a snowman. And I did build one of sorts. The world is so incredibly beautiful again that I want to—no, I have to—believe that goodness and kindness will prevail.

The new unit in which I work deals with diplomatic mail and Red Cross correspondence, as I may have mentioned. It belongs in the category of "Preferred Mail." And guess what? My boss's first name is Kurt! So whenever I lift my eyes, I see his name plate, his desk being across from mine. It's like a greeting in the flesh, because you are constantly on my mind. Quite a bit of Polish mail crosses my desk these days, mostly dealing with letters sent from camp to camp. The writing reflects so much misery, and in it you find thinly veiled references to poems or sayings,* which usually are not difficult to figure out. Can't help thinking it's an intrusion into the privacy of others' thoughts and feelings, though. In some instances the letters contain information that I'm supposed to stamp "Condemned," and I agonize over those. It's a case of duty versus emotion, and there are some things I simply can't get myself to do.

All my love,
Gerda

*Possible attempts at encoded messages.

My dearest, dearest Gerda,

Your gorgeous Edelweiss is right next to me in order to trigger inspiration.

Today I visited the JDC,* and a great weight has been lifted. They believe that they can be of help in cases like yours. I was advised to dispatch the completed papers to their office, and they will see to it that you will get out of Germany. What they know about Switzerland, on the other hand, is not supposed to be so good. Once in a while there are allegedly cases where exceptions are made, but in general, entrance to that country is not granted, except if you can prove that you will get the American visa immediately.

So that is the exact opposite of my assumptions thus far. But I don't really care, as long as the JDC can truly do something, perhaps by way of France. Of course, all means would then be at your disposal there as well. If I'm not mistaken, the Joint is represented at the German Museum in Munich. Why don't you explore whether you can get some information there. In the meantime I'll issue the affidavits and send them to you. Actually that'll take a few weeks, because I'll have to go to Buffalo for them, and I also want to be able to prove that I have a job, what my salary is, etc. In that regard, it looks as if I'm going to have a starting salary of fifty dollars per week, which is neither bad nor exceptionally good. I want to cast about to see whether I can find something better, or at least a job with a future.

Congratulations on your promotion! The letter containing the details has still not arrived, but you did mention that apparently they had you earmarked for a promotion from the start. That probably means that you'll have to work harder, quite aside from the extra hours they are forcing on you. Is it at least more interesting than the previous work? You know that I want you to withhold absolutely nothing, including anything that is unpleasant or too difficult. By the same token, don't think that in such a case I would exaggerate your difficulties in my mind. If I recommend that it's time to give up the censorship position when it gets to be too much, don't let that keep you from mentioning further details about it in the future. Once the disadvantages outweigh the advantages, let it fall by the wayside.

Barbara was sitting on my lap while I was reading your lines. She's a real doll and tells me stories for hours about her adventures. Although

*Joint Distribution Committee.

she is terribly shy with most people, once you win her confidence, you have her complete devotion and can gain many precious insights into the world as seen from a child's vantage point. That reminds me of a children's book, a fantastic satire on the puzzling goings-on in the adult world that can only be fully grasped by adults. I'm talking about *Alice in Wonderland*. That book is merely one of the minor miracles that await you once you've perfected your English. Isn't that an incentive for you to bone up on it?

Incidentally, don't think for a moment that we'll speak one more word of German than absolutely necessary. And no moaning or groaning will help you. In that matter I'll be quite unmerciful. You know I love the English language so much that that alone is sufficient reason why I find America so beautiful.

Can I say how much I am in suspense about the photos you mentioned. I hope I'll get them soon.

And now, good night, dearest.

All my love,
Kurt

New York City, November 14, 1945

Hello Darling,

I do wish I could wake up each morning like this. The first thing I noticed was that Barbara had moved close to my bed, had gently shaken my shoulder, and, beaming all over, was handing me an airmail envelope. Naturally that could only mean one thing, and it tore me from my state of dazed sleepiness without further ado. It turned out to be your detailed and beautiful reports of October 16 and 31.

Your writing is of such timeless content that I'm convinced I'll be able to read it over again ten or even fifty years from now and get the same enjoyment out of it. Fashions may change but your soul, never!

Let me start with the matter I consider most important. You mentioned the story of the ID card. It goes without saying that you'll need to have some sort of citizenship and, as mentioned, the Polish quota is allegedly quite favorable.

I'm glad, by the way, that in general you don't tie yourself up in self-imposed conventions. Please know that for me something is always "right" if it stems from spontaneous emotions and as long as it does not harm others. I consider it a healthy sign that you sometimes—or even frequently—rebel against all-too-stupid constraints imposed by the world around you. What's wrong with breaking into laughter if something strikes you as comical? If it's a prerequisite for adulthood to maintain a stern exterior at all times, and under no circumstances give your sense of humor free rein, then I prefer to remain childish. Are we more mature because we have learned to repress the spontaneous in ourselves?

You write so negatively about the possibility of my coming to Europe. It happens to be true that I myself wouldn't like to see you being alone in the States in such a case, but I can't agree with any of the other reasons you give. I made some inquiries in Washington, however, and the State Department claims that even wives of American servicemen wanting to leave Germany cannot be processed any faster. In other respects they will get preferential treatment, as will fiancées. Although the start of processing may take a considerable time yet, let's wait for further developments. We might still consider it.

Good to hear that you have occasion to visit nightclubs. I regret not being able to accompany you; the atmosphere does appear to be most amusing and entertaining. But I'm sure that we'll find appropriate substitutes here in time.

A few days ago I too attended something special. I went to the marvelous theater I raved so much about to you, namely Radio City Music Hall. That will be among the first things you'll have to see. There was an excellent film playing; followed by a symphonic program; then a dance troupe that performed with incredible precision; finally there was a variety show, including a ventriloquist, dancing horse, and what have you. The whole thing was staged with fantastic light effects, and I could see shows like that time and again without ever being disappointed.

Tomorrow Max is slated to be discharged from the army, and I should finally get to see him then. There'll be a big "welcome home" dinner for the family on Sunday, and next week, he and Sue will take a vacation, sort of a second honeymoon.

Enough now, more tomorrow. Let me embrace you and kiss you,
Your Kurt

Buffalo, November 17, 1945

My darling Gerda,
In case you are startled by this and similar forms of address, I hasten

to declare that it's high time to begin your "transition." I was delighted to hear that you are all geared up for America.

Don't ever think I can no longer put myself into your situation. I remember only too well how I felt before coming to the States and for the first time seeing an American travel brochure advertising a railroad trip from New York to Buffalo and on to Niagara Falls. Everything came across as so "American," from the paper to the print, color, and design. Here was the America I was soon to see with my own eyes. And that's what happened to me later, even with the smallest things, normally too trivial to mention. They were all a part, however minimal, of that "land of miracles."

The matter of your Swiss acquaintance needs immediate discussion, because such a connection cannot be underestimated. Regardless of whether he has influence or not, the least he can do for you is to get the necessary information. Should an opportunity present itself through him that promises any chance of success, do immediately avail yourself of it, if common sense and logic so dictate. Even if such a chance should deviate somewhat from my previous suggestions as to temporary stay there or anywhere else, please don't wait for my answer, if at all possible. I can modify the formalities here according to any changing situation. Don't miss any chances simply because you wanted to consult me first as to whether it's okay to do so.

How can I thank you for the very last souvenir from your autumnal garden? This rose signifies all that is beautiful. It grew and blossomed while we, only a few yards away, bantered, understood each other, danced, forged plans, and got to know each other better. In that sense it is like all we discovered in each other, that sprouted and blossomed until it came—just as did these deep red petals—to full bloom. And now winter has come for us as well, but a winter that already holds the promise of a new spring.

I do want to wish you a most pleasant Hanukkah. Too bad we can't celebrate together, but I've tried to convey my sentiments in a more graphic manner in the shape of a thin, longish parcel [an umbrella], although I'm hoping you won't have to make all-too-extensive use of it.

My emotions know no limits, and we don't have to put any constraints on the number of kisses we're sending each other.

Kurt

My very best little Gerda,

Just got back from downtown and found an envelope stuck into the door frame. Thought instantly that it had to be something special. It turned out to be a cable from Istanbul with a heartfelt message that put me in a splendid mood. I will transmit it verbatim and should you, contrary to my assumption, experience any difficulties with it, there'll be enough people around you who can help with the translation. So then, here goes:

MY HEARTIEST CONGRATULATIONS AND WARMEST WISHES FOR YOUR FUTURE STOP GOD WITH YOU STOP DETAILED LETTER FOLLOWS STOP PREFER GERDA'S TRANSFER SWITZERLAND STOP WILL INTERVENE CONSULATE HERE STOP MEANTIME PLEASE DO UTMOST YOURS LEOPOLD.

In regard to you, weather is a major concern of mine. You will let me know what winter clothes you really need, won't you? Otherwise, I'll only be forced to send things at random, as I had to do thus far.

Last night there was a big "welcome home" supper for Max, who looks terrific, which is unusual for him. Even as a child he never ate properly. Although that improved with time, I remember that he never really knew what he had eaten, because he was always too busy telling tales at mealtime. Can you imagine what yarns he was able to spin about Berlin on this occasion?

Tomorrow morning it will be back to camp for me, and I can only hope that this time I'll be discharged. If not I'll get a pass again, because this coming Thursday is a double holiday: Gerdi's birthday and the American national holiday Thanksgiving. It's traditional to have a noon meal of turkey on that day, although this year we may have to do without because, incredible as it may sound, a few diverse things are still rather scarce. Naturally they are ludicrously unimportant things compared to your situation. No, your ration coupons are not valid here, so don't bother sending them to me! But seriously, do tell me what's lacking on your end. Perhaps I can send something special.

You know, as touching as it was to see your happiness over my safe arrival, I couldn't fend off a slight smile when I read about the alleged "dangers" I escaped, according to you. You, of all people, are talking about me in that manner! Compared to your experience, my sojourn in Europe was more like a field trip to the botanical gardens by students at a girls' finishing school.

If all goes well I'll be in Buffalo by the end of the week, where there is a considerable amount to be done related to your emigration. I don't suppose I'll stay there longer than a week.

Barbara just called out a "good night" to me and asked me to give her regards to Aunt Gerda. I'm wondering whether she hasn't assessed you correctly, because when I answered her question as to whom I'm writing at the moment, she came back instantly with "Can she read?" Far be it from me to judge that, but perhaps you could prove that "she can write" by magically getting something into my mailbox by tomorrow morning. How about it? Your reward will be a few dozen kisses.

Love,
Kurt

Fort Dix, N.J., November 21, 1945

Gerda dearest,

So far every day seems to bring something new, some diversion. Otherwise the waiting for you would be unbearable. I wonder what frame of mind the monotonous rhythm of the hours must be putting you in. Actually I shouldn't write like that. After all, we also have moments to chat every now and then, and that ought to help us pass this trying period of waiting. It's just that sometimes a feeling of loneliness overcomes me quite suddenly and then I can't always be sensible.

I returned to the hospital yesterday and immediately received my discharge, although I do have to stay here at the Separation Center until tomorrow, in order to say good-bye to the army once and for all. I'll be separated from the service on Thanksgiving Day, giving me even more reason to be thankful. Don't misunderstand me: In America, people don't particularly like to play at soldiering, none of which is to say that I'm not immensely proud to have been allowed to wear this uniform and to have been of some service, however minimal, to the country that gave me infinitely more than I can ever repay. At any rate I owe the army a huge debt of gratitude, in view of the fact that without it, I never would have met you!

Naturally I forgot to mention the main thing in my last letter; that is to report on my brother's reaction to our engagement. As far as he was concerned, I didn't quite succeed in springing a big surprise. He claimed to have surmised something to that effect at our meeting in Frankfurt, when I apparently talked about you, so this turn of events finds him quite prepared. I accepted profuse congratulations on your behalf, and can only say everybody is very eager to see and meet you.

Listen, Gerda, could you find out how far along Captain Presser is with her points for discharge? I'm thinking that important mail might be lost for an indefinite period of time in case she should suddenly depart. Is there nobody who has signed up for a specific length of time and therefore would know exactly how long he or she will remain there?

An ardent kiss for you, from your
Kurt

Munich, November 22, 1945

My dearest Kurt,

I know that today's letter will not make much sense. Forgive me, but here it is. First, concerning our situation: Wherever you look, whatever you read, the word "help" jumps out at you. Yet all the organizations you approach seem dedicated to anything but rendering information or help. Starting with the Polish Legation and Consulate, which is in operation, to the Red Cross and UNRRA,* no one can help me to obtain a certificate of my Polish citizenship. The Polish Committee is again closed for several days, and I am supposed to write to Bielsko, although no normal mail service exists as yet. They do claim that the city hall or Bureau of Vital Statistics will have my birth certificate. Personally I wonder whether those records were destroyed or not. The officials make everything quite difficult under those circumstances. They know very well what the situation is, that we got out of camps, that so much was destroyed. They can question me in the language, in history, or whatever. It really is upsetting, but there is some hope along another avenue. As I told you, one of my coworkers here in the diplomatic section is a Swiss citizen and can travel back and forth to Switzerland—lucky man! He told me that I could get a transit visa through Switzerland because they do have an American consulate.

As you wrote, my uncle has my birth certificate. How wise my father was to have had the foresight to send it to Turkey. With that in hand, and if my uncle could deposit some security funds for me, that should

---

*The United Nations Relief and Rehabilitation Administration, an organization set up by forty-three nations, was active during the years 1943–1947. As its name implied, its aim was to bring relief to war-ravaged Europe, and in that role it performed its greatest service during the two years after the end of World War II. Food was distributed to millions of starving people, and the agency provided livestock to devastated areas and helped revive agriculture.

make it possible to get permission to enter Switzerland. He has been offering financial help all along. Naturally I won't use the money, it's just so the Swiss have the assurance that I shall not become a burden. But I'll need to see the American consul in order to get a visa for the United States. With your papers, stating that you will marry me immediately, there should be no trouble. I am told my stay in Switzerland would only be for a few days. If that should work, I pray it may take only four to six weeks until it goes through. Although I don't dare to let my hopes go too high, I foolishly do so all the same. Please cable Uncle Leo and send me the papers. I think my birth certificate should also allow me to obtain a Polish passport. I am so sorry to trouble you with all that. You have enough to do to find a job, to get back to civilian life and have some rest, instead of taking care of all the details concerning me. I hope that I will be able to make it up to you.

Now another chapter: I heard that some girls who were in camp with me have found temporary shelter at the German Museum. They were the ones from the transport that split from us last January 29. I have not seen them for almost a year and was so anxious to learn who survived. Early this morning I took off from work to go and see them right away. It didn't take long before I found them, but in what condition! You simply can't imagine what shape they are in. Three girls are seriously ill and have no one who cares for them, no place to stay. They arrived from Poland a short while ago, and in their condition have to stand in long lines to get food stamps and acquire accommodations.

I had just read a long article about the Bayerisches Hilfswerk* and the Red Cross, attesting to how eager and well-prepared those two organizations are to help all in dire need. That really got me going. Clutching the address in my hand, I was on the next streetcar headed for the Bayerisches Hilfswerk office. More than anything I was driven by outrage over the injustice of it all. Here it's months after the end of the war, and still nothing is being done for them. Once at my destination, I asked to see the person in charge. Naturally I was challenged as to whether I had an appointment. I laughed and announced that I was from the American Civilian Censorship Division, there on a most urgent mission. As soon as he heard the word "American," I was instantly ushered into the inner sanctum. I still can't get over my nerve. The official in charge seemed surprised. But before he had a chance to quiz me, I thrust the

*Bavarian Aid Soceity.

article in his face, putting it to him, "Do you or don't you want to hear about the deplorable conditions of people who were in concentration camps for years?" That got his attention, and he immersed himself in the article. I pushed my advantage by spilling out details of the situation I had encountered. The result? I gained admission for the three girls to the Schwabinger Hospital, along with emergency ration coupons and the necessary accommodations.

The official was eager to learn how I had gotten to him without an appointment, and I repeated my story about working for the Civilian Censorship Division. He seemed impressed and asked me what other languages I spoke, then offered me a job on the spot. I said that I would have to think it over and would come back. "Without appointment?" he inquired, and we both broke into laughter and shook hands. I hardly recall how I got back to the museum with my glad tidings. Quite likely I must have sprouted wings!

I also learned that Escia, a friend from Bielsko, just came to Munich. I have known her from earliest childhood, and in those days was closer to her than to Ilse. Throughout our time in the camps, she had been helped by her sister-in-law's friend Sabina, who is considerably older. They, too, had paired up, as I had done with Ilse. I am excited about seeing Escia tomorrow; she just got back from Bielsko, and I can't wait to see someone who knows my parents and Artur. I pray she has some news of them for me.

What a long and turbulent day this has been, how full of emotion!

Good night, my love; may tomorrow bring happy news.

Gerda

Munich, November 24, 1945

My beloved Kurt,

I can't believe it yet. I do not dare think about it, but my heart is bursting with joy. Artur is supposed to be in Turkey with Uncle Leo! I can barely write, I am so excited, so full of gratitude. But my first thought, of course, is to share my happiness with you, my beloved.

Here's how I found out. We had company tonight, and in the middle of our animated conversation, the doorbell rings and Mala goes to answer, then calls up to say that there is someone who wants to speak to me.

I run down, and a man stands in front of me. He looks familiar; where do I know him from? His lips tremble, and for a moment he cannot utter a word. Finally he says, "Don't you recognize me?" The voice brings back a memory. He was not a close friend, but nevertheless a friend of Artur's. They were taken away on the same transport.

"Where is Artur?" I ask.

"Don't you know? He's in Turkey!" And he proceeds to tell me that he just arrived from Bielsko, where he learned only last week that Artur is in Turkey!

I am almost afraid to express my elation, but it overwhelms me. It bursts forth from every pore of my being. I can't get a hold of myself. My prayers are answered! I hope, God willing, that in a few days I will hear from him through you. You can't imagine my state of mind, my happiness, and, to top it off, five letters from you arrived. You are with me, you share my joy. My happiness is complete.

Oh, I wish I could embrace you now and whisper, "Kurt, do you know, do you know how much I love you?"

Yours,
Gerda

Munich, November 27, 1945

My dearest Kurt,

Today I can at least render an exact account regarding the matters that I accomplished. I don't want to keep you in suspense too long and want to tell it exactly as it was. I can only say that the consulate turned out to be more than favorably disposed, because I'm now in possession of a Polish ID certificate, including photo, fingerprints, and other personal data. It's signed by a Polish liaison officer from the newly formed government and is embellished with so many stamps, eagles, etc., as I haven't seen since my school days when the Polish emblem was displayed everywhere.

Once I arrived at the Polish consulate, I saw the Polish flag waving in the breeze outside. A feeling of nostalgia overcame me. After all, it *is* the language that I command best, the literature I know best. I loved Poland, despite experiencing some dark aspects of my life there.

My initial interview at the consulate was with an engineer, and when he found out that I'm from Bielsko, he couldn't express his enthusiasm effusively enough. He studied there, and the conversation got off to an animated start, after which I was able to get to the point.

I had come to get proof of my Polish citizenship, and one of the officials did indeed recognize it. He promised me a document that would allow me to apply for entry into Switzerland, not without pointing out, however, that only a committee such as the Joint can represent my interests. I saw them too, but they don't handle such matters for the time being, and nothing at all can be accomplished there. So I decided to try my luck with the Polish Committee, but had to get a certificate from the Joint that I am not under their care. In that manner I was able to get a Polish passport, issued in my name. They advised me to see the Swiss consul, and speculated that with a bit of luck I should be able to gain entry into Switzerland within a week. Can you believe that?

They wished me every conceivable type of success and offered their help, in case I should have difficulties with the Swiss authorities. The next stop is the Swiss consulate. I'll try it tomorrow.

I would only ask that you send me some sort of paper attesting to the fact that you are trying to get me to the States. That will prove that I do not intend to stay in Switzerland. Please ask my uncle via the fastest possible way to let you know by cable where funds are at my disposal (including the address), which I can refer to in my application. That's all I should need. Then we can expect things to proceed without a hitch within days.

Kurt, I can hardly believe that I may see you soon! Can you imagine that? I'm trying to ward off thoughts of Artur; I fear getting prematurely excited, but I'm so ecstatic because of the news that reached me three nights ago, that I can hardly think straight anymore. Just imagine, he may be in Turkey!

Recently you said that you intend to have a headstone set at the local cemetery here in behalf of one of your relatives, and that you need exact details as to how to accomplish that. You were going to send me the particulars, and I've wanted to ask you about that before. Now that it's probable I'll soon be leaving here, I'd like to see that matter taken care of.

So my dear, now I sit here all alone, although I feel I've had a tête-à-tête with you. How awful that I had to fill these pages with nothing but formalities and such. I wish that would already come to an end.

You again mentioned packages that you sent off to me. Listen, Kurt, I really don't need anything. You seem hell-bent on leading me into temptation by making me eat chocolate! The loss of my slender figure will be on *your* conscience! You may laugh, but I don't want to hear your reproaches later.

Keep well, my dearest Kurt, and excuse the scribbling. We have constant power outages here, so don't ask how I managed to get this down.

> With countless kisses (who's counting, after all?),
> Your Gerda

Although the sudden hope held out that my brother Artur had made it to Turkey threw me into a state of elation bordering on hysteria, those feelings were tempered by a gnawing suspicion that my euphoria might be unwarranted. When the first message from my uncle in Turkey reached me after the war, I was devastated to find that he was asking me for news of Artur.

My family had agreed early in the war that in case we should ever lose touch with each other for whatever reason, we would contact Uncle Leo for news. That was exactly what I had done on being liberated. When I had last heard from him, Artur was living in Russian territory that had been overrun by the German army. Toward the end of the war, the Russians retook that zone, which led me to believe that he would have been liberated months before I was, and would meanwhile have gotten in touch with Uncle Leo. The conclusion was obvious, but while I could absorb the real reasons for his silence on an intellectual level, I could not come to terms with them emotionally. Even while lighting memorial candles for him and reciting the Kaddish, the Jewish prayer for the dead, my fantasies still centered on my finding him someday. That would persist over the decades to this day, and I never cease to look for him in hotel lobbies and at airports whenever I travel.

The loss of Artur has been the hardest to bear, and was most keenly felt at the time a few years ago, when I stood at Auschwitz, where I could experience a closure, because that site represented my parents' graves. But what happened to my brother, and where is his grave? That pain will be with me until the day I die.

My beloved Kurt,

Escia was in Bielsko last week. Unfortunately—always the word "unfortunately"—she brought the confirmation that I could not bring myself to utter in regard to my beloved parents. I had a bitter struggle with myself as to whether I should tell you everything. My dearest, if we are going to be totally honest with each other, then you must know it. There is no longer any doubt about the fate of my parents. Escia got it from a reliable source. Even while I write these words, I can't accept that, I just can't. I begged her to tell me the entire truth, also about Artur. She was hesitant at first, and said she didn't know, but finally admitted that she had heard from a friend who was with Artur that he and others—I can't write it, I can't say it—were shot. I can't picture it; I refuse to believe it.

Escia had three brothers. The oldest made it to Palestine before the war. He was with the Palestine Brigade of the British Army in Africa, where he was seriously wounded. Her youngest brother, Sam, was hidden as a Pole, together with her middle brother, Michael, who was Artur's best friend. Someone betrayed Sam, and Michael found out about it. Although he could have stayed where he was, he went in search of Sam, and that's how both died horrible deaths. I can't describe it, can't come to terms with it. I knew both boys so well, especially Michael. He was always at our house, and they were so funny and so exuberant. He and Artur were always playing practical jokes on each other, often on the phone. Their phone number happened to be 1622 while ours was 2622, a difference of just one digit. What fun they had when someone dialed the wrong number.

I just can't believe what I heard; it's so difficult, and I keep thinking it's surely a nightmare from which I will soon awake. Escia told me so much; we talked all night. She went to see my house in Bielsko and it's still standing, but is in sad disrepair. The garden is overgrown, and strangers live within its walls.

During a visit to the cemetery, Escia found my grandparents' graves. I'm immensely grateful to her for that gesture. Everything that Escia learned amounted to nothing but sad news. Abek, the boy I told you about, died in the vicinity of Regensburg. Nothing, nothing but terrible news.

I sat listening, overwhelmed by grief and in disbelief, learning with horror what the girls in the other column of the original transport went through even *after* liberation. I shuddered to hear all that. They were liberated by the Russians, and most of the girls were repeatedly raped. It drove two of the girls whom I knew quite well to suicide. Imagine, suicide, after the war, after the camps, after liberation!

Please, Kurt, forgive me for writing you all that. I had resolved numerous times before that I wanted to shield you from the horrible truth, but am doing this today for a reason that I will explain.

In my long conversation with Escia and the other girls, I found myself totally bewildered. My friends tell me that I am different. If I had not been with them, they would doubt that I went through the camps at all. When they asked about my life and I told them that I was happy and spoke about you, they thought I was crazy—and perhaps I am. They say that after what we went through, we can't be happy, we are only deluding ourselves.

But I conjure up your image in my mind's eye, then run toward your embrace, and feel that, yes, I can be happy as long as I can be with you.

All I want is to leave this hateful place, be away from Germany forever. Right after the war was over, in the hospital when you left and I thought I might never see you again, I thought that God had punished me by leaving me alive. I didn't want to go on living. And during the night of my crisis, when they thought I would die, you came and pulled me through. Since that day I have known that I am no longer alone, and now I have your love. I feel so blessed, so privileged, so grateful. I don't know what you will say regarding these words; they don't belong in your world now. Therefore please don't answer them with bland assurances that are meant to make things easier for me, to assuage my pain.

I am exhausted now, but will continue to write, because I have more to say and I must say it tonight. It is like a confession on a dark, tormented night, while ghosts try to smother me in their embrace. I know that dawn will come soon, and everything will look better, brighter in the light of day. But my pen keeps on writing, impelled by my anguish, driven to spell out my most painful thoughts. I know that no matter what promise I might make now, and no matter how resolute I may be, that this be the last letter in this vein, I can never be sure of what other monstrous truths I will learn, or that I will be able to cope with them alone.

I must tell you that I question my right to tie my life to yours, which to me is the most precious on earth. Will my past, the loss of my family, my own nightmarish memories overshadow our life together? I know of your pain and loss, so akin to mine, and only want to bring joy and sunshine to your life. I pray that our love may permeate our beings like gentle harmonies that will soothe our pain and transport us to a realm of peace. I pray so ardently that it will be possible once I'm on the other side of the ocean.

There is a storm brewing outside. I look at your picture, my love, and think of the coming of spring. A spark of hope enters my being. It is like a metaphor: the storm outside our lives, but together we'll find shelter in our love.

I embrace you,
Your Gerda

᙮ ᙮ ᙮ ᙮ ᙮ ᙮ ᙮ ᙮ ᙮ ᙮ ᙮ ᙮

I met Abek in September 1941, almost two years to the day after the war began. He was twenty-two to my seventeen, an artist of great talent. Because the Germans had warehouses full of furnishings plundered from Jewish homes, they established a small camp whose inmates were Jewish artisans who would restore what were at times valuable pieces of furniture and art objects. Nazi officials from all over Germany would visit the warehouse and select items for their personal use.

Abek's special skill was the restoration of canvases, and he also had a fine hand for painting portraits. He was introduced to me through Ilse's mother, who knew someone in that camp. Because of his skills, he had the freedom to roam the city, often working in municipal buildings. It meant that he had a less restrictive life, which allowed him to visit our home at regular intervals. That is how our relationship began; though for me it was a pleasant friendship, for him it was love. He would prove to be incredibly kind to me, trying in every way to ease the hardships that would follow for me in the slave labor factories. Thus, he would paint portraits of German guards and their families in his camp so as to be able to send me items of clothing, food, or other necessities. For all he did for me, I will always owe a debt of gratitude to his memory.

᙮ ᙮ ᙮ ᙮ ᙮ ᙮ ᙮ ᙮ ᙮ ᙮ ᙮ ᙮

Buffalo, November 30, 1945

My most beloved Gerda,

I feel as though I'm engaged in a game of "musical cities," and this week Buffalo is the "seat" I'm occupying. The outcome of my seesaw attempts at finding the right job is still undecided, so it could be either

New York or Buffalo. It's also impossible to figure out what's happening to time. It seems hardly longer than an hour since I last wrote to you, and yet two days have passed. And I'm by no means finished making the rounds of people I know. Presumably I will have to stay longer than expected in order to do it all. My head's buzzing like mad. New York was never like this. I had no idea I knew so many people here, and it goes without saying that each and every one of them would be offended if I didn't visit them. By the look of it it'll be another week before I return to New York.

This morning I received the enclosed letter from Istanbul, including a few lines to my sister-in-law, through whom I was in touch with your uncle until I got back to the States. Those lines repeated once more all the cables that are already in your possession, so I won't enclose them again. What was interesting was that they were written only four weeks ago. That makes it clear that my letters from here reached their destination and that we can soon expect to get a direct answer from your uncle. I find that Leo writes in the most touching fashion; he absolutely has his heart in the right place!

A number of the papers you require will be made out by my cousin today. At the same time my uncle in St. Louis wrote that he will expedite the matter on his end and that the documents will be in my possession soon. All that's needed after that is proof of my employment. In that connection I looked up my former employer here, who seemed to regret seeing me settle in New York. He offered to provide references I can present to firms there, which may or may not help.

My friends are trying to persuade me to stay in Buffalo. After surveying the situation here, however, I find that my chances appear to be better in New York. Naturally there are disadvantages to living in the big city because, in general, life is much more pleasant here, quite aside from the fact that the scarcity of apartments has assumed serious proportions in New York. Despite that, the advantages ought to outweigh those disadvantages. Finding a job there shouldn't take more than a week or two. Wish me luck.

I wonder if you're aware of something that was in the newspapers recently. It allegedly will be possible to correspond with displaced persons via UNRRA, but you would have to initiate the process on your end. Are you familiar with that? It might be a good thing, because then we could be sure that mail would arrive. Perhaps we could try it alternately one way, then the other. What do you think?

At last I've acquired some civilian clothes, a suit, which ought to enable me to send you some photos soon. It was no simple matter to get this suit. These days you have to take what there is. Imagine, I went to the very large clothing factory owned by my relatives, and they had nothing in my size. They had to refer me to one of the retailers with whom they do business. Naturally, as soon as things start rolling, there'll be more of everything available than anybody might need. For the moment, though, everything is at a standstill, due to the countless strikes, at a time when there are masses of returning servicemen. Also, it seems that manufacturers are still geared, at least in part, to military orders and are only gradually converting to civilian needs.

Buffalo can be quite ugly in winter, stripped down to a bare and gloomy appearance. So I expect the white stuff will last till the weekend, when we'll take some photos. You see, right now the snow has turned everything into a magnificent fairy-tale landscape, even though it is so deep that cars are forever getting stuck in it. No change there since I went away.

I feel it's ludicrous to write such nonsense to you, but I'm thinking that you too might be interested in what I'm observing since my return.

Love,
Kurt

Munich, December 1, 1945

Dearest Kurt,

Above all I have to report what I accomplished at the Swiss consulate. All I found out was that admission to that country is totally blocked for the time being, and that a transit visa is completely out of the question. At any rate I'm supposed to come back in three to four weeks. Although it was conveyed to me in the nicest possible manner, it means the doors remain closed.

Following that, I went to the Polish Committee to learn more about the stuff they filled my head with before, but unfortunately couldn't see the gentleman who two or three days ago promised me Switzerland on a silver platter. Another one suggested Paris, as before! Next I'll have to visit the Polish Military Government on Monday, and subsequently the French one. He promised to discuss the matter with a French captain who is a good friend of his. Despite all that I haven't altogether given up hope regarding Switzerland, because my Swiss acquaintance with whom I discussed the matter—I've written about him before—was not the type to make empty promises.

In any case there is a lot of running around to do. If it keeps up like this I should soon be able to take an exam as a tourist guide for Munich, and you can probably do the same in New York! Kurt, don't we have marvelous occupations! Actually there's nothing I like better than to flit about like that. Peculiar pleasure, don't you think?

To be honest I can't really focus on my work these days; my thoughts and worries do distract me a great deal. It's true that the office can be quite amusing at times, but it's the environment that is so, rather than the work itself. Actually they've now given me greater responsibility and independence, a wider circle of autonomy, yet there are always constraints and regulations, as a result of which the inflexible point inevitably wins out. Initially I thought it was just what I had longed for, that it would give me a measure of satisfaction, but even when you were still here I already realized that it would turn into failure from that point of view.

I discussed it recently with various people and had to listen to their advice: "Do you want to expend all your heart and compassion on each and every case? Soon you'll be shattered by it." I see the logic of it and realize how immature it was to harbor unrealistic expectations along those lines, which held within them the hope of preventing something "big" from happening. I think I've come down to earth since then.

All my love,
Gerda

∞   ∞   ∞   ∞   ∞   ∞   ∞   ∞   ∞   ∞   ∞   ∞

Soon after I started my work at the Civilian Censorship Division I realized that my naive hope of finding and exposing a giant plot, something that would substantially aid the American authorities in the pursuit of their postwar administration, was nothing but a pipe dream. Instead I began to see that my role was of very little import, and that the voluminous, painstaking reports I handed in at the end of each day would at best get no more than a cursory reading. I could see that, by and large, there was little of significance in them, and that the American personnel wanted nothing as much as to be relieved of their duties so that they could realize their hope of going home. And I could hardly blame them for it.

Among the letters were those from prisoner-of-war camps, which dealt with pain, longing, and tragedy, which I took all too personally, identifying with some of those feelings. My state of mind at that time was that of someone looking for a home where I could emulate the model of my mother, immaculately dressed, aproned, and setting a table with flowers, immersing myself in cooking, baking, and entertaining a host of guests. In view of my impending marriage, that was the vision that beckoned.

Once I was able to realize this dream, it turned out that I fell woefully short of the ideal, at least by the standards my mother maintained throughout my childhood. Eventually I was to fulfill my early hopes of someday becoming a writer; nevertheless I like to think of my ultimate achievement as having been able to create a warm and loving home for my family.

෨෮   ෨෮   ෨෮   ෨෮   ෨෮   ෨෮   ෨෮   ෨෮   ෨෮   ෨෮   ෨෮   ෨෮

Munich, December 2, 1945

My beloved Kurt,

What could possibly have happened now? you will justifiably ask. As soon as I put down my pen last night I went to sleep, and now am picking it up again during the first moments after waking up, for I must share something rather beautiful with you. Yesterday I wrote you so much because my thoughts of you permeated every waking hour. And blessedly paper is so patient and my pen did not run out of ink, although I wouldn't be surprised if you ran out of patience by now.

Last night transported me back to a child's paradise, a colorful fairytale world, filled with faith in everything that is good and beautiful. At the same time, I saw the reality of life, but was unable to dismiss the legends that have nourished me. Are there, after all, no fairy tales for grown-ups? Yet, I know that there are wonderful, magnificent miracles, if only you open your heart and mind to them, instead of being oblivious to that part of life which lends meaning to our existence and which seems to elude so many.

I fell asleep, a deep sleep without dreams. Suddenly, something very soft and gentle woke me up, and my startled eyes looked straight at the moon, which hung smack in the center of the window. It somehow struck me as a question, a pleasant though eerie feeling; a message no doubt from you.

Were you just looking at the moon as well, and did you transmit that

Kurt and friends, emulating their "Western heroes," 1932 or 1933. (Kurt is far left.)

Mountaintop near Oberammergau, Bavaria, which Kurt climbed in 1933 while vacationing with Richard and Klärle Mayer.

The same spot, twelve years later, when Kurt was stationed at a U.S. Army post near Munich.

Julius and Helene Weissmann, circa 1920, in the garden of the Weissman____ home, Bielsko, Poland.

Kurt's family in the yard of his family home in Walldorf. *Front*, Ludwig (father), Alice (mother); *back*, Irmgard (sister "Gerdi"), Kurt, and Max (brother).

Needlepoint made by Gerda's mother, Helene Weissmann, for her brother, Leo, in 1937. It took five years to complete.

Gerda and her brother, Artur Weissmann, circa 1936.

Gerda's father, Julius, at her uncle Leo's wedding in Turkey, 1937.

Artur at Krynica (a Polish resort) in 1936, with his maternal
grandmother.

Artur at Krynica in 1936.

Gerda and her mother at Krynica,
1939.

Kurt in Walldorf, 1937, in front of memorial honoring John Jacob Astor, a native of the town.

Gerda's brother, Artur, 1937.

Gerda at Krynica, July 1939.

Dorle Ebbe at her home in Wiesbaden (late thirties).

Gerda's mother, Helene, at Krynica, 1939.

Gerda's ID photo, 1940, used during the war.

Gerda's maternal uncle, Leo, in Istanbul in the early forties.

Kurt studying a map during an advance across France, July 1944.

Gerda photographed by Kurt in Munich, summer 1945.

Kurt at Freising, Bavaria, army post, summer 1945.

Kurt in Metz, France, autumn 1944.

Kurt in France after the
American breakthrough,
1944.

Kurt in Buffalo, New York, December 1945.

At engagement party,
September 14, 1945.

Kurt in France, 1944.

Gerda in Perlacher Forst, the woods near the house she lived in (outskirts of Munich), summer 1945.

Gerda convalescing in Volary, Czechoslovakia, army hospital, June 1945.

Gerda in Munich, September 14, 1 the day after her engagement.

Gerda in Paris, June 1946, around the time of the wedding.

Kurt at the Albright-Knox Art
Gallery, Buffalo, New York,
spring 1946.

Gerda and Kurt's wedding
day, Paris, June 18, 1946, in
hotel lobby.

Gerda in Paris, June 1946,
around the time of the
wedding.

Kurt in Paris, June 1946, before the wedding.

Gerda in Rochester, New York, 1947.

Gerda and Kurt at the Lilac Festival, Rochester, New York, May 1947.

Gerda with *(left to right)* Leslie, Vivian, and Jim, taken by the Associated Press in 1957, the year Gerda's first book, *All But My Life*, was published.

Las Vegas, 1990.

Gerda acknowledging the Academy Award for the documentary *One Survivor Remembers*, in 1996. © Copyright Academy of Motion Picture Arts and Sciences.

Gerda and Kurt's entire family of sixteen in Aruba, June 1996, on the occasion of their fiftieth wedding anniversary.

message by the sheer magic of our love? I felt enveloped by a sense of well-being and total bliss. The entire experience took perhaps just three seconds; then it was over, and I fell asleep again. Does that sound strange?

What I had been hoping for was a marvelous fairy tale, one that comes true, like the one about a prince in uniform, coming to the rescue in a Jeep just in the nick of time. Do you know it? Please tell little Barbara many fairy tales, so that you won't get out of practice.

But truly, Kurt, the above was not a figment of my imagination; it really did happen last night. I think that for the first time the name you gave me, Miss Moonbeam, fits. And that creature from out there in space loves you very much.

Gerda

Munich, December 3, 1945

My dearest Kurt,

Well, I went to the Polish military authority and found it to be the best and most reliable source. I must say that the result of my inquiry looks promising. Unfortunately—there is always an "unfortunately"—I find different sources daily and am sorry to drive you crazy with all those possibilities. The Polish officer in charge here wore an American Third Army uniform—the same as yours—and spoke Polish. Since I have an affinity for lieutenants in that uniform, I felt very much at home. The only thing missing was the diamond of the Fifth Division. Listening to my story, he exclaimed, "And you are *still* here?" He assured me that all I needed was the certificate of my admission to the United States, based on your assurance that you will marry me upon my arrival. If I could produce that, he would be able to take care of the matter immediately. When I asked him how I could get out of Germany, he laughed and assured me that he would take care of it for me once the required documents are here. So please send them as soon as possible. I really have high hopes, and seeing the Polish military working alongside the Americans, I'm sure I won't have too much trouble.

I have met with some of the girls I knew in camp and am rather depressed and keenly disappointed. Some seem extremely enterprising and are flourishing, in a wild drive toward material success, which is easily available here, what with the black market, etc. But most of them are in a state of abysmal resignation, pain, and loss, without any aim. When recounting the past we have a bond in common, but when it comes to the future, we seem to dwell on different planets. Everybody thinks I am insane to work, but I would go out of my mind if I didn't. Have they changed so much or have I? I am certain, though, that my anchor to normality lies in rejoining you. The core of my focus is our love and our future, but I do wish that others would have that too. I hope there is mail from you tomorrow and that it will include mail from Uncle Leo— and I pray, oh, God, I pray so hard that it will bring positive news of Artur.

Love and kisses,
Gerda

Buffalo, December 3, 1945

My very dearest little Gerda,

Your much-longed-for letter was received with great delight. It was good to get mail from you, even if its content didn't exactly evoke undistilled joy. The lot of the girls who wound up in the German Museum is particularly heartrending in view of the many promises made by the various organizations that appear to have neither the understanding, intent, nor the imagination to alleviate those indescribable conditions to the least extent. Please do report more about that. I'm interested in what *isn't* being done, in cases where, as I only know too well, it would be relatively simple to render assistance. The fact that the rest of the girls had to leave Volary under such circumstances and once again had to face an absolute blank is a striking example of the criminal stupidity and impotence of the appropriate authorities. I was extraordinarily moved by the death of the girl from Wiesbaden, who seemed to have a good chance of survival on liberation day. At that time, she left a profound impression on me, because of her youth and (still) good looks. She was so terribly young, only seventeen, from what I remember.

I'm quite curious about what they told you at the Joint Distribution Committee, or at UNRRA. It just has to click with Switzerland, and I believe I'll hear something soon from Turkey about that. Buffalo is getting a bit too much for me. But before I leave I want to investigate a few more possibilities. Although I intend to go back to New York before the week is up, a few job references were made available to me by people who advised me to remain here. I want to follow those up because they sound interesting. I'll keep you current.

If only you could hear some of the comments I get regarding your photos. Everybody insists that I should take the first opportunity to bring you to Buffalo. Some of my friends plan to attend the University of Buffalo by January. As for me, I'll presumably attend night school in New York, something that's been made quite easy due to my army service. It seems like a really good opportunity.

I've wanted to write you for a long time regarding the engagement ring. What I found was that it's not possible to insure parcels to Europe. Thought I'd better not take the chance on sending it off to you without the assurance that it won't go astray. May I therefore keep one for you until you get here? A proper ring will await you at your arrival! Should I learn of a foolproof way of sending it, well, all the better.

Do you have as much snow as we do here? It's gradually melting, but could come back at any time, creating the greatest slush, as is common in Buffalo.

Hope you'll receive the winter coat soon. Do let me know how everything fits.

Ardent smackers from your
Kurt

Among the 120 young women I encountered at the time of their liberation in Volary, Czechoslovakia, was one who startled me by her fragile youth, natural grace, and beauty, even under those diabolic conditions. In speaking to her I discovered that she was sixteen, the youngest among the group, an anomaly in the process of selection the Nazis had methodically employed. As I was to learn later, she had beaten the odds thanks to the sheer persistence and resourcefulness shown by her three sisters. They had managed to shield her by hiding her from the malevolent eyes of the SS inspectors who would make their periodic appearances at the work camps.

Dorle Ebbe was fourteen when she, along with her three sisters, was deported to the work camps, and somehow her siblings had convinced the camp authorities of Dorle's ability to perform the hard labor required of her in the spinning and weaving mills. She had indeed measured up to those demands, and when freedom finally came, she appeared to be in better health than many who had gone through that ordeal. It was therefore an especially bitter blow to learn that Dorle had succumbed now, six months after liberation, to the barbaric treatment to which her oppressors had subjected her.

Hello Dimples,

I just got back from a concert and am still under the spell of the music. Oh, how I missed you there, Gerdush. The orchestra has improved incredibly since I went away, and was under the direction of a famous Canadian conductor. The soloist was an enchantingly beautiful Negro soprano, who sang in flawless German and French. I'm enclosing a clipping that cannot, however, give you an idea of her voice or graceful presence. I can't adequately describe how moved I was by the entire atmosphere and the countless nostalgic memories it evoked.

After an absence of three years, I ran into many old acquaintances, one of them a girl who for a time lived in the same apartment with my relatives, as did I. She is now a member of the orchestra. I found that the same people who had always been active in musical circles were still around, and I recognized many faces of people I only knew then because of their regular attendance at concerts.

Although all that made me aware that I'm truly back, I could only think of you. I know how much you belong to this and are needed in order to make my inner rejoicing and contentment complete. You are a very necessary part of my life, Gerda, because without you, it's only half a life.

If for no reason other than to show you this building and all that goes with it, I want to take you to Buffalo. Even in New York, you won't find anything like it for concerts. Although I always dreamed of the times I had visited that concert hall, tonight turned out to have surpassed all that I imagined.

Where you are it's time to go to work, and I'm wondering what the new day will bring. I looked around for a job today, although I had actually decided to settle in New York. I don't really believe I'll find anything halfway decent here, and nothing has come of my search so far. That is to say, jobs can be had, but it's important to me to find the right one. I'm reluctant to pounce on the first thing that comes along. Right now I have a real opportunity to look around for something most to my liking.

No mail from you—or from anybody else, for that matter. Must be due to the holiday rush. Hope you'll be able soon to confirm receipt of a package that went to you—if only one could ship them by air mail—and I know you can use the items well because it must be very cold by now. You'll be able to identify this package by the sweater it contains.

Regards to all and my own kisses to you, along with lots of love,
Kurt

Buffalo, December 7, 1945

Gerda dearest,

Today it's four years since America got into the war. How long ago that seems, and how that cruel conflict has unraveled meanwhile! Yes, it came out the best we could have hoped for, but why can't people bring as many unselfish sacrifices in the name of peace as they do in war—constructive, bloodless sacrifices? Most people are too indifferent to devote themselves to the world they live in with wholehearted effort. Does anyone ever learn from experience?

Your mail arrives here only slowly and sporadically. I received two of your earlier letters, one of them addressed to your uncle, and the one to me dated November 15. Naturally I forwarded the former immediately to Istanbul, along with the photos you requested, which I was going to enclose anyway. Unfortunately I had nothing decent to send of myself. Guess we'll have to wait and see how the first civilian photos turn out.

Actually I have to explain why I'm still in Buffalo; I'll be returning to New York in two days. After looking around here, the situation is as follows: I could get a job in a printing plant here for approximately fifty dollars. If I'm not mistaken, it would be ten to fifteen dollars higher in New York, but as far as I can determine, that would be absorbed or even surpassed by the higher cost of living there.

My friends advise me to stay in town for at least a year under any circumstances. Room and board would be available at an attractive price. As for me, I feel very comfortable in this environment and prefer living in one-or-two-family houses to being cooped up in New York's apartment buildings, which turn into virtual ovens in the summer. Here, everything is greenery, wide open, and tree-lined. Winters usually do bring a lot of snow and slush, but in summer you simply hop into a car and in no time at all you are at a beach.

New York is a fantastic city, but some of its charms are bound to pale after commuting twice daily to and from work, sardine-fashion, in the subway. That's only one small example. It definitely has many advantages as well, but in general the city is too large to do all the things one intends to do. It's the most interesting city you can imagine, for a visit. As for living there, that doesn't hold much allure for me. Quite aside from that, it's nearly impossible to find an apartment at the moment (a single room is somewhat easier). You don't even get a chance to discuss the matter without first bribing someone. And if you get something in that manner, you naturally take anything, no matter how bad.

On the other hand, I don't want to depict New York in darker colors than it deserves. After all, in all probability I'll wind up there anyway. But with you in mind, I believe you'd get to know America much better if you didn't live in New York. In particular I'd shy away from the neighborhood in which my sister lives.* Wherever you go, on the streets, in stores, in parks, or among acquaintances, you hear nothing but German. It's hardly surprising, then, that this part of the city is known as "the Fourth Reich."

Whatever may happen, you must know this: Once you are here and accustomed to the country, you'll be able to decide at any time which city you'd rather live in. Don't think I wouldn't also enjoy and be happy in whatever appeals most to you and gives you pleasure. I'm only writing *my* opinion at the moment, and expect that in due time you'll give me yours. At any rate, part of that decision is still hypothetical. I'm only trying to plan ahead as much as possible.

A parcel containing overshoes got off on its unfortunately all-too-slow trek to you yesterday. If only they were already in your possession. You just have to write and give me your shoe size; it's so important!

I'm immensely eager to find out how your new dress turned out. Do bring me up-to-date on it, and show it to me in person soon.

> Keep well—lots of love, darling [in English],
> Your Kurt

---

*Washington Heights, still a haven for immigrants today, has become home to many Dominicans.

Dear Mr. Klein,

or my dear, dear Kurt, the civilian!

Well, at last. I thought the army would never let you go. Congratulations! All the dangers inherent in being a soldier are over. (I know you don't like to hear that.) I am trying to picture you as a civilian and find myself unable to do so. I can only say that I did love you in your uniform and will fall just as much for that guy in civilian clothes, I'm sure. Unfortunately that new status brings me to another point. I dread the thought that because of it, your mail will not be forwarded as fast as that of military personnel. I'll just have to try and fill that void by picturing the day of our reunion!

I was lucky today, because four of your letters came. I enjoyed the description of Barbara and the baby ever so much. I will have no problem communicating with the baby, I guess. At four months his vocabulary must about match mine. With Barbara it's another story. I will study hard to be able to talk to her on many subjects. What puzzles me about her, though, is that according to what your sister writes, she is crazy about you. How can *anybody* be crazy about you?

As to your dilemma—that is, the decision of whether Buffalo or New York City should be our home—I can't render any intelligent comment, since I know neither. Obviously I would opt for New York because of the family. But you must make that decision, and I will be happy with your choice as long as we are together.

Many kisses and love, yours,
Gerda

New York City, December 10, 1945

Gerda, my dearest,

If my mail reaches you in the manner whose reverse is true here, then I can well imagine why it seems so interminably long until each letter arrives. What I'm not delighted to gather is that this is such cause of concern for you. You see, I'm used to similar inexplicable intervals, through years of previous exchanges of correspondence with my parents, something I should have pointed out to you in order to avert your groundless worry. Well then, Dimples, cheer up; how could something happen here that would be cause for concern?

Now the countless visits, parties, and job interviews are behind me, and I am once again in New York. The main problem at the moment is something I already touched on in my last letter: Where finally to settle down? I have a job offer in Buffalo, which is tempting. On one hand, I do have my next-of-kin here in New York and there is perhaps more to do and see; on the other hand, the apartment situation is nothing short of catastrophic. It's a difficult situation, but I believe I will opt for Buffalo, at least for a year.

When I arrived in New York, I immediately set to work to follow up a few leads I was still in doubt about, but didn't find exactly what I wanted in advertising. In Buffalo there is a good opportunity to work my way up to it for about a year by holding a job, as formerly, in a printing plant.

Up to now all you've heard about is "me, me, me," and that sounds especially hollow when I reread your latest three letters. I refer in particular to the content-heavy letter of November 28, after you spoke to Escia. Gerda, I feel so tiny, so terribly insignificant, while I try to absorb those lines and imagine their full impact, as they must have fallen on you with merciless force from your friend's lips. What can I say about that? Words of banality meant to console? You're quite right, I must leave unsaid all that touches me the most profoundly, but not for the reason you mention. If I were with you, I could perhaps indicate my feelings through my presence. After all, you always—and without exception—understood my feelings.

Gerda, I have never known a human being who in any way came even close to having your courage, your faith, your resolve, your confidence, and your selflessness! I don't know how that's possible, I only know it is so. Everybody has his or her weaknesses. In you I could only discover rock-solid principles so far, and it seems like a miracle that I found you. I can never aspire to reach your heights, but I can attempt to shape your life in the manner that you desire. Love will replace all that we do not possess. Yes, you will bring sunshine to my world, so much of it that its rays will warm you as well!

I do have to ask something of you, my love. Never say that what you write doesn't belong in my world. That's not so, for *you* are my world. I hope that in the end I'm not so superficial that I only know how to chase after pleasure and that I force myself to look at lighthearted things, while the somber simply doesn't exist because it would be too "inconvenient" to be reminded of it. I don't mean to say that I want to indulge in fruitless complaints or wallow in negative self-pity, but in order to live fully we have to be able to face existing facts.

Gerda, I'm so proud of you, of everything that you always accomplish when you see others in need. And the fruits of your self-sacrifices are always so rewarding; it's just marvelous what you achieved on behalf of your friends! Do keep me abreast of their progress.

Hope these lines will speed toward you, driven by trade winds.

I embrace you,
Your Kurt

New York City, December 12, 1945

Gerda darling!

Now I've reached a firm decision to return to Buffalo and accept the job offer I have. It was difficult in view of the many pros and cons, but I believe I am doing the right thing.

There's no doubt that we'll be able to live much nicer and more comfortably in Buffalo, no matter how modest the first apartment may turn out to be. By and by we'll create a home exactly as we like it.

I'll be taking the train this coming Saturday evening and will start my job the following week. Your papers are all ready, except for the ones that depend on my having the job. I visited the Joint offices once more yesterday, and was told I should wait with the booking of ship's passage until you are in either Switzerland or France. Once there you should go to that branch of the Joint (in Zurich or Paris) and get information on how to go about the next steps. They will then cable their home office in New York, which in turn will notify me that passage has been booked.

No answer so far from Istanbul, which leads me to the conclusion that you have to count on a period of two months until you get an answer if you write through me. It'll probably be faster by way of Switzerland. I do hope, though, that air mail service will gradually improve. It should take only a few days from here, after all. Once the necessary documents get here from Turkey, much can be accomplished.

Were you able to see *Madame Curie*? I certainly hope so, because it's very, very good. The actors are fabulous, only I imagine that a lot of the English dialogue fell by the wayside, even if it had subtitles.

I saw a musical called *Oklahoma* yesterday. It's a type of operetta, but I was somewhat disappointed. It's been playing for a couple of years to enormous acclaim, but I thought the reviews were exaggerated to some degree and the "hoopla" too much. Other than that, it made for good, light entertainment.

How are the girls doing? Do they still live in the museum or have they got private accommodations? Were they able to recover from those terrifying experiences?

Do make my day soon with your eagerly awaited lines,
Your Kurt

Buffalo, December 13, 1945

My dear little Gerda,

Your honorable fiancé has turned into a real goldbrick. The year is almost over, and he can only go on record as having been a lazybones. I've got to put an end to that vice. Am really impatient now. High time that I get acquainted with work once more. Oh, well, in a few days.

I had hoped to find something from you in this morning's mail. What came instead were my discharge papers from the army. At least I now know that the officially sanctioned period of loafing is at an end. By contrast, if I imagine your labors, I get a peculiar feeling. It seems to me that you have to work much harder than is necessary. Think about it some more. I would so much like to make things easier for you. How do you manage at all financially? Please don't hesitate for a moment to tell me about it. I can't bear the thought that you might lack things.

Gerdi is very sorry that I'll be leaving New York, and I myself have gotten used to having members of my family around me again.

The temptation was great to stay in New York for another two days. Imagine what's playing at the Met next Monday: yes, *Fidelio!*—my favorite. Too bad, but I'd much prefer to see it with you anyway. Instead was able to get tickets for an operetta, called *Song of Norway*, based on Grieg's music. It turned out to be overwhelmingly beautiful. You'll get to see it, too; I could watch it dozens of times. Magnificent music and a great deal of humor thrown into the bargain. I think that even Grieg wouldn't have any objections to having his music used in ways not originally intended.

Enough for now. I'm thinking of you and am sending many, many kisses.

Lots of love, your
Kurt

Munich, December 15, 1945

My dearest Kurt,

It must have snowed all night. Fluffy pure white snow covers everything. I had the desire to go to our woods again and knew that no one would be there to disturb my thoughts, my memories, allowing me to commune with you.

I trod with reverence on the untouched snow, along the path we used to take, engaged in our long talks and once, during a long silence, just holding hands. I stopped, and had the feeling I was not alone, then found myself looking into two huge, soft, gentle, brown eyes. I held my breath and we looked at each other mute, the deer and I. When I took two tentative steps forward, he sprinted away in a flash and was gone.

It was so beautiful, so pure, so wild and free that I was overcome by a deep desire to pray. It was a strange prayer, a prayer of three words only: Thank you, God. I somehow needed to express my boundless gratitude for the happiness I felt at being able to see such beauty, and that this feeling had not been extinguished within me.

It was only then that I realized that today is Saturday, a day when many Jews go to synagogues to worship. I recalled how I used to attend services back home, but often was bored, occupying myself by counting the ornaments on the ceiling and walls, and how I had mouthed prayers I did not feel. It is in nature that I can sense the presence of God, feel the awe of the divine, can truly pray.

I am sending you this tiny branch from "our woods" and hope that I will dream of you tonight. I love you.

Gerda

My feelings about God and prayer must have lodged early in my mind, awakened by tales my father would tell about his own father. That grandfather was to become the strongest influence in my spiritual life. I never had a chance to know him; he died when I was a year old.

Grandfather Yosef was a pious Jew who was in the habit of reciting his morning prayers while walking in the woods that surrounded the shtetl, *the small then-Austrian town that was Chortkov, close to the Russian and Romanian borders.*

My own memories of Chortkov crowd my mind like a painting by Chagall, whose hometown of Vitebsk was only a short distance away in Rus-

sia. I see sunflowers towering over small houses, huddled together; horses that, by a slight leap of the imagination, could jump over rooftops; and when Sabbath evening would fall on the hushed, tiny hamlet, crooked fences that seemed to bow in deference to the Sabbath queen.

That was my father's native town, a place he left as a young man to further his education in Vienna. Meanwhile World War I broke out in 1914, which meant that Papa and his three brothers were inducted into the Austrian Army.

Before long Chortkov was occupied by Russian enemy troops, cutting off Papa's family, which also included a sister, from contact with the sons and brothers serving on the Austrian side. I would listen over and over to the tale of how Grandfather loved walking in the woods reciting his prayers. No doubt he also faithfully attended synagogue services, but he apparently found a close connection with God in the realm of nature. In retrospect I realize how much I followed in his footsteps.

One day, because of his great love for animals and all growing things, he came to the rescue of a small bird that had fallen out of its nest. Knowing that the mother would reject it if he touched it, he fashioned a type of cradle from a forked tree branch, with which to lift the bird back into its nest. Just then, he was intercepted by two Russian soldiers, reeking of alcohol. They hauled him before the Russian town commander, accusing him of having attempted to lay telephone wires, considered an act of sabotage. Without trial he was banished to Siberia for life.

During my summer visits to Chortkov, I would always cry after pleading with Grandmother to recite the well-known tale of the heartrending farewell from her husband, a parting that she thought would be forever. All that he chose to take along were the Bible, his tefillin (phylacteries), and his tallith (prayer shawl).

During the period that followed, Grandmother received no news from her husband or from her sons at the front. My father, meanwhile, had met my mother when his unit came through Bielitz, as Bielsko was then called. He had been in search of quarters, and the Jewish family he happened upon had a young and beautiful daughter. They fell in love and married as soon as the war was over, after it was decided that the young couple would settle in Bielitz. More than a year later, after my brother Artur was born, dramatic news came via a telegram: Grandfather had returned from Siberia! The end of the war had brought release for the czar's "political" prisoners.

To the best of my knowledge, it took Grandfather almost two years to make his way back home, a trek during which he traveled on riverboats, *horse-drawn carriages, or even sleighs, whenever possible. He also covered much of that distance on foot, stopping to work for peasants in return for meals that consisted of little else but vegetables and potatoes. That allowed him to adhere to his strictly kosher observance, and he would fully comply with it by cooking this food in the embers of a fire. He also lived on fresh fruit, whenever available. Of course he never traveled or walked on the Sabbath or on Jewish holidays.*

That was how he staggered into his home one day, a frail, bearded old man, aged beyond his years. After embracing and kissing his family, as well as his beloved sacred books, he broke down and cried on hearing that he had a grandson. After that, Papa, Mama, and their small son set out on the long, arduous train ride, my father eager to show off his beautiful wife and their small son. Mama, fashionably dressed, undertook the journey with some trepidation, aware that she would be a stranger who spoke only German, rather than Yiddish, the language current among Jews of that region.

When Grandfather greeted the young couple at the door, it was with the words Israel spoke to Joseph, as set down in Genesis: "I had not thought to see thy face again; and, lo, God hath let me see thy son also." Mama bowed to Grandfather and kissed Grandmother's gnarled, work-worn hands.

Among the gifts they had brought, Mama innocently offered Grandfather some of her mother's justly famous chicken. While the other family members held their breath, he fixed the daughter-in-law he just had met with his beneficent gaze and said simply, "That chicken looks delicious, my daughter." With that he went to wash his hands, broke off a small piece of the poultry, and, reciting a blessing, ate it.

For years I did not truly understand the implications of that story, but I loved it, wanted to hear it again and again. It moved me in a strange way until I could fully grasp the nobility of his spirit. His orthodox discipline applied only to himself, and he never wanted to imply that others' standards were beneath his.

There was another revealing story about Grandfather that Papa told me while sitting on the time-worn stoop of his birthplace in front of the house. It was there that Papa had sat as a young boy, when one Friday morning a pale-faced wisp of a girl had appeared, carrying a small bowl containing an egg that had been broken open. In a shy voice she inquired of Grandfather whether the egg was kosher, because it had a blood drop on it. Young as he was, my father knew that the egg was not considered as meeting kosher standards. To his amazement, though, his father held the bowl, letting the egg white wash over the offending blood spot, finally pronouncing the egg kosher and declaring that it would make for a fine challah, the bread used to welcome the Sabbath on Friday evenings. Gratefully and much relieved, the girl ran home.

Seeing how incensed Papa was over this obvious breach of tradition, Grandfather explained that the girl's mother was a widow with six young children, and if she wanted to praise God by baking a challah in honor of the Sabbath queen, that egg was pure. He went on to say that if his verdict were to be considered a sin, he would gladly bear the consequences.

During the difficult years of slavery, whenever the going got rough, I would think of my grandfather and vow to myself that if he, in his old age, was able to cope with the ordeal of his internment in Siberia, then his endurance would become my lodestar.

When our son was born, his Hebrew name became Yosef, after my grandfather, and his middle name Arthur, after my brother. He embodies the best of human values left to him by both.

∞   ∞   ∞   ∞   ∞   ∞   ∞   ∞   ∞   ∞   ∞   ∞

New York City, December 15, 1945

Gerda, my very dearest,

I want to let you know right from the start why the enclosed letter from Istanbul, which just arrived here, is being "censored" by me. Following your uncle's wishes, I'm deleting one paragraph, in which he reports with exceeding modesty all he attempted to do for you during your camp years. Perhaps you can see why I don't want to deny his very first request, after the type of touching welcome into the ranks of your family he accorded me. May I ask you not to mention anything to that effect in your next letters to him, because it would after all be extremely embarrassing to have violated his confidence. On the other hand, I have no desire to harbor any secrets from you, and realize that it would trigger all sorts of thoughts and apprehensions if I left the matter unexplained. Okay?

Although this letter clarified a lot of things, a lot of misunderstandings linger due to the slowness of the mail. Unfortunately I didn't have the foresight to explain to him why your first lines to him were of necessity so brief. Meanwhile he must certainly be in possession of your detailed report, which I'm sure has helped him to understand. Mail service has in fact improved considerably; today's letter from Turkey was in transit for only two weeks. I'll answer immediately and will furnish the necessary dates.

It does show that your uncle unfortunately knows nothing concerning Artur's whereabouts. But who knows, he may well surface in the USSR. I'm not saying this to console you; I believe you're beyond that, but in his case there exist so many possibilities, while in the case of our parents it seems clear beyond doubt what transpired.

Are you surprised at Turkey's peculiar attitude regarding refugees? I believe that business plays a decisive role in this, but wonder whether the attitude of the Turkish government has anything to do with Leo's contemplated move to England? I don't mean that one can expect to be harassed in Turkey. After all, your relatives must be citizens there, but apparently England offers a more promising future.

Now that you know the number and address of the account in Switzerland, let's hope that your uncle's friend can achieve something concrete.

As you can gather, the question of your uncle's possible visit to the United States has been answered. The way I see it our wedding cannot be scheduled for a specific date, but in a way it would be even more beautiful if your family could visit us *in our own home*. In general I'll answer all those inquiries, including the matter of being in "full accord" with Leo's suggestions in the manner you would like. It's too bad, but that's the disadvantage of this correspondence. Both sides must, of necessity, appear too stiff and formal, instead of being able to broach matters closest to their hearts, as they could in a personal relationship. However, I do find your uncle's sentiments far beyond all that you can expect by way of words straight from the heart, and the friendship he displays is obvious. I can only hope he'll gain the right impression from my naturally more reserved lines.

I just want to mention quickly that I'll be leaving for Buffalo tonight and hope to start work next week. There I expect to find the type of calm and quiet that should enable me to write in much greater detail.

My ardent kisses, Dimples, from your
Kurt

∽ ∽ ∽ ∽ ∽ ∽ ∽ ∽ ∽ ∽ ∽ ∽

It was at this point that we got a first inkling of Uncle Leo's tenuous position regarding his lack of Turkish citizenship. Although he was a successful businessman, providing employment for many workers, the Turkish government had thus far refused to grant him citizenship. Despite the fact that his wife and family were Turkish citizens, it had been his misfortune to have been born in Austria, in a territory that subsequently became Poland. As a result he was considered "stateless," because he had left his hometown soon after the end of World War I without having acquired Polish citizenship.

As we were now finding out, that prevented him from traveling to any country, a handicap for which he compensated by sending his father-in-law, Mr. Louis, as his "roving ambassador" throughout Europe.

&ed; &ed; &ed; &ed; &ed; &ed; &ed; &ed; &ed; &ed; &ed; &ed;

Buffalo, December 16, 1945

Gerda, my dearest,

It's only a few hours since I arrived in Buffalo, and that gives me the chance to use the weekend to report to you. Surprised as I was the previous time by the snow flurries that greeted me, that paled into insignificance by comparison to how it was this time. The entire traffic was temporarily paralyzed by the blizzard, which hit with full fury. After an interminable wait, I just barely caught a bus that took me to my friends' where, as mentioned, I'll be staying.

I'm so curious to know how everything is going for you, how the Swiss matter is progressing, what difficulties work and weather are imposing on you, and what's doing in general. Mail service, unfortunately, seems overloaded, due to the holiday rush; it's a long time since your last letter came.

Leaving New York was especially difficult this time, considering the bonds that had been renewed with my family.

Tomorrow I'm going for another meeting with the people who made me an offer, after which it should go fast; I figure one or two days. I want to use the time, meanwhile, to complete all your papers and get them into the mail. As I see it, Switzerland offers the best prospects. That means then that I'll send duplicates of everything to the American consulate in Zurich. That will actually be done by the Joint Distribution Committee, and I'll give you all the details later.

If I also enclose an ardent kiss, can I induce you to pay a visit to my mailbox by tomorrow, or at the latest the day after? All my love,

Kurt

P.S. Wonder how long the package containing the sweets will take to reach its destination. What other wishes do you have that could be taken care of that way?

It felt comfortable to be back in Buffalo among my friends, in the familiar surroundings I had dreamed about during the two years in war-ravaged Europe, a continent with which I could no longer fully identify.

One of those friends was Arthur Rothschild, a lawyer who earlier had played a pivotal role in my life. He and his wife urged me now to make Buffalo my residence once again, generously offering to make their home available for the duration of my bachelorhood. Then, too, there was his brother-in-law, Howard, a friend through whom I had originally met Arthur, or Art, as we called him.

Art easily fit into a "most unforgettable character" category, a study in contradictions and someone who had a powerful impact on my life and assimilation to the country that was still very new to me when I first met him. He possessed a brilliant, encyclopedic mind and was a man of scintillating wit, which led to some of the cleverest repartee I have ever come across. For me he bridged the gap between my European upbringing and the mores of the new country, having himself attended school in Germany for a short while. Although a native-born American, he spoke colloquial German, a language that had actually been his mother tongue. He was first-generation American on his father's side, who as a German Jew had come to this country before the turn of the century, though second-generation American as far as his mother was concerned. He appeared to have inherited a certain rigidity from his father, who was a martinet, along with some other rigid traits. In general he did not suffer fools gladly, was impetuous and possessed of a low boiling point, while giving most generously of himself and his worldly goods when it came to people he liked. He could display infinite patience, explaining some intricate or abstruse points that would puzzle a newcomer like me; he was also exhaustively well-versed in history, literature, music, and the arts and sciences in general. He could arouse instant antipathy or great enthusiasm among the people he met, and it was always possible to disagree violently with some of his unconventional theories while carrying on the best of friendship.

Art was responsible for filling in many of the gaps in the education that circumstances had prevented me from gaining, and in that sense he was my mentor. It was always stimulating and usually a great deal of fun to be in his presence, and due to his language proficiency we would amuse ourselves for hours on end, coming up with literal translations of colloquial English into German or vice versa. His life and career were of a turbulent nature, and it was only toward the end of his years that he found a certain tranquillity. That, in short, was the man in whose home I now awaited the unscrambling of my own life.

✂━━━━✂

Munich, December 17, 1945

Kurt, my love,

Our work hours have changed, and this has been a long day. We put in more than two extra hours a day and have only forty-five minutes for lunch. But that way, we get every Thursday afternoon off. That means that I leave in the morning while it's still dark and return in complete darkness at 7:30 P.M. Anyway, I went to the Bavarian Aid Society to see about my new job, and it looks promising. I know that I will like it because I will be dealing directly with people and, I hope, will be of some help to them. I thought that they might not hire me if I tell them that I would leave as soon as my papers for the States will be approved, but fortunately, my new boss does not regard that as a stumbling block. I am to start work on January 1.

When I got home, my landlady held me to a promise I had apparently made, to help with the baking for Christmas. I feel pretty strange about that. I love to bake, but obviously have not been able to do so for the past six years. My God, was I only fifteen years old then? When I agreed to help her, was I driven by nostalgia or the chance to "nosh"?

It didn't take long before the kitchen was permeated by the smell of cinnamon and cloves. To my mind, smell is the strongest of our senses when it comes to evoking memories. There is something so warm, snug, and comforting in the aroma of baking. I found that even the shapes of the cookies were the same as at home: hearts and stars. I could close my eyes, inhale the fragrance, and be transported back to my childhood home again. Impulsively I let on how I used to come home from skiing and sledding, the smell of cookies baking filling the air, and how that was heaven as far as I was concerned.

Without much ado the Bäumlers' son went into the attic and brought down his old sled, and so I went sledding under a starry sky. Once more I was able to fly free, exuberant, unshackled, over the untouched snow, brilliant as spun sugar. Where was the bitter, biting cold, the cruel elements, the hunger? Had it all been a nightmare? Was I really alive and enjoying this?

Now I am alone in my room and have time to reflect, to confront what I have just done. For a few blissful moments I recaptured what I had yearned for all those years. But how could I have done that? I actually went sledding with my landlady's son, a former German officer. I only know that for a little while I recaptured a moment of my carefree childhood and could forget with whom I was sledding. I know that I should hate him and his parents, but find myself unable to do that.

How I hate Germany! And yet here I am in a German home that undeniably evokes memories I treasure. I know I don't belong here, and when I visit Landsberg, the DP camp where my friends are staying, I can't stand that either. It reminds me too much of other camps, except that these days there are no guards, there is no hunger. I can't stand the din of so many people, the commotion. I have an irresistible urge to escape, but escape to where? Back to Munich, to my quiet room, the room in a German home. Why? Just to recapture a moment of childhood, to revel in the fragrance of cookies baking.

I feel so torn, so guilty, so disloyal. But I *am* loyal to the past, to all I loved and lost, and this is only a fragment of memory, just a part of the mosaic of my childhood. I am holding your photo in my hands. You are my only reality, my only escape. Only in your arms will I be at home again.

Gerda

(The day after)

The morning renders my thoughts clearer. I am not as upset as I face the day, and my hope is high that there will be mail from you, something that always restores me. Tonight I am going to Günther's engagement party. I told you that he met his brother's widow and had her come to Munich. It is such a terribly sad story. I had a long talk with him.

He told me that he had been engaged before the war and that he understands the depth of my love for you, because that's how he loved that girl and always will. He knows that such love comes only once in a lifetime, but realizing that she is gone, he has an obligation toward his brother, who had been married only a few months before being sent to Auschwitz. And so he is going to marry his brother's widow, whom he likes and respects enormously. I do hope so much that he will be happy. He is such a fine, sensitive, decent human being. And we must live with the consequences of such and similar tragedies every day. It is terrible

169

to have to snatch fragments of happiness from the ruins of such loss. Now I must be off to work.

Love and kisses,
Gerda

ℰ   ℰ   ℰ   ℰ   ℰ   ℰ   ℰ   ℰ   ℰ   ℰ   ℰ   ℰ

I do vividly remember Heinz Bäumler's homecoming and the bitterness it caused me.

There was his mother's boundless joy, bordering on hysteria, when he first entered the house, followed immediately by her preparation of his favorite food, Pfannkuchen,* *filled with jam. It brought back how my mother had also hoarded a little jam from before the war, awaiting a special occasion, and then gave it to me on the day she was sent to her death. And there I sat, upstairs, listening to Frau Bäumler's rejoicing. Soon thereafter I was introduced to him and he was most polite, jumped up from his chair, and I heard the clicking of his heels, my eyes riveted to the dark spots on his uniform where the insignia was missing.*

The following morning I woke up to the sound of his shouting and the shattering of crockery. In a wild tantrum he was venting his anger and frustration. "Don't you understand, Mutter, *we lost* the war?! We lost *the* war!" *And I, who* "won" *the war, was cowering upstairs, trembling, my tears staining the flower-patterned pillows in which I buried my face so that my sobs couldn't be heard.*

Somehow I never wondered how he must have felt when Kurt would come to visit me. He, the former German officer, the fading of his uniform showing the outline of the swastika, and the traces of his rank, which had been torn off. And there was Kurt, the American officer in full uniform, with his shining bars and multicolored ribbons.

I haven't thought about that until now. Did that thought comfort me then? I just don't know.

ℰ   ℰ   ℰ   ℰ   ℰ   ℰ   ℰ   ℰ   ℰ   ℰ   ℰ   ℰ

Munich, December 18, 1945

My dearest Kurt,
It is Sunday and a bright sunny morning. Completing all the household

*Pancakes, German-style.

chores made me feel well and joyful. Opening the window wide and inhaling the crisp, clear air gives me a sense of youth and strength, and makes me want to embrace the entire world, especially the one across the ocean.

Let me tell you about a preliminary meeting in regard to my future job. I was hired and, having been asked to attend one of their sessions, was rather nervous, being the only girl in the company of six distinguished gentlemen. I would guess that most of them are my father's age. The meeting dealt with the stance the Bavarian Aid Society should adopt and what responsibility it should accept vis-à-vis all the needy cases in Bavaria. I was deeply distressed and disappointed when it was decided that the operation would fall into three categories: care for (1) Jewish survivors of concentration camps, (2) part-Jewish concentration camp survivors, and (3) politically persecuted people. I posed the question of whether the care and help within the framework of the three groups would differ? The answer was: "No!" Why, then, must there be three divisions? Obviously all of our clients have suffered; why must we create differences and splinter groups? Why can't we band together and use our resources to help them all?

I looked around me slowly, all the while wondering whether they were aware of a radio program I had listened to a few days earlier. No doubt some of them had attended the event that had been broadcast. It was a program that created widespread discussions about the Munich radio transmission of a special Christmas/Hanukkah observance. First a Catholic priest spoke, then a Protestant minister, and finally a rabbi. All focused on how we must strive to forge a better world together. I was moved to tears as the choir sang of how all humanity should be united by a "divine spark" of brotherhood.* But only yesterday I learned how far we are from the realization of that lofty ideal. As you know I feel very strongly Jewish, and only God knows how much our people have suffered. But perhaps because of that I can't bear segregation and discrimination in the rendering of help. That is why I asked the questions, only to be met with silence.

No, Kurt, the world, at least this one, stands on a pretty shaky foundation. I guess with that attitude I am not going to advance here very fast or too far.

*From Friedrich Schiller's "Ode to Joy," the text of the last movement of Beethoven's Ninth Symphony.

On my way home after the meeting, I bought a bunch of fragrant greenery. It was clean and sweet and most refreshing. I found it soothing to arrange it in a couple of vases. That certainly was preferable to meeting with people who think of themselves as standing at the apex of so-called justice. I will work there. I will and must, and it will give me some satisfaction to help a few, I hope. At the same time I do realize that I will not be able to render help to all those who need it most, nor will everybody be satisfied with what I am able to do. I guess there can be no absolutes; therefore I can't be totally satisfied.

And so my eyes wander elsewhere for a more complete fulfillment. I'm looking at the future, to the one with whom I can find it. You must know him well, since you have been with him since July 2, 1920.

Have to leave now to attend an engagement party.

Till later,
Gerda

Buffalo, December 19, 1945

Gerda dearest,

Let me get right down to answering your two letters of late November, which arrived simultaneously. How good that you repeated the matter of the certification, because the letter in which you originally detailed it is still outstanding. I can only hope now that the enclosed document, a sort of affidavit, will be found to be adequate by the Swiss consul, inasmuch as it makes my intentions unequivocally clear. I also stated in it that you are only visiting Switzerland as a tourist, and that means are at your disposal through the account in Zurich, that no American consul in Germany can issue you a visa, and that that is the only reason why you are going to Switzerland.

Immediately on getting to Buffalo, I called the Swiss representative and, as a follow-up, went to his home, explained the whole matter, and asked that he cable the Swiss consul in Munich, stating that he's checked over the substantiating papers here and found them to be okay. Meanwhile he is also sending copies of that to Munich by diplomatic mail, something he declared himself willing to do. Now I'm curious whether the Swiss consulate notified you of the matter.

You really achieved quite a lot on your own. I thought it was impossible to obtain a Polish passport, and now you mention that you have one without saying how you managed it. I assume that those are some of the details that are still on the way. At the moment the mail service leaves a lot to be desired, but the situation ought to improve after the New Year.

Good luck in your interview with the Swiss consul. I just know you'll pull it off without any difficulties. So far you've certainly handled it fabulously well. You're going to have to tell me a whole lot more about it once you're here.

Now, more than ever, I'd like to be near you, because I can imagine what you're going through. What an emotional upheaval it must have been to get the report of Artur's being in Turkey, something Uncle Leo subsequently didn't confirm. I can only hope that the rumor was based on fact all the same, and that an error was made only in reference to his exact locale. Can you track down the report in greater detail? The question of whether or not I'll remain in Buffalo isn't entirely settled yet. I can only say that one of the job offers fell through, but a few other possibilities have surfaced meanwhile. I'm sorry to have to spend so much time on it, but I realize that for this search it's tremendously important that I find the right thing. I know from experience that once I start a new job it's not that easy to break away, if it happens to be a bad one.

I'm awaiting good news from you, but would much prefer to take you into my arms and hold you tight!

Kurt

Buffalo, December 22, 1945

My dearest Gerda,

I woke up this morning right next to your beautiful Hanukkah letter, containing the news of your success at the Polish Committee. First off I want to give you the name and address of a cousin of my father. She and her husband live in Basel, and you can use them as a reference when you go to the Swiss consulate. They have been of great assistance to other members of my family regarding emigration. I don't know them personally, but you can count on them in every respect. You might even prefer to stay in Basel, in which case I know they'd be happy to help you find a room. Above all they could acquaint you with everything you'll need to know there.

I can't wait for their answer because speed is of the essence in your matter. I assure you you don't need to have the slightest qualms about contacting them.

It's fantastic how you conquer wherever you go. It seems you're able to turn all difficulties to your advantage. All it takes is your wish, your willpower—the determination to act—and the world is yours. Your personality emanates so much that is good that obstacles simply evaporate.

Incidentally we might consider the Paris alternative, but only if Switzerland is out of the question. If the Polish Committee should succeed in getting you to Paris, then all you'd have to do is to see the Joint Distribution Committee. I wouldn't worry about a possible conflict. They wouldn't care *who* got you to Paris, as long as you were there.

Your thoughts on Hanukkah were magnificent. How great that you could enjoy a preview of things to come next year. Yes, we'll see to it that everything the lights promised will come true.*

I've been anticipating getting a few good photos, but they are not quite ready yet, so instead, accept some bad ones today; they were taken a few weeks ago.

Let's hear from you soon; I'm looking forward to it so much. All my love, Kurt

Munich, December 23, 1945

My dearest,

I had a very satisfactory meeting with the overall head of the Bavarian Aid Society. He couldn't have been nicer. We discussed my salary, and I told him that it really doesn't matter, inasmuch as I could easily have been on the receiving end of such a service myself. I suggested he should give me what he thought was right because I am pleased to be working for such an organization and all it stands for, even if it is far from perfect. Please, Kurt, don't think I disdain the importance of money. I know that it provides some security, but I also know that by itself it doesn't make

---

*We wanted nothing so much as to be reunited, and Hanukkah seemed like a good time to express our hopes for the future. After the unsettling and tragic period we had lived through for so many years, we craved stability and the freedom to build a life of our own choosing, which we hoped would be a fulfilling one. Our most ardent wish was to reestablish continuity, becoming links in the chain of family progression after the losses we had sustained.

people happy. He suggested a starting salary of two hundred reichmarks, to be raised each month (I hope not for too many months, in this case), and I'll be able to eat free of charge in the same building and receive free tickets to all cultural events. But above all he indicated that he would introduce me to the person in charge of the Joint who could help me get out of Germany. That's decent of him, considering that he just hired me. Maybe he wants to get rid of me?

Went to the circus tonight, and there was a delightful bear riding a motorcycle. Also lots of clowns, who brought mountains of hay to the arena, assuring the audiences that it was not for the horses but for the asses who believed in the One Thousand-Year Reich.* Got back late, about 10 P.M. Lots of Christmas activity. I hope I don't have to participate too much, but how can I refuse, being a guest in this house? Margaret, my English friend, invited me to her parents' home for plum pudding. She explained the significance of that flaming delicacy, and I am extremely eager to go there. I was able to buy a pretty wooden candlestick for her. I found it among a mountain of the usual kitsch for sale.

I wrote a few notes to people who work with me and drew some decorations around the borders of my cards. They came out quite well.

It's 3 A.M., but I still had to write to tell you that every stroke of my paintbrush was accompanied by thoughts of you. You know, I don't recognize myself. How did all this come about? During my entire girlhood I always kept silent about my feelings concerning affairs of the heart. I had crushes on some of Artur's friends and never admitted it to anyone. What would the nuns in my convent school think of me now? Throughout our early relationship you never betrayed your feelings, and neither did I. Now the floodgates have opened, and it seems we understood each other even in that silence.

Good night, Kurt; ten thousand kisses,
Gerda

Munich, December 25, 1945

My dearest Kurt,
Whenever I start a letter to you, I let my thoughts go back to the moment

---

*Refers to Nazi boasts that their regime would last one thousand years and more. The clowns' "joke" must be regarded with some skepticism as to its sincerity.

when I put my pen down at the end of my previous letter, then try to review what happened in the interim.

I have been seeing my friends Esther and her husband, and another couple. It is so very strange to hear them constantly referring to each other as "my husband" and "my wife." The last time we lived a normal life, we had hardly outgrown playing with dolls, and now we are somehow grown up. I guess because all normalcy was arrested, there was no period of transition allowing for social development between the ages of fifteen and twenty-one. So here we are with a hundred years of life experience, consisting of unmitigated horror, but what happened to our normal growth and maturity?

Esther told me some news that really sent me into orbit. It's about a friend of mine, Tania, from Bielsko. We were together until the time of the death march, when she was chosen to go with the other column, which took a different route. Well, she got married three weeks ago, and I simply can't imagine her in that status. She was such a tomboy and whirlwind, so much fun. Hearing that triggered a long-forgotten memory.

Tania was in love at age twelve, or at any rate had a crush on this boy. Her heartthrob was seventeen, one of Artur's friends, by the name Kubi. He was one of the best-looking guys in our circle in Bielsko, and naturally was oblivious to her infatuation with him. I had to swear not to tell anyone about it, not even Artur. The only reason she took me into her confidence was in order to find out diplomatically where their usual hangouts were. It goes without saying that at their ripe old age, the boys would look with disdain at twelve-year-olds. However, I did find out that Kubi, in turn, had a crush on a girl with whom Artur's girlfriend was close.

Tania was inconsolable. She made me get paper, pen, and sealing wax, then proceeded to write down her resolve never to trust men again and never to get married. Needless to say I was touched to the depth of my soul by her nobility and self-sacrifice, and that prompted me to add my signature to her vow. Afterward we attached this "sacred" document to a kite and let it soar to the skies. I can't help but wonder who found it and what they might have thought of such self-denial? Now that Tania has broken her oath, I think it may be okay for me to do likewise. She is coming to Munich with her husband, and I can't wait to see her.

Much, much love. I miss you so.

Gerda

Hello, Miss Moonbeam,

Well, I've never been so well compensated for a long period of waiting. First came three of your letters, dating back to the beginning of December, followed by others from November. You write so beautifully; every small detail, every seemingly trivial incident takes on a special significance because of the way it flows from your pen and touches my senses, which in turn magically conjure up the shape of your thoughts for me. It shows we have to be capable of being moved by small things in order fully to enjoy the big ones. I feel sorry for people who can no longer believe in fairy tales; they miss a lot.

That reminds me of a book by the Chinese writer Lin Yutang, who lives in the United States. His theory is that we are all born sentimental, but that we gradually repress such sentimentality, something we may even boast about in the erroneous assumption that the less sensitivity we display, the more "mature" we are. That is our way of "steeling" ourselves against life. What peculiar notions people do have!

But to get back to the mundane: I was so disappointed about the negative answer by the Swiss consulate. I hope something can be done. I don't understand this attitude at all. Perhaps your Swiss acquaintance can intercede. When do you expect him back? I read in the papers that President Truman came out with a statement that help will be rendered to "displaced persons" to the limit of our ability. Of course it's going to be done within the framework of existing immigration regulations, but it's supposed to be made easier, and all those who became homeless are to get preferential treatment. Sounds beautiful, but let's see what comes of it.

If it weren't for the new job opportunity that came up for you, I would have to persuade you to give up your present one. I just can't continue to watch you being exposed to these spiritual conflicts, to see how you regard each line you are reading in the light of your own experiences, thereby letting the past well up in all its pain and bitterness. I know only too well from my own emotions how limited and futile thoughts of retribution can be. It will never replace our losses. Vengeance is something toward which every human being is inclined, but it must never be allowed to degenerate into senseless hatred because it consumes and shatters us. Gerda, let's be done with the past and where the wounds are deepest; they should be replaced only by respect, by reverence, and

177

by the gentle pain that is a symptom of the healing process. Yes, Gerda, please do it for me, but above all for yourself!

The matter of the Bavarian Aid Society appeals to me. It's always a daring step to venture into something like that, but it does take courage to try what is uncertain. Should it turn out that the people you have to deal with are not the right ones, then you can always give up that position and devote yourself to the study of English. I'll take care of the necessary financial arrangements. By the time this letter reaches you, most of these matters will quite likely have been resolved. Let's hope that, meanwhile, either Switzerland or France will have come through.

You really stuck to your writing quite assiduously. I was so happy with your "Daily Journal," and think that such a sacrifice deserves a better reward than I can provide with my inadequate correspondence. Even I have to recognize what an achievement it is to concern yourself with me from early morning till late at night. But your lines fully accomplished their intended aim. Cupid, irresistible as he is, really did it to me. His arrows unerringly found their target. Yet I have unlimited confidence in his playful pursuits.

I'm still without a job, but expect to have definite word about it by tomorrow. I'm so sick of this uncertainty; it gives me a lot to think about. If nothing comes of it, I'll stay in Buffalo until New Year's, then go to New York to find something concrete.

Regards to all your friends, and do let's hear something favorable from you. That's when your much-maligned "iceberg" will melt with joy. Despite your impudence you'll get a kiss, and just you wait for the punishment that will follow once you're here.

Kurt

Buffalo, December 26, 1945

Gerda, my beloved,

The dreariness of this winter day in no way matches my mood. In reality I wish I could embrace you and shower you with countless kisses, while conveying the big news to you: I have a job! I'm not entirely certain whether all the euphoria isn't somewhat exaggerated; nevertheless I was gradually getting concerned that the matter took so long to be settled. Let me share the details with you.

I'm going to start working in a printing plant as a typesetter. What's especially favorable about it is that instead of the year-and-a-half training period that was technically still ahead of me, it will now only take another half year. At the same time the starting salary of fifty dollars is quite decent compared to that for other jobs, and if all goes according to plan, it will soon increase to sixty dollars (per week, naturally). This being Buffalo, that's more than adequate to get along. Certainly a lot more than the same in New York. Actually I consider it only a springboard toward something better, and within a few months plan to take an advertising course at the university here, concurrently with my work. That's made quite easy for qualifying veterans (how peculiar to hear myself so described), inasmuch as the government will subsidize tuition and board. I can't see myself spending a full four years at the university, though.

To answer your inquiry regarding your possible occupation once you arrive here, let me tell you first of all that I hope to let myself be simply intoxicated by the magic of your charms for a considerable period. Should any time be at our disposal after awhile, I will leave it to your judgment to select something to your liking. I feel that after so many years of forced labor, you should only be aware that you can do anything you have an inclination to pursue and that you find stimulating. If you're asking my advice, I'd like to suggest that you do something along the lines of arts and crafts, providing that still interests you, while at the same time you learn the language. If I suggest this as a daytime endeavor, it's only because I can't quite picture evenings spent without you, after all this unnecessary involuntary separation. But let's discuss that more later.

In my next letter I'll enclose a copy of Truman's speech, according to which I've reached the conclusion that, despite all predictions, American consulates will nevertheless open in Germany by spring, that the granting of visas will be accelerated, and that the transportation problem will be solved by then. That means that if all else fails and you can't get transit visas for either Switzerland or France, there is a good chance that a get-together by May 8* will yet be a possibility.

> Hoping that these lines will reach you much faster than all that preholiday mail, I am with much love,
> Your Kurt

---

*Refers to speculation that Gerda would be in the United States by her birthday.

Munich, December 26, 1945

My dearest Kurt,

Well, it's done. A chapter of my life lies behind me again. Perhaps that statement is too strong, but my work at the Civilian Censorship Division, my first real job, can be called the end of a chapter. My leaving there is definite. I found it hard to resign after all, and devoted a lot of thought to it before I did. I hope that you know me well enough to realize that it was not a spur-of-the-moment decision, and trust you are in agreement with my step. Once we are together, I shall tell you in greater detail exactly why I left there.

I hope that the new job will let me do something more positive. There should be satisfaction in being able to aid people in need, and that is really what I aspire to do. Now a new chapter is about to start.

I never got around to finishing this letter, then forgot about it, and now have a few days on the new job behind me. It's quite a change from what I was doing. Just to give you an idea, I had an interesting case today. You wouldn't believe this one. A man came to see me because he has "a very strong feeling" that he really was born Jewish and might therefore be entitled to receive help. I asked the usual questions and stopped cold when he told me that he had been a member of the Nazi Party since 1927.

"Why were you in such a hurry?" I asked. He had an explanation.

"Well, you see, look at me. Don't you think I look Jewish?" Indeed, he had a strong Semitic look about him, I had to agree.

"That was my problem; people took me for a Jew, so I thought if I wore the party badge early, that would take care of it. And it did."

I had my fun with that one, only he was dead serious.

We come again to the question of my emigration. When you sent me the needed papers I was told that I'll be able to get out of here. But how, without a consulate being open in Munich? There seem to be nothing but endless difficulties. I have gone from office to office in every conceivable organization, only to conclude that these days we are engaged in another war, a battle to scale the walls erected by hostile authorities. But in the end we will win!

And what then? We will get married and be very happy. Seriously, I am starting to think about what I will be doing besides cooking and loving you. Do you have any idea what you would want me to do? I would like to study, if that's possible. Perhaps I could begin by taking some courses here, but my work hours are so long and I don't want to give up my job, which keeps me busy and independent.

I can't wait to hear what Uncle Leo thinks about our engagement. If only Artur could be there, my beloved big brother. I dare not think about it, but I pray hard.

My thoughts turn to you again and again. I try to imagine so many things that may have happened moments after your return home. Then I focus on the instant you took off your uniform jacket that you wore "cum laude" for so many years. What was that like? Filled with gratitude, relief, and some nostalgia, perhaps? You must have taken it off very slowly, didn't you? Did those colorful civilian ties feel strange after being used to nothing but khaki for such a long time? But please do take good care of your uniform; I shall always remember it with love and gratitude.

Perhaps someday our children might want to play "soldier." No, better not, but by all means let them see it. May they never have to wear one like it again. But you should keep the uniform for some future reunion of "Old Veterans." We should reserve a place of honor for your old helmet with the red diamond of the Fifth Infantry Division. I shall dust it carefully each day. And please do promise me that you will acquire a net* for it. I must have the net you wore over it when I saw you for the first time. Please, even if you have to buy it on the black market!

Many kisses and much love,
Yours, Gerda

Munich, December 27, 1945

Dearest Kurt,

Sorry I had to stop yesterday; I had 1,001 things to attend to. But today my thoughts are on a different plane, and my sorrow blots out everything else. It is my empathy for Günther, a friend whom I value and admire, a most decent human being, finding himself tested to the limit of his endurance. I told you about his engagement to his brother's widow. Today he got a letter from the love of his life. She survived the war and is in Australia. She has waited for him for seven years, despite the fact

---

*Nets were meant to facilitate attachment of camouflage items, when needed.

that she knew he was in Auschwitz. Seeing him today, I found that he appears to have aged overnight. Witnessing his suffering is the most heartbreaking thing I have done since the end of the war. So far his decision is to stay with his widowed sister-in-law. Can you imagine his dilemma, his pain?

This damned war has left so much sorrow and pain in its wake. I hear about such a multitude of individual tragedies every day. So many survivors are being asked to make incredible sacrifices. What a price to have to pay for a little happiness! I can't bear to see so many people unhappy. In light of all that, my not having seen you for three and a half months seems very small.

I love you,
Gerda

In the course of a visit to Australia in 1998, we were to find out that this story had a happy ending. The resolution of Günther's dilemma was told to us some fifty-three years later by Stella, who had befriended me while we were both working at the Civilian Censorship Division. She was the one who, much to our relief and gratitude, had helped us forward our correspondence to each other through army channels after our initial contact person, Captain Presser, returned to the United States.

We learned that once Günther discovered that the love of his life was alive and had waited for him steadfastly, despite the odds against his survival, his sister-in-law released him from their engagement. In due time they both emigrated to Australia, where he was able to realize his dream by marrying his former sweetheart.

Unfortunately Günther was no longer alive by the time we made our journey to Australia, but we took great satisfaction in hearing how well disposed providence had been to all concerned: His sister-in-law found happiness as well by meeting and marrying a decent man.

Munich, December 28, 1945

Hello Kurt,

Outside spring is undeniably in the air, because there is a lightness and transparency in the atmosphere that allows my hello to be heard in New

out the help of the postal service. I think nature has heard my
d was kind enough to move ahead of itself. Unfortunately it
o have affected Captain Presser in just the opposite way. She is
ill, perhaps I should say "under the weather," which could well be the
cause of it all.

I met an American woman at work who is about to leave for Paris in
order to meet her husband there. She seems to know someone in that
city who finds herself in the same predicament as I but who will soon—
or has already been able to—leave for the States, thanks to the favorable
disposition of her case by the American consul. Do you think that might
perhaps work for me as well? Do you want me to pursue it?

Now something in a lighter vein. The Munich streetcar system has
become the butt of all sorts of jokes. Most people are terribly upset by
it, and for good reason. All the same I find it amusing most of the time
because of all the characters you see and the way people hang from
those straps, like bunches of grapes. Well, this morning I acquitted
myself nobly. It was more crowded than a sardine can, with people
standing on each other's feet. Just then a really jolly-looking woman
pushed herself into the center of this mass of humanity, carrying on her
head—you won't believe it—a rocking horse! You should have seen the
disgust and indignation that registered on a sea of faces. I couldn't help
but visualize how they had looked in uniform not so long ago, so arrogant
and self-righteous, and that gave me an idea. Making my way around
the mass of people, and in the process stepping on many toes, literally
and figuratively, I managed to add to their wrath by getting close to the
lady and allowing her to put the horse on the floor.

Now a caustic voice, dripping with venom, was directed at me. "Why
don't you ride that horse to where you're going?" "An excellent idea!"
I retorted, and much to the chagrin of many, but also to the amusement
of others, I rode in great style to the Sendlinger Tor, on the back of a
rocking horse!

Enough for today. Many kisses,
Gerda

Munich, January 1, 1946

My dearest Kurt,
I can't in good conscience say that I had much sleep—about three

hours—but I don't mind at all, because the most marvelous news jus.
came as a morning greeting, on the first day of the new year. What a
good omen!! It was announced that emigration to the United States is to
begin soon!

This month the American consul should arrive in Munich, and the
American ships are to start operating, with transports of about one thousand people to leave twice a month. American citizens have priority, of
course, along with their wives, even if noncitizens. But I hope that my
chances are good as the fiancée of a serviceman. Can you believe that?
I am jumping with joy at the very thought! It seems you were right in
your estimate that it should take between four and six months. I can't
write much more, am truly overcome by the thought that it is for real.

What all is going to happen during the interval until this letter reaches
you? Tomorrow I hope there will be mail from you. Tomorrow also I will
be starting my new job. During the past few days, I have met a lot of
people. For years now, people have confided in me, although I don't
know exactly why. I am privy to many secrets, so many wrenching life
stories, and the more I hear, the more I marvel at my good fortune and
realize how lucky I am. What enormous happiness was given to me
through you!

Yours,
Gerda

Munich, January 2, 1946

My dearest Kurt,

I had a strange and uneasy premonition today. I got home rather late
with a gnawing feeling of uneasiness, apparently unfounded. On my bed
I found your two letters of December 15 and 16, containing two photos
of you. It gave me so much pleasure to see your image, and now they
bear some lipstick stains.

Now, to my premonition: Uncle Leo's letter. It is touching of you to
have deleted a reference to "something" that you felt would upset me
and from which you want to spare me pain. But you know, dearest, what
I seem to gather from the rest is worse than the bitterest reproaches. I
do prefer the unvarnished truth, whatever it may be. I can't imagine
what I am to make of the fact that my uncle accuses me of "coldness"
and of keeping a distance. How could he possibly be angry with me for
the brevity of my letter to him on the day of our engagement! Does he

have no idea what it was like? A few hours earlier, to my inexpressible joy, you had asked me to marry you. Then, a short while later, I had to part with you, my most beloved being on earth, not knowing when I would see you again. I love my uncle very much, now more than ever, since he appears to be the only one left from my family. But I can't understand him. I have not seen him in eight years. I was thirteen at the time. Doesn't he know what happened during those years?

You sat next to me as I penned those lines to him, informing him of my engagement to you. I could barely restrain myself. How could I have imagined what approach he expected at a moment when everything was churning within me? Had I truly given free rein to my emotions, I might have lost my self-control completely and made our parting even harder. You, my beloved, are trying to spare me, though I do know that my uncle is angry that I did not ask his permission to marry. Does he think that I just came out of my convent school and because my parents are not here I owe this to him? I am so sorry to have upset him and caused him pain. It certainly was not intended that way.

I am touched by his goodness, love, and concern. Is it because I am his beloved sister's child? Does he know that I am ashamed to have stayed alive while she did not? Were it not for you, I would ask myself why I survived and what for. You are the center of my life and the hope of our future together. Were it not for that, I could not go on living in this place. You are the anchor to my normalcy. The thought of you dispels my terrible loneliness, which I confess, despite everything, overwhelms me at times. Then all I have is your picture.

I shall write a letter to my uncle. Please read it and forward it or withhold it, as you see fit. In time to come, once I can do so face-to-face, I might tell him what I tried to spare him. I know how much he loved my mother. He does not know the truth about the terrible years in the basement of our house and later in the ghetto. He knows nothing of the deprivation, the pain, the illness, Mama's suffering, and her constant worry about Papa and Artur.

Please forgive me for the burden I must be imposing on you, the concern I am causing you. I promise I shall try to repay you when we are together.

So I am sitting here reliving the day. After only one day on my new job, how much have I seen! I ask applicants the usual standard questions: "Where were you born? Where did you spend the war years? Have you lost family members?" Invariably I will look into tear-filled eyes and receive answers from trembling lips. So far it's been most difficult to keep my own emotions in check, and it took every last reserve of strength to hold back my own tears at some of the stories that unfolded. I found myself saying meaningless pleasantries to people I encountered, all the while longing to get to my room, to be myself, to let go and hold your picture, read your letters. I promise I will be brave and endure the loneliness, as long as you are there for me.

Gerda

Munich, January 4, 1946

My beloved Kurt,

We had a meeting today at my new office at the Bavarian Aid Society, and I think it rivaled what I read about meetings in the British House of Commons, both in length as well as boredom. I sat among forty men and four women, all very old, I assume between forty-five and fifty. A man from the Central Committee was present, and there was an awful lot of talk about the desirability of a merger between this agency and the Joint Distribution Committee. They would work hand in hand, with the idea of gathering all loose threads into one united, strong, and meaningful strand.

But, as you might guess, they are not going to do it. The ladies, matrons in long sleeves, dresses buttoned to their throats and some wearing pince-nez glasses, looked so forbidding and accusing that I felt it would be construed as a criminal act if I crossed my legs. I felt very uncomfortable under their scrutiny, certainly intimidated. Then I started to wonder where they had been and what they had done when the people who are now their clients were in the camps. I gather those women are Germans who would probably deny ever having been card-carrying Nazi Party members. They exuded a lot of authority, but I don't think much understanding or compassion.

Suddenly I felt that a new era was dawning in which it's possible to offer help without being stern or severe, but simply by displaying understanding. It's sufficient to offer your hand and tender whatever help is possible. In that way we can ensure a better future. I said little, merely expressing my opinion that we should work together harmoniously. In that way the fruits of our work would become evident and reflect our success.

That's about it for now. Good night, and all my love,

Gerda

What had swayed me to accept the job offer from the Bavarian Aid Society was the prospect of having some one-on-one dealings with people in need. I was glad to abandon the sterile world of agony and suffering, as observed from a distance at the Civilian Censorship Division, after reading what people had been compelled to commit to paper. It had often left me helpless and distraught at my inability to be of direct help to others, as would not be the case at the Aid Society. Included perhaps in my motivations was also a naive concept that all efforts would be directed toward the most expeditious way of alleviating the plight of the needy, some of them Jews or half-Jews, mostly refugees from countries that were at least in part German-speaking, such as Czechoslovakia and Hungary.

Thus it was my hope that I would be able to interact with a variety of people and be able to render them a measure of help.

The Fifth U.S. Infantry Division took the city of Frankfurt on March 30, 1945, at which point we did not move on as usual but were held in reserve. That afforded me the chance to search for a cousin of mine, a physician who had a German Christian wife, Leni, and two daughters, Wilma and Charlotte. Although contact had been lost with him for most of the war years, there was a slight chance that he had been allowed to live with his family, and I set out to see what I could find out about his fate.

Ludwig Reinheimer had served in the German army with distinction during World War I and had always been a fervent nationalist. On the occasion of my bar mitzvah in 1933, he had included in his congratulatory letter to me the admonishment, no matter what might lie ahead during these uncertain times, always to remain conscious of my German heritage. It had had a hollow ring at that point of the Nazi power seizure.

Now word had reached me that precisely such survivors of mixed marriages were in fact drifting back to the city and were gathering at what had once been a Jewish community center. This lead put me in touch with a handful of people, perhaps a dozen, but my inquiries initially yielded only blanks. However, one of the last women I spoke to immediately burst out, "Oh, yes, I can tell you how to find Leni and the girls!" And she proceeded to explain that Leni had moved in with a farmer and his family some forty kilometers outside Frankfurt, suggesting that I contact a friend of hers who knew the exact address.

I wasted no time getting that information and subsequently was able to locate the farmhouse, where, sure enough, I found Leni and her two pretty, blond daughters, aged thirteen and eleven. Remembering the dozens of photos I had seen of her during my formative years, she appeared much aged and did not look well. She soon brought me up-to-date on all that had transpired. Quite late during the war, Ludwig had been sent to Flossenbürg concentration camp, in northern Bavaria, and while she was without news of his whereabouts, she clung tenaciously to the hope of his survival. As for her the report was not good. She was suffering from cancer, needed better care, and very much wanted to move back to Frankfurt. As far as that desire was concerned, I was able to procure an apartment for her and the girls before I had to move on with my unit. When I returned once more in August, I found the Reinheimers doing as well as could be expected, but I was oblivious to the fact that Leni had only a few more months to live.

Although exact details remain obscure to this day, it appears that Ludwig died in Flossenbürg as late as March 1945, in all likelihood after having been taken to another camp, only to be marched back to Flossenbürg. The city of Frankfurt has recently named a street in his honor.

Wilma and Charlotte were initially sent to an orphanage, while their relatives in the States tried unsuccessfully to get them into this country. Later they were brought up by their mother's family in Germany. Wilma followed in her father's footsteps and became a physician with a practice in Frankfurt, and in the course of her medical studies spent some time at a university in West Virginia.

Charlotte married an Englishman and has been living not far from London ever since.

My beloved little Gerda,

A few hasty lines before I'm off to a cocktail party. It's Sunday, and I slept till noon, as usual. Tell me how you're going to like that habit once we're married. Quite likely I'll be torn from my slumbers around 6 A.M. by means of ice water. One thing I can promise you: During the summer it's "up-and-at-'em," into the green environs, regardless of whatever sacrifice that'll require. It would be such a waste of time, after all, as long as the beach or tennis courts beckon.

Despite the fact that it's only January, you can almost sense the first harbingers of spring. It's warm enough so you can easily go outside in your shirtsleeves. No doubt there'll be a terrible snowstorm by tomorrow, but that's Buffalo. Totally crazy climate, and that's why I fit so well into this milieu. And where two weeks ago there were mountains of pristine snow, all that remains is ice-encrusted dirt. Anything can be expected here.

Still no mail from you. I hear that there are raging storms in the Atlantic, so that various ships couldn't dock. What a consolation! I'm so curious about what all happened on your end meanwhile. And I know how easily you jump to conclusions if nothing reaches you for a while. I can only hope all is well with you.

Do you remember the wife of my cousin, whom I found in the Frankfurt area when the Fifth Division took the city? She is Christian and remained inconspicuous for part of the war by staying on a farm. I visited her again later on my return trip from the Riviera. She had two very nice girls, ages eleven and thirteen, and had still not given up hope that her husband, a doctor, would turn up alive, because he was sent to the camps at a late stage. Inasmuch as she never got a sign of life from him, she had to assume the worst. What has come as a total surprise now is the blow that she too died in Frankfurt a short while ago. She was no longer very young, had various kinds of major surgery, and apparently succumbed to her afflictions. It's very tragic for the kids, who had to be sent to an orphanage. The girls have an uncle and aunt here in the States, who want to find out whether their nieces can be brought to this country.

So you see there is much tragedy around. Apropos such unpleasant news, I can only ask you again and again not to hold back but to write me everything. Don't think you ought to spare me certain things or that I want it that way.

From time to time my mail reaches me via my old army address, and I just received the enclosed money that an army friend of mine is putting at my disposal. He claims he found it among his things after leaving Germany, and says it'll see its very best use in this manner. If anything else should be lacking, please let me know immediately at any time.

More soon, have to leave now. Keep well; it won't be long before we'll see each other again.

> And here is an attack of kisses from your
> Kurt

Munich, January 7, 1946

My dearest,

Rita is still here and I am delighted. Wouldn't it be heavenly if she too came to Buffalo? I like her so much, and we have gone through all the nightmare years together. We both went to Notre Dame,* were in the ghetto together, then in the camps. She had two aunts with her (her mother's younger sisters), while I had Ilse, Suse, and Liesl. Now that she is here, I can talk with her, really talk.

Though the time goes by slowly, it moves me toward my aim: May 7. I have it firmly fixed in my mind and heart. Captain Presser will be leaving in four to six weeks, and I shall miss her very much. It also means that your mail may be coming by "snail back."

I must share something with you that has been troubling me a great deal. I thought I could resolve it without giving you concern, but I really don't know what to do. Two days ago, the head of the housing commission called me to his office. He came right to the point, asking for my address, and when I gave it to him, he said, "Ah, I thought so." Then he opened a ledger filled with lists of people who had been Nazis and whose homes were being confiscated in order to find accommodations for the masses of displaced persons who arrive in Munich daily. I did not understand at first, then he pointed to my address and let me read it. I learned that my "kind" ailing landlord, who sees to it daily that my shoes are warmed next to the kitchen stove, has been a party member since 1933. I was assured, though, that he and his wife would

*Catholic girls' high school in Bielsko.

not be thrown out as long as I continued to live there. That left me speechless for a few moments, and I guess my eyes filled with tears. He looked at me and said rather harshly, "Fräulein Weissmann, who had pity on your parents?"

I want to leave. How can I stay, Kurt? What am I to say to people who treated me civilly, no matter what their motives might be? I can hate Germany and all things German with a passion, but I can't hate individuals. Am I too much of a coward? What is wrong with me? Or am I so comfortable that I am becoming complacent? I don't know what to do. Rita is urging me to go with her to Regensburg for a few days. I long to go in order to sort myself out, but can't leave just now. Thousands of DPs are arriving, coming back from their former homes where they found a bitter welcome awaiting them. Now they have no place to go. I have been working from 9:00 A.M. to 9:30 P.M., with only a ten-minute break for lunch. The misery is indescribable. I see two worlds here, a few figures dominating the arena. On the one hand, I can avail myself of the theater, the opera, art galleries, and restaurants, on the other, I see what goes on behind the scenes, where there is only misery, pain, despair, and sorrow.

I see dozens of people daily, and my card file is a virtual chronicle of agony. What am I to do? Please forgive me for burdening you with this. Is it wrong of me to want to escape? I want so much to go to you, where together we can build a new life.

Please write about you, what you think, what you feel, what makes you happy, what gives you pain. Let me share your joys, your sorrows, and the little daily disappointments. I want to be at your side for it all. Even if everyday cares should come knocking at our door, I am not worried. We are so young, we can face life with all it may bring. We'll enjoy its beauty and treasure those small, seemingly insignificant moments, simply because we can share them together.

Sleep well, my love. I hope I will dream of you.

I love you,
Gerda

Rita turned up at my doorstep in Munich one day, after having scanned the lists of survivors at the German Museum, and we had a delirious reunion. She hailed from my hometown, and we both attended Nôtre

Dame, a convent school a notch above high school level. It was only after we were forced to live in the Bielsko ghetto that we became close friends. That friendship was heightened further when we suffered the common fate of the Jews of Bielsko: deportation and, for our age group, slave labor in German weaving mills.

The last time I had seen her was one evening in April 1945 in what was the final stage of the death march we had been on since the end of January. She had looked for me to let me know that she had found a way out of the barn into which our SS guards had herded us, and that she and her young aunt, who was her constant companion, were about to make a break for freedom. I could not join her in this risky venture because my friend Ilse, from whom I had become inseparable, was no longer able to walk.

It was wonderful to know that Rita and her aunt had indeed made it to freedom, and on bringing her up-to-date on my recent engagement, I naturally spoke of nothing but Kurt and where he was living then. It turned out that she had just found some of her father's relatives in Buffalo, and that is where she was to settle a year after my coming to that city. Later she met and married a German-Jewish young man who had lived underground in Berlin by his wits, resourcefulness, and daring during the war years. His brilliance stood him in good stead in the building of a career, and in time Steve and Rita moved to Detroit, where he eventually became executive vice president and a board member of the Chrysler Corporation.

∽ ∽ ∽ ∽ ∽ ∽ ∽ ∽ ∽ ∽ ∽ ∽

Munich, January 8, 1946

My beloved Kurt,

Again there is so little mail from you. During the past three weeks I received only three letters. Please don't take that as a rebuke. It's so frustrating, because you report the same problem, yet I do write every day.

Fortunately Rita came to visit. Too bad that you were not here, or maybe it's better, because you might have thought us completely crazy. Rita is a serious, composed, quiet girl, but when she gets into a silly mood, there is no stopping her. We really cut loose yesterday till two in the morning. First we had a fashion show and draped every conceivable type of fabric around us. Then we got into gymnastics (we had attended a gymnastics class as children). After that, we reconstructed a long-forgotten dance. We even managed a lively mazurka.

Rita declared that you are the only American she ever addressed as "Sie," simply because she has not met any Americans who speak German.* Please don't be angry that I have not done well in English, although I do know the most useful and important phrases, like "I love you," "Okay," and "Leave me alone; I am engaged." You will have to be a very patient teacher. It does not seem all that difficult, even though you spell English in the most peculiar way, pronounce it differently, and think in it differently. Don't construe the last statement as being arbitrary. Just one example: when I write "Darling," I think "Kurt." Well, I have had some much-needed fun, and if all else fails as far as work is concerned, I can always get a job in a circus.

Love,
Gerda

Munich, January 9, 1946

My dearest Kurt,

A red-letter day! Four of your letters arrived together. I shall answer each one in detail, but must first share some new developments with you. Apparently Switzerland does not look too good. There seems to be a chance that I might be leaving directly from Bremerhaven within a few weeks. So please don't worry so much; it will work out for the best, I am sure.

Your bachelor days may be numbered, I warn you. I have so much to tell you. I looked at your photos before reading the letter and was startled, for I did not realize they were taken seven years ago. I like you better older and wiser! You must not worry so much. We are free and that is the greatest treasure on earth. What's more, we're also young and healthy. We'll be able to take anything that comes along.

All my love always,
Gerda

*She was to get the chance to address Kurt in English in the course of a long-standing friendship that began when she moved to Buffalo as well.

Munich, January 13, 1946

My dearest Kurt,

I just got back from Regensburg and wouldn't want you to think for a moment that a three-hour ride in a Jeep during a snowstorm can intimidate me. I had the choice between a private car or a Jeep, and which do you suppose I preferred? I'll report in greater detail on last night's magnificent party, where I met people from Bielsko in American uniform! For now, I only want you to know how overjoyed I was to get your five letters (with photos) of late December, along with a truly moving letter from Gerdi. I'll answer that one right away. Kurt, I'm totally taken with Gerdi and can hardly say more. You can't imagine how fortunate I consider myself that she is the type of human being I've always dreamed about as a big sister!

Now to your letters. My darling, I congratulate you on your—I mean *our*—position. May it be the right beginning of our lives. Do tell me every last detail about it. I do like you a lot in civilian get-up, Kurt. I might "almost" fall in love again!

Don't worry about me as far as finances are concerned. I assure you that I have sufficient funds to manage easily. Does that calm your fears? Please don't send anything; everything can wait until we're together, okay?

I'm enclosing a snapshot, which I regard as very bad. As you can see from my hair in the enclosed photo, I got caught in a big snowstorm.

My dear counselor, I am following your advice. So it's handicrafts and English! Good God, if you only knew how poorly I speak English. But you'll teach me, won't you? If only I had applied myself more while you were here, I wouldn't have to disgrace you now. "*Nix* comprehend!" That's about the extent of my proficiency at the moment. Much as I try, I can't muster enough concentration to learn anything at present. Do tell me that I'll master it one day!

Gerda

Buffalo, January 13, 1946

Hello Dimples,

The past two days have been most rewarding because they netted a total of seven long-awaited letters and an abundance of news. Your letter from before Christmas came a few days ago, while the others that reached me after that dated as far back as December 8. At last the missing pieces are now in place, even if they turned out gloomier than I had hoped.

I haven't read anything as beautiful in a long time as your reflections on the walk through "our" woods, which I can hardly imagine draped in a garb of snow. What moved me especially was your symbolic interpretation of the "gate." Only you can do it in that manner. I'm so glad that I could experience it with you. Life has a more transcendent meaning if one is capable of viewing it through the eyes of the soul. It requires a certain sensitivity. Joy in nature is part of it, but not the entire perception. I feel sorry for anybody who can't feel that way.

I hesitated to send off papers this week because I'm expecting a raise next week. I'm fed up with all this waiting, and so I'll send off the entire batch of papers in my possession, thinking they'll do, even without the additional certification. At any rate it can always follow later; it's not worth delaying the matter any longer.

I'm racking my brain to get an idea of what you look like with a loose hairdo. You're well acquainted with my mania regarding the style and length of your hair, so it shouldn't surprise you if I permit myself to say a word of two if I don't like it that way.* Not that such expressions ever have any effect, coming from men; in the end we always dance to your tunes anyway. If Ulysses had encountered a siren like you, history would never have been written like that. In spite of that, a kiss from one who always—and gladly—succumbs to your siren songs.

Your Kurt

Munich, January 14, 1946

My dearest Kurt,

I just came home, and have to write to you immediately to report what I was able to achieve, or rather not achieve, at the Polish Committee. The sum total is zero. After the great build-up and high hopes I was given the day before yesterday, I am sorry to have sounded so optimistic in my last letter. I must tell you now that I was sadly mistaken. It would be funny, were it not so sad and upsetting. They know very well that people in my position have no papers; we were merely numbers under the Nazis. I suggest that they question me about Polish history, literature, or whatever. If I had been born elsewhere, would I claim that I was born in Poland? They claim that if the Swiss consulate would issue a

*Subsequent photos managed to calm my fears that Gerda might cut her hair because "it simply is too loose."

transit visa, the Polish Committee would give me a citizenship certificate.* On what basis are the Swiss going to give me a visa, if the country of my birth won't first recognize my citizenship? By the way, that consulate is not open every day, so I will have to see when I can go there, knowing that I'll probably be turned down anyway.

My boss shows a lot of understanding by letting me take time off to run all those errands. I make up for the hours by working evenings, which means I usually don't get home before 10 P.M. That presents problems, because after 6 the streetcars run infrequently. I am sorry not to be able to paint a rosier picture, but I guess the wheels of bureaucracy grind slowly. It would be ever so much better not to have such high hopes held out to begin with. Surely the picture will have changed by the time this letter reaches you. You can be sure that I will leave no stone unturned, and that everything will come out all right.

What pains me most is that I came out of this horrible war, expecting normalcy and peace—and now this.

For me it's simply agony to be in Germany. I hate this country as I have never hated anyplace before. I have ample reason for that, not only for obvious reasons, but based on many new observations. God willing, once we are together I will tell you about it. When I get out of here, I will only be able to think of Germany as an inferno.

I am greatly concerned about the fate of your cousin's children. I've heard so many similar stories. Here you have a father killed in a concentration camp, someone who felt himself so deeply German. And now the mother, a good, caring woman who was German also died. Is there anything I can do? I would be glad to go to Frankfurt or wherever. As you know I work with cases of that nature and will do anything possible. Please talk to their aunt and uncle in America and ask them what they want me to do.

I am able to borrow books now, that's my greatest pleasure. I'm reading a very good one, Klabund's *History of Literature*, and enjoying it very much.

Good night, my love. You must be getting sleepy reading these boring, endless letters. They are my lifeline, though. Many gentle good night kisses.

Yours,
Gerda

*I had only a temporary, personal certificate.

Munich, January 15, 1946

Dearest Kurt,

Although I had no intention of reporting to you about my session with the Swiss consulate, I find I have to do so anyway, because it requires your help. So let me start with the early part of today. The force that seems to determine the favorable outcome of my plans, or the lack of it, is, of all things, the streetcar I take. Once I miss it by seconds, all else goes awry as well on that day.

Today the tram materialized, as if on order, and so I rode it in the best of faith. Then, at the consulate, I see that they only admit groups of ten people at a time. Being the eleventh, I hear the man in charge announce, "This time, eleven will be admitted." So far so good. I inquire how I can go about seeing the consul in person. "Out of the question," comes the answer. Undeterred, I fill out a form that will announce me. The wording I chose sounded as though I had been sent by some diplomatic corps to negotiate war or peace, but I got action only three minutes later. No less than a reception by the consul's private secretary.

Unfortunately nothing had come yet from Buffalo, but he heard me out, then handed me an application form for a transit visa through Switzerland, despite the fact that they do not issue them at the moment. Nevertheless he assured me it would be sent to Bern and could be approved within six to eight weeks, provided all necessary documents are in order. Everything had to be filled out in quadruplicate, along with four copies of your letter and four other supplementary forms and explanatory documents. And I literally sweated over a typewriter for the next four hours. Have pity on me—imagine me typing, and in English yet!

In it I furnished my uncle's account information, and I must ask you to cable him to that effect, and please stress that he should notify the bank once more, so that they will be familiar with my name if and when such an inquiry is made. Next I listed your relatives as "relatives in Switzerland" (there is actually such a question on the sheet). Again, it would be good if they were notified about it. It's extremely important that you send a message to Bern via the Swiss representative in Buffalo, stating that you will obtain American immigration papers for me. It's the *most important* thing you can do. You see, I need to have proof of the duration of my stay in Switzerland.

Another thing: The American consulate is supposed to open here sometime this month, and it's entirely possible that might work faster than Switzerland, although I find that country quite promising. Please, Kurt, do this as quickly as possible, so that the papers are here to substantiate the matter once it's my turn. My Swiss acquaintance at work is terribly nice and ready to help. He'll travel to Switzerland within a few weeks (couldn't do it last time, due to pressing family matters) and will personally investigate what can be done to expedite matters.

How's your work going? What progress are you making with your bachelor shack? Is it nearly ready? Will you let me have a look at it? Of course I'm going to insist that there be flowers in it. It wouldn't do to let you become a typical bachelor! Can't wait to save you from that fate. But before we get into a dispute about that, a thousand kisses and much love,

Gerda

Buffalo, January 15, 1946

My dearest, dearest Gerda,

Quickly a few words to you during my lunch period. My evenings are pretty short at present. As you know, I attend night school twice a week,* that is, I come home from work, gulp down supper, and immediately leave again. I'm usually back by 10:15 P.M. and naturally that doesn't leave much of the evening.

I'm getting used to my new job in a hurry. It's not hard. For now it's an advantageous position, but I can't see myself doing it for the rest of my life. I realize how much the army has changed my thinking. That multifaceted life has certain repercussions now. It'll be a while until I'm used to regular hours again. I imagine that most of the guys must feel like that.

Painting my room seems to take forever. Actually I don't care in the least how it looks; I would much prefer to have *our* apartment already. As soon as I have some indication that your prospects for a visa look good, I'll make a search. Sometimes it's possible to find something quite

---

*A printing course, interrupted by the war, that allowed me to become a journeyman typesetter.

by accident. At any rate the situation here is incomparably better than in New York.

I've thought about what would be best and would like your opinion on it. Because in all likelihood we initially won't get *the* home of our dreams, it might be good to live furnished for a while. It would be best if I didn't have to make those choices alone before you're here. It would be unthinkable for me to do it without being able to consult with you. Besides, that'll give you time to get used to American tastes and styles. Then you'll find it much easier to decide. At the moment, all that's available is ersatz war goods, or nothing at all. In any case, most of what's available for purchase is junk. So, my dearest Miss Dimples, let's have your valued opinion and, please, no "I leave that to you." In that case I would only give you 999 kisses instead of a round thousand.

Your Kurt

Munich, January 16, 1946

My dearest Kurt,

I am thinking how topsy-turvy our lives are. I am sleeping while you are awake and vice versa. I think we need to get on the same time schedule as our thoughts and hearts are.

I do spend most of my days running to the Swiss consulate. Fortunately my working hours are flexible, so I can make up the time. I hear that people are easily able to obtain transit visas for Switzerland. Please send me a notarized letter in English stating your intentions, along with a copy to the American consul in Munich. The consulate, it is rumored, will open here soon, and by all estimates that will take another six to eight weeks.

If all that comes to nothing, we'll have to try something similar with France. It is so sad that after this horrible war we are now engaged in a paper war. All the same I am hopeful that we will win this one as well.

How are we going to celebrate that victory? I took out a 1946 calendar, trying to guess which will be the golden, happy day of our reunion. I am fervently hoping that our meeting will again take place in May.

I got the strangest "invitation" today, if you can call it that. It asked that I appear in the former concentration camp Dachau to witness the prosecution of some of the guards from Flossenbürg. The paper nearly burned my fingers. My first impulse was to go see those murderers being brought to justice. But what is justice? What sentence could ever right those wrongs? As to revenge, perhaps God can think of some just punishment, because I can't. Everything pales in the light of what they have done. Can I sit in the same room with them, breathe the same air? No, I won't go—or am I just looking for excuses because I don't want to be hurt? Am I afraid that they still have the power to hurt me? I just don't know. There are so many incidents of which I have perfect recall, but to my amazement, others now seem to elude me. I wonder, Will there ever be a day when I'll have forgotten most of it? Perhaps we shouldn't talk about it at a time when you and I are standing on the threshold of our new life together.

It's time to tell you "good night." Many tender kisses—

Yours,
Gerda

Munich, January 20, 1946

Dearest Kurt,

Two letters arrived today and brought much joy, but also some concern over the fact that you have had no mail from me for two weeks. I write faithfully every day.

Now to answer your questions. I don't think that you need to send the original documents; copies should be sufficient. It would only further complicate matters. I have my Polish identification papers now. The situation here looks as follows: I applied for permission to enter Switzerland on a transit visa, merely for the purpose of seeing the American consul there. I was told that if all goes well, I might get the visa in about six weeks. They held out high hopes that this will work in my case. The Polish officer in charge of travel affairs assured me that under the circumstances this is the best way, inasmuch as he thinks general emigration will probably still take a considerable number of months. Were I not an optimist, I could be very depressed by this time. You see, I am not much favored by Swiss authorities as a Polish national. It is so strange that when I appear in person, things seem to go quite well. But then you have to fill out endless questionnaires in quadruplicate, after which the process usually bogs down and the answer is inevitably no! If only the American consul were here and I could see him.

Please tell me more about your daily life, your work, and everything. I somehow feel that I have deprived you of your inner peace, that your concern about me has disturbed your vision of the peaceful civilian life for which you yearned while you were in the army. I hope so very much that this will be restored for you soon. My work does give me a measure of satisfaction. In some cases I attempt to play "doctor for the soul"; or do detective work that gives me a glimpse into people's lives. You cannot imagine what goes on beneath a seemingly "normal" surface in some instances. A true drama of life, except not played on a stage but rather behind the scenes.

There are so many unhappy people, young people like us, with so many complicated miseries. I don't know how to thank providence for having spared me much of that. I was brought up in a normal, happy home, with a loving, caring family, and I am struggling to re-create that with you. Oh, yes, I must tell you that your picture got a beautiful decoration. It is graced now by a marvelous blooming cactus. I have never seen one in bloom. It arrived today without any accompanying words save for the name and address. Naturally I have no idea who sent it, but must chide you for being a very bad boy. I always did have a penchant for bad boys!

Good night, many kisses,
Gerda

Munich, January 21, 1946

My dearest Kurt,

I do believe in premonitions. I worked till 8 P.M. tonight and on the streetcar home was overcome by such a strong longing for you that as soon as I got off I started to run, as if you were there to meet me. Well, in a sense, you were. Your three letters arrived. It compensated for the long, arduous day. Your thoughts on New Year's are so exactly like mine. In the interim you must have gotten my letter. It made me feel that our thoughts and emotions met in some unimaginable celestial sphere, convinced that this year will bring our reunion and happiness.

Captain Presser thinks that she will be here for about another month. Tomorrow I will send you an address to which you can mail future letters. Considering that they usually take three to four weeks to reach me, it could delay receipt of important documents from you. If only the day would come when I could know for sure how many weeks or months it will actually take until I will see you. Then I could start to count the days and hours. You probably think I'm crazy, but if one concentrates all one's thoughts and actions on one point only, then hours seem to stretch into years. I look forward so much to our life together.

You suggest I might be disappointed that we will not be living in New York—you silly man! I only thought of New York because your family is there, and I admit that I have grown extremely fond of Gerdi. Her letters exude an undeniable warmth, and I have already begun to think of her as a sister. You must decide what is best for us, and you chose Buffalo, so Buffalo it will be! I think of it as a small paradise. You have to begin teaching me English immediately. Your friends will consider me terribly ignorant, and I don't want you to be embarrassed by me. Now I really must turn in. It's a beautiful, starry night, very clear. The snow glitters in the moonlight like a storybook scene. I do believe in fairy tales. Sometimes, they become reality.

Yours,
Gerda

Munich, January 22, 1946

My dearest, beloved Kurt,

You have really spoiled me now. Your letters arrive in batches of five! I'll settle for one a day as well. Before I answer your questions, I'll share with you some interesting cases I handled today. First there was this Christian couple who converted to Judaism in 1930. They suffered as Jews and spent some time in the camps. Their papers corroborate their statements. Anyway, they want to belong to the Jewish community officially and devote their lives to studying the Talmud.

Then, early this afternoon, I thought a movie star had come calling. Here was a most attractive, dark-complexioned young man, exceedingly well dressed, in what seemed a flawlessly tailored suit. Adding some dash was a colorful silk foulard, casually wound around his neck. Not only was he a vision to behold, but an example of elegant manners, speaking in faultless High German. I had to ask the usual questions: "Jewish?" "No." "Part Jewish?" "No." "Are you a non-Jewish marriage partner?" "No." "Perhaps you came to the wrong agency?" I suggested.

"No, I don't think so. I was persecuted under the Nuremberg Laws because I am a Gypsy!"

I was touched and a bit ashamed. One pictures Gypsies in dilapidated wagons along dusty roads, with lots of unkempt children, barking dogs, and greasy frying pans over campfires. Instead, here was this impeccably dressed young man with an aristocratic bearing! He needed to have some papers notarized, a service our agency provides, to allow him to resume his architectural studies at the university, which he was forced to give up because of his origin. So, you see, I met an original Gypsy baron!*

My superiors informed me that I will be working in the field quite a bit from now on. I welcome the idea of calling on clients outside the office. I'm eagerly awaiting your papers and hopeful that the consulate will open here soon. The letter you mentioned, containing detailed information regarding a visitor's visa, has not arrived as yet. Oh, well, as long as it comes. And soon, I pray.

With much love,
Gerda

Munich, January 23, 1946

My very dearest Kurt,

I am at work and it is 8:00 A.M. We start early, but I have a few free minutes and want to use them wisely, as you can see. You are still sleeping, and I hope the thoughts I try to transmit will not wake you up too soon. There is something important I need to ask you, but of course I know that it will take at least six weeks before you can answer. I'll have to make up my mind about something important.

The American consul is supposed to arrive any day now, and I will try to get the earliest possible appointment. But I doubt I will succeed if I go to the consulate alone. As you know, my English is practically nonexistent. Will I spoil my chances that way? Is it best to say as little as possible? I have your letter and the papers; perhaps that is the best way. It is so frustrating not to be able to say what one feels. But I do

---

*Reference to popular operetta, *The Gypsy Baron*, written by Johann Strauss, Jr., in the late nineteenth century.

have this strong hunch that the next few weeks will be decisive in some way. This seemingly endless waiting is very hard to take.

Gerda

Munich, January 25, 1946

My beloved Kurt,

What do you think your Dimples is doing right now? I pushed away all the papers I am working on and decided to take a break by writing to you. Unfortunately no mail from you this morning, but I hope for some tomorrow to brighten my weekend.

In talking to Captain Presser just now, I found out something of great interest. Apparently there is a possibility of marriage by phone, which might be recognized as being legal. If that were the case, it would take me out of the quota system. Have you heard about it? It would be fun and so very American!

As you know, our captain will be leaving next month, and I shall miss her terribly. After this weekend I'll be able to give you Stella's address. She is the person who will be the go-between for our mail and is coming to spend Sunday with me, at which time we will arrange everything. I am also eager to hear more about her life in England.

I did something else today that weighs heavily on my conscience and wonder how you feel about it. I was given tickets to see a concentration camp film called *Mills of Death.** After agonizing over it, I decided I would not go and tore up the tickets. Actually I feel terrible about what I did, which was to shield myself from seeing the horror again. Please don't think ill of me, but I wouldn't feel right if I didn't tell you about it. Is that cowardly of me? My whole being wants nothing more than a new life, so I'm reluctant to see those scenes on the screen again. Perhaps I fear that I might recognize someone and not be able to persist in my fantasies, which have helped me to shape a new beginning. I feel better now, having shared this with you. Back to work then, but my thoughts remain with you, as does my love.

Gerda

P.S. Somehow I can't let go of this letter; there is still so much that I want to share with you. Perhaps one reason I feel so negative today is

*Produced by Billy Wilder.

that my boss has just left this agency. I had worked so well with him, and he was open to many suggestions. He truly had only the welfare of our clients in mind. Unfortunately, he was replaced by an impossible person who has worked here before and who is the exact opposite of his predecessor, goes strictly by the book, no matter whether people are starving or find themselves in some other horrendous predicament.

I had seen him at an earlier date, at which time we all made fun of his pomposity and unvarying adherence to routine. Let me give you an example. At 12:30 P.M., not 12:29 or, God forbid, at 12:31, he takes out his buttered roll and cuts it into sections, which he proceeds to eat clockwise. Honestly! And nothing on earth can stop him from varying that routine. By the way, his parents and brother are in America, but he will not go there, because his heart (*what* heart?) lies in this city. He proudly proclaims that it belongs among the ruins of Munich. Naturally he is not overly fond of me, because of my impatience to get out of Germany.

The fact is that all the people I know—even those who have been able to forge a fairly good life here by finding opportunities—want to leave, without exception. Illegally if necessary, such as to Palestine, or they take a chance on being admitted to the United States later. For that matter, they'll take any country that will have them, even though it means facing a difficult life and once again learning a new language. Anything seems preferable to remaining here. That moron is the only one who wants to stay here, and to think he has his family in America! What bothers me most is that people's welfare depends on someone like him, and I shudder to think of the degree to which their lives will be affected by his decisions. I watch and wonder what I can do to help those in real need. I'll have to think of something.

Right now, I'm thinking of you, though, and send all my love.
Gerda

Munich, January 28, 1946
Kurt dearest,
Am just preoccupied by a most interesting thought: Will there be mail from you today? Am in bed, nothing serious, just bashed my elbow into a door, and am running a bit of a temperature. Had a cheerful letter from Rita, urging me to come to Regensburg again. Rita is lovely, and

we have a wonderful time together. She claims I owe her four days, and I am tempted to go but can't do so right now.

Munich is gradually turning into a very unsafe city. I constantly hear about "those foreign elements" that are taking over and have the run of the place. The German Museum has become a virtual den of iniquity, and of course I cut a wide swath around it. Wherever you go, you are challenged to produce your ID. Raids are the order of the day, and the most painful part is that they are carried out by German police. My point of view on that uniform has remained the same as it has been for years: I distance myself from it and harbor my own thoughts.

Some people at the office tried to persuade me to write a few articles for the *Münchener Zeitung* [a daily newspaper], in order to rebuke the op-ed voices that cry out against foreign elements. I tried, but then I threw the pages into the fire. No, Kurt, those who were trained as criminals and enthusiastically degraded other people aren't worthy of gaining an insight into the very source of our suffering.

Many of those individuals don't deserve to be called human beings, and these days, far from feeling chastised by their comeuppance, they merely proceeded to perfect their manifestations of brutality. They come in all guises, but it's fairly easy to spot them, and I often put that to a test. So far the results have usually been successful. All I do is pose ten questions and often get to the root of their perceptions that way. In general I'm embarrassed to see how base and petty people have become—or perhaps have remained?

I have a lot of dealings with people of that ilk, some of them my contemporaries. Initially they are shy, betraying a combination of reticence and hostility. You have to know how to deal with that. A matter-of-fact tone that conveys interest, followed by a warmer, straightforward attitude, usually assures success.

A few hours have passed since the above, and the doctor was here and found me okay, even recommending that I get out of bed. No mail from you, unfortunately, and the other news is that Captain Presser announced she'll be leaving in four weeks. So do write to the address I gave you previously, which I'm repeating herewith. . . . On the other hand I did get a letter from your relatives, the Sigaloffs, in Basel, which made me very happy. They write in so nice and warm a manner as I can hardly convey to you, at the same time asking me to stay with them as long as necessary. Their letter is full of loving sentiments toward you as well. They also declared their willingness to vouch for me and do all that may be required. The letter reached me by a detour, via the French zone, and of course I'll answer it immediately. I certainly hope things will materialize as far as Switzerland is concerned. It looks like a country full of sunshine, an antechamber to my future life.

Please excuse my scribbling, but as you know, electricity only goes on at 7 P.M. in Munich these evenings, and I'm writing this in semi-darkness.*

Kisses,
Gerda

Munich, January 29, 1946

Dearest Kurt,

I came across a letter today that I had written to you during the first weeks after our meeting. A formal letter: "Dear Lieutenant Klein," or something to that effect. The style is so guarded, so distant. I am trying to put the two "yous" together, vis-à-vis the two "Is," but find it impossible. I simply can't get back into my skin of eight months ago and wonder whether you feel the same way. No mail from you the entire week, so let me resort to telling you about some of the people I have encountered.

A young man came to my office a few weeks ago. He's Jewish, born in Munich, lost his entire family. He spent three years at Auschwitz and has tuberculosis, diagnosed as incurable, so he told me. He appears every few days under some pretext in order to see me. Feels that I am the only one he can talk to and who understands. Perhaps that's true to some extent, because I am so close to his age. He is twenty years old, and I am only one year older, while everybody else in the office is twice that age.

Anyway, his biggest concern is not his illness but a romantic involvement. He is in love with Marta, a sixteen-year-old girl who also has TB and is willing to marry him. She is Hungarian and went back to her

*Because of the curtailment of electricity during the winter of 1945–1946, I would usually try to stretch the daylight hours to the limit when dealing with my correspondence. Beyond a certain point I would write letters to Kurt by candlelight; in that way I could write in a more intimate manner and feel that it brought me closer to him.

home to find her family. She has not returned so far, and he is frantic. He tried several agencies, and I also gave him some leads, all to no avail. Marta has not been found yet. Poor guy, I can feel for him. He came to the office in a very determined mood and declared that while he has not given up hope of finding her, he must look elsewhere for a girl. "You understand," he declared resolutely, "that it's high time I get married. I can't wait any longer." I wished him luck.

He showed up again later and told me that he found a girl, that she is German but willing to enter into a relationship with him (by the way, he is extremely good-looking). He told her that I'm his friend, and I must meet her first. I became very uneasy with that situation and pointed out that it was highly unprofessional and that I shouldn't be involved. He informed me that he knows where I live, and if I didn't agree to see her in the office, she would come to my house. Then he added that, inasmuch as he was one of my cases, it was my responsibility to look after his welfare in every respect. He was dead serious about it. Lo and behold, this young Brünnhilde-type appears, straight out of a BDM* poster, and tells me her tale of woe. She has no news from her fiancé, an SS man she says was forced to join that brutal organization, and she wants me to help her. Help her with *what*? Well, she was not certain, but it was quite clear to me, and I offered my candid opinion regarding their relationship. Without a moment's hesitation, he declared that he would resume his search for Marta in Hungary.

I wonder what I am doing here?

I did have another "funny" case. A very assertive woman appeared and informed me in no uncertain terms that she is entitled to receive help, inasmuch as she is one-eighth Jewish. At the same time she admitted that her husband had belonged to the Nazi party for thirteen years. Suddenly she feels very Jewish: "It must be the Jewish blood in me that has awoken," she says. I swear to you, that is exactly how she put it. And what does she want from us? A certificate that she is one-eight Jewish, to send to her son, who as an officer in the *Wehrmacht* is still in captivity. Then she could tell him about his heritage, because he doesn't know that he is one-sixteenth Jewish. There are some even more bizarre cases, but I'll save them until I can tell them to you in person.

Love and many kisses,
Gerda

*Bund Deutscher Mädchen, a Nazi girls' movement, equivalent to the Hitler Youth.

Dearest Kurt,

Just kissed your picture "good morning," and despite that you don't seem to be in a happy mood. Why? It's really I who should be angry, because two weeks have gone by without mail from you. It's Sunday, so perhaps you're upset for the same reason I am, that is that we are not together. But cheer up. Much as I normally dread Mondays, I don't in this case, because it might bring mail from you.

What stories I hear almost daily! Recently there was one about this young woman who had lived a rather ordinary life. She expected me to commiserate with her because her parents are so old-fashioned and protective. In her words, she simply had to leave home to be on her own, to do what she pleased, instead of having to give an account of all her activities.

I asked her what she would do if she couldn't get a job and her money ran out. Without batting an eye, she came back, "Then I would go back home." Independence: What do they know about that? How can they understand what it means to have parents? So many thoughts cross my mind, and there is much I must sort out about myself. I'm often torn by these thoughts. I mean, I'm able to act on my convictions, and my values have become even stronger, taking on fuller shape. Only my relationship with you remains unchanged. There are no shades of gray in it and the boundaries are clearly drawn. There is only black-and-white when it comes to us—period. But all around me swarm so many emotions— questions, doubts, apprehensions—so that when things really get to me, I retreat to my sanctuary and let nothing follow me. I embark on a letter to you and feel whole and safe. Then, no current, no matter how strong, can sweep me into different waters. Please don't mind my ramblings; I just love to "talk" to you.

I'm still trying to get used to the type of greeting I get when encountering people I knew elsewhere. The other day I ran into a girl on the street, and she cried out, "Gerda Weissmann, you are alive!" Then the usual questions followed, which led to the same sad tales: the assumption that everyone is dead and the genuine surprise and delight to hear that someone has survived.

Recently I also bumped into two people I knew from Bielsko. The young woman was the most timid girl I had ever met, and the man, now her husband, had gone to school with Artur. I remember him as sort of loud and overbearing. The odd thing is, she became a major in the Polish army, and he refers to her as "my wife, the major," or just "the major." How amused Artur would be!

Love,
Gerda

Munich, February 5, 1946

Kurt dearest,

It's only a few hours since I started to work, and I have a few free moments. As always I use them to write to you. I had a wondrous moment as I started the day. There was this incredible sunrise, and a soft breeze was blowing, rather warm for this time of the year. I felt as if it were a greeting and promise of a new spring. I experienced a liberating lightness within me, a need to be unfettered, an urge to run. I couldn't possibly board the lumbering, crowded streetcar, full of weary, exhausted people. So I decided to run the distance between two stations, my hair in disarray, tousled by the wind. The morning was getting brighter, and my spirits soared with the rising sun.

Now I look through the windows, and from the tall building across the street, waving gently in the breeze is the American flag, its forty-eight stars beckoning with bright promise. How different it was when I saw it for the first time, how different *I* was. How marvelous for me that I'm healthy now, that I can stretch out my arms toward it, that I will be a part of what it represents.

There was yet another wonderful experience in store for me. Two of my coworkers heard that a certain indoor pool was open again. I could hardly believe it, but sure enough, when I went there it was true. I had always loved swimming. It was my favorite sport of all, and I had not been able to go for the past six years. Here was a dream come true. I jumped into the cold, refreshing water and cut the surface with strokes that instantly came back to me. It was so easy, so free, so liberating, and my tears of joy mingled happily with the twirling water around me.

So much for today.

My love and many kisses,
Gerda

My beloved Kurt,

Quickly guess what just arrived? Your photos and the documents! You look like a very handsome stranger. I am going to fall in love with that man all over again. You do know of course that your uniform had a very special significance for me. Please introduce me to that "other" person—and soon.

On the way to work this morning, I saw an old woman selling pussy willows. Couldn't help but get a big bunch of them and am looking at them now. I love to touch their soft, gray buds because they remind me of the fur of my kittens at home. There is something very special about pussy willows. It seems that nature dresses those first harbingers of spring in fur coats to ward off the cold. I always loved them, and now more than ever.

Again I have to resort to reporting the vexing problem of the consulate here. Unfortunately nothing is working yet, despite a lot of promises. I try to be patient.

For the moment I would much rather answer your challenging question of how I visualize our home. Whatever and wherever it will be, it seems like a remote paradise from here. We can't afford much, and you say very little is available, so that is good in a way. It will double the fun to be able to get things once they will be within our reach. I have lived in so much austerity and among such a hodgepodge of furnishings that I don't think my taste has at all been developed. Yours is likely to be so much better. In the meantime I can dream.

I like modern things, light and bright. Above all I love flowers, which lend so much warmth to a room. I like to put vases with flowers on the floor to create the feeling of a garden. I love paintings with a light background, in narrow frames to give the illusion that they are coming out of the wall. I also love small flowers in shallow bowls and lots and lots of soft pillows thrown around. What do you think of that?

Whatever it may be, it will be *our* home; that is all that matters, however small or simple, and it will be filled with our love. I love you so much.

As ever,
Gerda

Gerda, my precious,

I suppose it's senseless to send this letter before you notify me of your new address. Yet I just have to chat with you, you who are so close to me. Today is my beloved mother's birthday, a solemn day that is much less sad when I think of your "presence." After all, you know how much I need you, how much your understanding and your nearness mean to me, and what a calming influence your simple, modest perception of life has on me.

Yes, you paid a steep price to gain the formula for happiness. And I? I probably would never have found it without you. United with you, I'll be able to face whatever may come, and together we'll create *our* world, our life, only as it has meaning for us.

You said before that "It is surely no coincidence that we met." No, there must be a higher design behind it all. I dreamed for years of the person who would be my partner throughout life, until I believed that I was pursuing an impossible ideal, was demanding too much. Time and again I turned away in disappointment, remained lonely, but couldn't accept the idea that my ideals were transcending reality. And now, all at once, entirely new vistas have opened up, new heights rise before me that I had never dared to hope for. Why that should have come to me I have no idea, for it is so much more than I deserve. I am only aware that it is so. I'm asking no questions, though, I only sense something intangible. I, too, feel that our meeting was as inevitable as the rising of the sun or the growth of a leaf of grass in the spring. Love is no coincidence!

Kurt

Munich, February 13, 1946

My dearest Kurt,

Today I am eager to share some really happy news with you. I came home from work and who was sitting in my room? None other than Hanka, who had come a great distance and could only stay a brief time. The reason? To invite me to her wedding! You know how much I care for her, how much she means to me, and how delighted I am to see her so radiantly happy. She said that she had found it impossible to simply send me an invitation by mail, inasmuch as she considers me her only "relative." So she felt compelled to come in person, and I am so glad she did.

Her fiancé hails from Poland, is thirty-three years old, and, judging by his picture, could easily make a career in Hollywood. He is editor in chief of the UNRRA magazine. His brother lives in Australia, where they hope to emigrate as well. It promises to be a great wedding. Hanka will wear a white dress, and you know how gorgeous she is! She asked me to be her maid of honor. I must somehow manage to have a long dress, too. That should be fun, because I have never worn one.

Hanka told me about another girl whom I know slightly, who will also be getting married. Her dilemma is that she has to choose among no fewer than four suitors. You see, there is a dearth of Jewish girls here. Any female who looks halfway decent can get married. Please take note!

There was one very poignant moment. Hanka and I sat across from each other and talked a blue streak until, suddenly, we both fell silent. We each knew what the other was thinking. One year ago, at precisely this time, we faced the bitterest, most difficult chapter of our lives.* And today? She is about to be married, and I have been engaged for five months. Life can be beautiful, and it is worthwhile to be alive. It even validates endurance and suffering.

Tomorrow I'll write a longer letter. I'm happy to see Hanka so joyous, but surely, our waiting period should soon be over as well.

I hope there will be mail from you, which I so anxiously await.

Love and kisses, yours,
Gerda

Munich, February 14, 1946

My dearest Kurt,
I withdraw all my complaints regarding the mail. *Five* of your letters arrived today! For all of them, and for each one separately, my thanks, accompanied by countless kisses.

---

*The march, which became a death march for all too many of the two thousand young women who were forced on it on January 29, 1945, began to take its toll almost from the start. Our inadequate clothes, especially the lack of proper shoes, decimated our numbers each day. Throughout there was the all-pervading hunger, and girls who could not go on under those conditions were shot or often died at night from exposure.

Now, back to our situation. I went to the Polish Central Committee today and spoke to the chairman. He doesn't hold out much hope for Switzerland, although I told him that I submitted my application more than three weeks ago. His advice is to wait for the American consul, who, if rumors are correct, should open the consulate in about two weeks. He was somewhat skeptical about the Polish quota. Thought I might have a better chance if I stress the fact that you are an ex-officer. He felt that the quota favors people in the States who are trying to bring over parents, spouses, or children.

I hope you are not too disappointed, knowing nevertheless that you must feel as let down as I do. I hate to have to write you that our hopes are dashed and the time we must stay apart is indefinitely extended. But I know that we will be reunited and that it can come quickly in an unexpected way. I'm still hoping for May.

You ask what I think of you in civilian clothes. Are you fishing for compliments? Do you by chance think I was blinded by the glamour of your uniform? I was. You do look a little strange to me and tired, and I hope that it is not on account of the worry about me. I have to say that you do look very handsome. You look *you!* Uniform or no uniform, I love you. I only hope that this does not turn your head—and toward those beautiful American girls. Just remember, there is an abundance of men around here!

I shall try to convey my feelings to you regarding the forthcoming marriage of the young woman you wrote about. It seems you are involved in a situation regarding her parents' opposition to her non-Jewish intended. My thoughts and sympathies are really with her. This friend of yours, brought up in the freedom and democracy of America, was indulged by her parents. Now she suddenly finds herself hemmed in by boundaries that relate to the very thing her parents always aimed to give her: happiness. I understand her bristling at the older generation's archaic ideas and intolerance, if not blindness. What must hurt her most is to hear the forthcoming marriage called a misalliance. In her eyes her intended must be a respectable, intelligent, honorable man whom she loves. I can imagine how she must question it all, and understand her well. At the same time, I have had a lot of occasion these past months to see the results of "mixed" marriages. Sadly, the best assessment I have heard was from one Jewish woman who was married to a German man and put it this way: "My husband was decent to me during the past twelve years." So you can see, I do understand her parents as well.

I must share something with you from my own life. Only now can I see what an incredible father I had. How wise, unselfish, and noble he was; what foresight he displayed, and how great was his love for me. During those long, bitter, hungry days, when we lived in the basement of our house and later in the ghetto, we talked about everything imaginable. Once, seemingly out of nowhere, I asked him what he would do if I married a Christian. He looked at me for a long time—I can still see him, gray and gaunt, his collar frayed, his eyes sad—then, his voice just above a whisper, "I would never deny you happiness, no matter at what cost to me." I was so touched that I impetuously shouted, "Papa, I swear, I would never do anything that would hurt you and—" He interrupted me, "Swear nothing, promise nothing; you don't know what life has in store for you. Just know that my only wish for you is that you will be happy." How wise Papa was, how wholeheartedly he would have approved of my choice.

I know deep down that, no matter what, I could never have hurt my parents, and that carries over, even now that they are no longer here. As long as we are fortunate enough to have parents, we can afford to be egotistical, counting on their love and generosity. Tell that girl that in the end, her parents will be at her side. I wish her happiness.

All my love to you, yours,
Gerda

Every so often I believed that I was coming to some better understanding of my past, that I could begin to handle the memories, that the pain of my losses was diminishing and would no longer intrude on the present, only to find that the scars of my experience would remain for life. I feel renewed pain and anger whenever I see refugees, identify with and recall pangs of hunger on seeing the emaciated faces and bodies of children. That pain is most acute whenever I see a lonely, crying child, even if that child is not otherwise deprived or abused.

I know from long experience that specific pain will lessen and ultimately pass, but I have never been able to free myself altogether of those emotions. The truth is that at this stage of my life, removed from the immediate concerns of raising a family or making my way in a profession, I have more time to reflect, and let the wanton suffering inflicted on millions come into sharper focus. The past remains vivid and the inhumanity an enigma.

∽   ∽   ∽   ∽   ∽   ∽   ∽   ∽   ∽   ∽   ∽   ∽

Munich, February 16, 1946

My beloved Kurt,

The weekend is here again, and I wonder what you are doing. Lately our office has been a veritable madhouse. Such chaos reigned that nothing whatsoever got done. You wouldn't believe how imbued our "higher-ups" are with their own prominence. And that includes yours truly, who is among the "privileged" class, according to my special pass. It gives me a number of perquisites, such as instant theater and concert tickets, for which ordinary mortals have to wait interminably, providing they can get them at all. I will never get used to receiving preferential treatment in Germany. I realize that it's only superficial and would love to leave this state of privilege, the sooner the better.

One of the most prominent members of this privileged class is leaving. He happens to be my boss and his impending departure is causing a great deal of commotion. I, for one, hate to see him go. He was very good and fair to work with and didn't take himself too seriously, unlike others who were pompous and given to set routines. I learned a lot from him, and he always allowed me a lot of latitude, so that I was able to work by myself—a challenge I tried to live up to.

Once the farewell festivities were over, my friend Heidi and I went to a movie. Actually a very silly picture that has already left my mind. But the newsreel surely was worthwhile. It showed a contingent of homecoming American troops. I looked for you in vain, but vicariously was able to experience those hours with you. Afterward we went to "Regina," the most popular restaurant/café in Munich, which made me feel very sophisticated and grown-up.

Heidi will be quitting our office as soon as the university sessions start. She will study medicine. I am leaving for Landsberg tomorrow to see Mala and attend her friend's wedding. By the way, weddings are the order of the day here. I often get the feeling that others are more mature than I in so many ways. Of course, I too am yearning to marry you, but my friends somehow take their lives in their hands more resolutely, while I go on as I did when I was a schoolgirl, daydreaming and leaving so much up to you. I think that's what it is; I lean on you. Thanks for your shoulder, your arms, and your lips. I love them.

Yours,
Gerda

Munich, February 25, 1946

My dearest,

I went to a wedding yesterday, and although my head is still spinning, I want to report my thoughts to you immediately. I didn't know the bride too well and the groom not at all, but she is a close friend of Janka, who was with me in Grünberg. It was such a large camp that I didn't know her too well either. Even the slightest shared experience seems enough to forge certain bonds. Few of those who survived the war have any family left, so that even the most casual acquaintances are invited to events like weddings, which take place almost daily. This one was truly lavish, considering the circumstances. There was a band, wonderful food, including delicacies I have not tasted since before the war. I marvel at people's resourcefulness and ability to provide, which is totally beyond my ken. Anyway I rejoice at their good fortune.

Believe it or not, I danced quite a bit and even tried to go along with the crowd by smoking. Everybody but everybody held cigarettes in their hands. It looked so grown-up and sophisticated that I simply had to try it too. But I paid dearly for my folly because it made me sick.

Again I found myself isolated in many ways. For some unfathomable reason, I always seem to be on the fringes of the crowd. This is not due to the war, although almost everything can be attributed to our immediate past. All the same I remember that even as a young child, when I would be invited to birthday parties, I could never fully participate in the merrymaking, could never quite fall in with the singing of songs, in reality a blessing, because I have no voice. I always felt self-conscious, a trait that has remained with me.

What I'm driving at, however, is something quite different. I found myself alone with Janka for a little while, and she told me exuberantly that she would announce her own engagement the following day. I was truly delighted, remembering that during a conversation we had had two weeks earlier, she had talked nonstop about Lolek, a boy with whom she was in love. She had expressed fear of losing him because, in her mind, he seemed to possess every virtue known to mankind. I hugged her and said, "Let me go find Lolek. I must congratulate him." "Are you crazy?" she came back, "I'm not marrying him. It's Iziu to whom I'm engaged!" "Who is Iziu?" I asked, startled. It turned out I did know Iziu, who seems like a nice guy. He's a little older, about twenty-eight, I would guess. Well, the wedding date is fixed, and I'm invited!

People appear to be swept up by a type of hysteria, throwing themselves into things wild and untested. Perhaps they do that in order to forget. But can one forget? And will marriage to just *anybody* help that?

A bit of other news. I was told by the Polish Committee that a Rabbi Blum is arriving in Munich as the representative of an organization called HIAS.* I will try to get an appointment with him; perhaps this agency can help me. I have lost nearly all hope for Switzerland. They are creating insurmountable difficulties, while my case is really so simple. I need just one day in Switzerland, so I can see the American consul. That's all—but, no, it can't be done, according to the Swiss authorities. Perhaps it will work with France.

I love you,

Gerda

Regensburg,† February 26, 1946

Dearest Kurt,

I've been reflecting on something I want to share with you. Most of my friends who are married are expecting babies. I find that rather incredible so soon after our ordeal, but it is exciting. No matter how well some of them manage to live, all of them hope to be able to leave here—the sooner the better. The language, the environment, and some of the people here are all-too-graphic reminders of the past. The way I feel is that even when surrounded by the beauty of nature, which is certainly possible in this setting, you may temporarily be able to push the past to the recesses of your mind. But before long an awareness of where you are

---

*Hebrew Immigrant Aid Society.
†Hearing of a chance to catch a car ride to Regensburg, approximately seventy-five miles from Munich, I decided to make a long weekend out of visiting two of my good friends from Bielsko and the camps, Rita and Ruth.

sets in. I love children, and above everything else, it is my most ardent desire to have children, as you are aware. But I would like their cradles to be bathed in the sunshine of freedom, so that from infancy it will be enough to fill their entire lives.

In the course of my long talks with Rita and Ruth, we remembered with a wistful mixture of amusement and sorrow that at the camp in Bolkenhain we had formed a loose association which we dubbed Club Olympus, an escape that gave us a temporary respite from the real world. There were six of us who, after long night shifts of exhausting physical work, would challenge our minds to remember tales of Greek mythology that we would discuss at length. Mostly, though, we used the inspiration from this intellectual stimulation to dream up insults and curses directed at our tormentors to bring them down from their self-appointed perch. Now we are able to have a reunion in Regensburg, and we mused that, sadly, three of those six young women are gone. They did not live to experience freedom. We sorely missed Liesl, Suse, and Ilse. We, the remaining three, once called ourselves Aphrodite, Diana, and Psyche. Can you guess which nickname was mine?*

I am leaving for Munich in the morning.

Much love,
Gerda

Buffalo, March 1, 1946

Dearest Gerda,

As usual I'm using my lunch break to "talk" with you. No further letters arrived from you this week, but I can't really complain because there's always the possibility that more will be forthcoming.

Because I know that Buffalo is a pretty hazy concept for you, I'm going to attempt to give you an overview of your upcoming home and its environs. In that regard, please overlook what I may already have told you about it.

One of the primary differences between this American city and its European counterparts is that the business district is distinctly different and separated from the residential sections. The center of business activity is the so-called downtown area (every city has one), a district that

*Psyche.

comprises offices and stores only. It's only a twenty-minute bus ride from where I live. We do have streetcars as well, but they are ancient crates that (gratefully) are gradually being replaced by buses. Anybody who hasn't been in Munich thinks that Buffalo has the world's worst transportation system. I find it adequate.

As I mentioned, almost no one lives downtown here, except in hotels of course. Most people live in residential sections, along streets consisting mainly of two-family frame houses, each with a little stretch of unfenced lawn in front of or behind their home. I'm only referring to the average, of course, so don't assume that there are no brick or stone houses or no fences whatsoever. Most streets here are planned in the manner of avenues. They look pretty bare and desolate at the moment, but with the coming of spring Buffalo assumes incomparably more beautiful proportions, to a degree that would totally surprise you if you had only seen it in winter. On the other hand, because of the multitude of trees, one street initially tends to look much like another.

Because most homes have no garages, or insufficient space for one, you'll find many cars parallel parked along the streets, the exceptions being main thoroughfares. There parking is either prohibited altogether or is allowed only at certain times and within prescribed zones. Traffic is enormous but easily regulated by means of numerous traffic lights and stop signs. The police are quite strict about that.

Each residential district has its own small business center, which means that it only takes at most a ten-minute walk before you reach a street where you can obtain the usual necessities of life. A variety of shops, such as a bakery, a butcher, at least one grocery, barber, dry cleaner, etc., cater to all your needs. On the other hand, larger department stores or clothing stores and such are all located downtown, as are most offices.

We do have a few skyscrapers here, as well as a display of neon signs at night, modest compared to a place like New York. The population here is predominantly of Polish descent, and it's quite common for various ethnic groups to be concentrated within certain districts of the city. The Polish population, for example, is so huge that it has its own large business section. It's not as expansive or beautiful as the downtown section, but on the other hand, it's reputed to have the largest retail turnover in the city. In general its stores are also cheaper than their downtown counterparts.

Geographically speaking, Buffalo is located at the Niagara River, adjacent to the immense Lake Erie, one of the so-called Great Lakes. Allegedly ours is the largest inland harbor in the world, but you know that sort of local boosterism. You actually can never be sure how much is based on fact and how much is promotion on the part of the Chamber of Commerce. On the other side of the Niagara and Lake Erie lies Canada, and it's about an hour's drive to Niagara Falls, where the Niagara gorge divides the two countries. Here in Buffalo you can be in Canada within five minutes. Big deal: You simply cross the bridge.

Enough about the city that will offer you a lot more than I can sum up here. You'll see it soon! My hugs and kisses await you.

Love,
Kurt

Munich, March 6, 1946

My beloved Kurt,

Yesterday three of your letters arrived, faster than ever. The most recent one was dated February 22. There was also a long and wonderfully kind letter from Gerdi, which gave me a great deal of pleasure and joy. She writes in such an open, friendly, delightful style, as if she had known me a lifetime. You must know how much it means to me that your sister, with whom you are so close, is extending this warm welcome into the family. I have always wanted a sister and now am fortunate to have one, obviously a very special one. Thank you for providing that for me.

I had a most happy letter from Hanka, telling me of all the exciting wedding preparations and also that the wedding has been moved up, at the same time urging me to come even sooner. In order to achieve that I have to work a lot of overtime. I have already taken off from work so often because of my running to consulates and all that I don't feel as if I'm earning my salary.

I had a stroke of good luck, due largely to your generosity and part of the contents of your package. Hanka implored me to wear a long evening dress for the stellar occasion. Sure, but under the circumstances, how do you go about that? I try to save most of my salary, spending very little. Still, fabric is extremely hard to obtain in stores. I made some inquiries as to whether I could possibly get some silk, explaining that I was going to a wedding. The woman wanted to know about my own marital status, so naturally I bragged that I was engaged to an American officer. She instantly perceived that I must have "connections." "Cigarettes, perhaps?" "No." "Chocolate, then?" When I admitted that, yes, you had sent some of that heavenly stuff recently, a length of exquisite light blue silk appeared miraculously. Enough for a long evening dress, and since I won't be eating the chocolate, it required less material. I just tried it on, and it does look very elegant. It goes straight to the floor, and attached to my shoulder is a spray of spring flowers. I wish I could model it for you. Imagine, my first grown-up evening dress! My hair is quite long; it falls to my shoulders. I know that you like long hair and am sorry that it was still so short when you left. I'm told that there will be lots of dancing at the wedding. Unfortunately for me, the arms in which I would love to find myself are far away.

All my love,
Gerda

P.S. I don't seem to be able to let this letter go. I forgot to take it along yesterday, and here I am again. Saw several of my camp companions tonight and came away feeling lonely and somehow bereft. We were in the camps together for years, and I find that as long as we talk about that experience there is a bond of understanding and similarity of attitude. As soon as we switch to the present, though, we face each other like distant strangers. It was different with Rita in Regensburg, but here I am painfully alone and again keep asking myself whether it's they who are different or I? I had that same forlorn feeling in Volary right after liberation.

꙰   ꙰   ꙰   ꙰   ꙰   ꙰   ꙰   ꙰   ꙰   ꙰   ꙰   ꙰

None of my closest friends survived the cataclysm. I cannot therefore claim to know how they would have reacted to the new postwar realities. In our minds we had associated survival with the restoration of the world we had known before, so it was especially difficult to realize that that world was gone forever. From what I could observe, it seemed to me that survivors who lacked great imagination, who rather faced this new world in a pragmatic way were far better off than the others. That was in sharp contrast to the war years, when the ability to let your imagination soar, thereby lifting yourself from the horror of daily existence, contributed considerably to your eventual survival—providing you were also blessed with a modicum of luck.

Just before the war I had immersed myself into the pages of Gone With the Wind, *just published in Polish, a volume that had fascinated me to the degree that I reread it countless times, little realizing that my own world was about to be undone. Now, only a few months after the end of the war, I saw a number of Scarletts emerging from the ashes and seizing opportunities open to them. On the other side of the spectrum there were far more confused, gentle Melanies, clinging to the past and all it held for them. No one was there to give us direction or ease us back into normality. By and large the world around us was uncaring, even hostile; it was as though a whirlwind had deposited us onto a desert island, and the task of surviving in such a harsh climate was up to us.*

I was more fortunate than others. From the outset I found an anchor in Kurt, one that allowed us to fashion a stable and meaningful life. Others made their way back, each in his or her own individual manner, some very successfully. But there were more who would never fully adjust to the new realities. So once the shackles of common slavery were cast off, we reverted to our original molds, much as (I gather) is the case with war veterans and their shared experience.

‿ ‿ ‿ ‿ ‿ ‿ ‿ ‿ ‿ ‿ ‿ ‿

Munich, March 11, 1946

My dearest Kurt,

Again there's no mail from you. I had a very nice letter, however, from your relative, Mr. Sigaloff, from Basel. Following your letter to him, he apparently initiated an application on my behalf for a transit visa through Switzerland to the United States. He writes that the papers are already in Bern and estimates that it should take about six to eight weeks. I dare not hope, but can hardly restrain my hopes. Mr. Sigaloff writes in such a nice, kind way, and his eagerness to help is deeply touching.

I had a very strange encounter this morning. While waiting for the streetcar, I noticed two men staring at me. It made me very uncomfortable, so I moved away, trying to avoid them, only to have them follow me. Finally one of them approached me, said that they had just gotten here from Poland, and asked if I knew the station where they should get off. Imagine the address he showed me: It was my office! I wasn't sure whether I would handle their case, because I only deal with Polish nationals who have some sort of German connection.

Nevertheless, when we arrived at the agency, I asked them which camp they had been in. Their answer made my blood run cold. It was

Janow, the same camp in which Artur was! That led to endless other questions, and yes, they seemed to remember an Artur Weissmann, but added that two of their friends who had come to Janow earlier would know him better. And those friends were now also in Munich.

Naturally I begged them to let me go see those people, and they gave me their solemn promise that I could do so the following day. They claimed not to have their address, but said they'd return with it to my office.* They did let on that, to their knowledge, nobody else got out of this hellish camp. The four of them had been in Janow until November 1943, then had escaped and spent the rest of the war with Russian partisans. The last news I had from Artur was dated May 1943.

Oh, if only it were tomorrow already. What will I learn?

Love,
Gerda

Munich, March 14, 1946

My dearest Kurt,

You describe Buffalo in such glowing colors and the fact that much Polish is spoken there gives me a great deal of pleasure. The other news contained in your letter has rekindled the hope that Mr. Louis† will soon be in Paris. I immediately went to the Polish Committee to see whether their representative in Paris could get in touch with him regarding my visa. Unfortunately they are closed for several days.

Now I must deal with a topic I'm reluctant to discuss, but I have to. You've asked me so many times about it, and in your last letter, dearest, you imply that I have become pessimistic concerning my emigration. You are quite wrong. You can't imagine how it is when you go to the authorities here and they build up your hopes to the point where you want to turn cartwheels, only to find later that all their promises are really based on nothing. People are kind and tell you what you want to hear, only most of the time it's baseless. I've had my hopes dashed too often and would prefer to be told the truth. Deep down I know that ultimately we will be reunited; it's only a question of time. Unfortunately

---

*I never heard from them again.
†My uncle's father-in-law.

I don't have anyone here who is close to me. Of course I could throw myself into a social whirl, but it's all so superficial.

Perhaps I feel so blue tonight because it's six months today that we spent our last evening together. *Half a year*, and I have absolutely no clue when I will see you again.

I remember the words you spoke at our parting: that I must believe, must remain strong and hopeful. I do believe in you and am strong, and I certainly have hope. I can cope with all that, as I did throughout the years in the camps. I was strong during the most trying times, and I can be again. But I'm vulnerable and weak when it comes to other obstacles. Bolstered by warmth and tenderness, I can go on. You do understand that for three long and bitter years no family member was near who might have spoken a kind word to me; no caring arms embraced me. After that, you came and gave me the love I yearned for. And then you left.

Please don't feel sorry for me; I couldn't bear it. Just understand that I get a little low at times, particularly in this country that bears the guilt for all the misery suffered by so many millions. Having said all that, I feel much better. I really do believe in the happiness that lies ahead for us.

Eternally yours,
Gerda

Landsberg [near Munich], March 17, 1946

My dearest Kurt,

I arrived in Landsberg yesterday afternoon, and you can probably guess why I'm here: Yes, Mala is engaged. I rejoice for her and hope that she will be very happy. Michael is such an exceptionally nice guy! In the evening we went to a makeshift synagogue because it's Purim now.

Landsberg seems like a mini–Jewish state, made up of six thousand survivors from camps all over Europe. All the houses and buildings are decorated with multicolored bunting in Polish, English, and Hebrew, and there are brightly illuminated Yiddish signs everywhere. Life-size straw effigies of Hitler and Goebbels in uniform hang from gallows, and music and songs are amplified over loudspeakers. Blue-and-white Jewish flags are everywhere, and I watch people embracing one another in a frenzy of unrestrained celebration. American flags are displayed in profusion, and they adorn the sports arena where last night the oldest Jewish survivor in this area, a seventy-five-year-old woman, burned a copy of *Mein Kampf* on a huge funeral pyre, right here in Landsberg where Hitler wrote it while imprisoned in the old fortress. It was that book that initiated the great tragedy, all the loss and pain. As it was being consumed by fire, there was an outburst of joy and jubilation from the masked, costumed crowd. It made me feel so strange, as if I were not a part of it at all. My mood is somber and detached. I keep thinking of all those who did not live to see this, who so desperately wanted to live.

Love,
Gerda

Munich, March 23, 1946

Darling,

Please don't be angry with me—I say it without rancor—but I miss you so each day, and more each hour. Now that I have found the person who means everything to me, the desire to be with you is overwhelming. In your recent letters you depict our future life in such glowing colors that my impatience reaches its zenith. I promise you to remain brave, however difficult that may be.

I've been struggling for days about whether to tell you, but unfortunately I think it best to let you know that the information you received on your end has no basis in fact. There is no trace of a consulate, although the American consul appears to be here. But nothing functions as yet. I do call the Swiss consulate almost daily and unfortunately get no answer there either. I also phoned Paris, and that branch of the Joint Distribution Committee is going to get in touch with Mr. Louis. If I can obtain some documentation from him and the French police, it will allegedly become child's play. Sorry to say I didn't get an answer on that either.

My coworkers, who initially promised to be of such help, are turning lukewarm and openly declare that they are reluctant to see me go.

I'm going to devote myself to the Paris matter and will also try to obtain a permit for a one-day visit to Switzerland. I hope that my luck will hold and not let me down in this case either. It's extremely difficult to tell you all this, but I hope I'll have good news for you soon. If only I knew how long Mr. Louis plans to stay in Paris.

Oh, Kurt, I won't permit you to shoulder all the troubles that life can bring. I don't just want to be your wife but your partner as well. Just know that someone is here who will wait for you, with passion and tranquillity, that someone will be with you in every conceivable situation, that I have strength through the feelings I harbor for you. After liberation I believed that God had left me on this earth in order to punish me, but I never became alienated from my faith because of the loss of my dearest ones. Rather, they were given back to me in you. When I saw the name of my beloved mother connected with the phrase "of blessed memory," in my uncle's letter, it paralyzed me, and my mind refused to accept it. No, Kurt, we will never think of our parents in that manner. They live distant from us, but nevertheless within us. We will love and revere them, not mourn them, but make them happy with our own happiness. I want to come to you free of all mourning and pain, able to share your life joyfully. I can be resolute and strong if I have a goal. And my gift to you is my love.

Your Gerda

Landsberg, March 24, 1946

My dearest Kurt,

Mala is celebrating her engagement, and there is additional cause for rejoicing. I got to Landsberg this morning in order to help prepare for Mala's party. Because she is working, her fiancé, Michael, is helping me with the arrangements. We expect between twenty-five and thirty guests, so I will have my hands full.

Shortly after my arrival this morning, Mala's friend, Franka, came to us for a "consultation." It seems that the chief of the hospital has been pursuing her for several weeks. I had met him before, and Mala knows him well. Knowing that, Franka approached us to help her make up her mind. Pointing out my limited acquaintance with him, I gave her a very positive picture of him, and Mala, knowing him better, really sang his praises. "Okay, then," Franka declared, "I'll get engaged to him this afternoon at three."

While I was preparing little sandwiches, the unsuspecting suitor happened to come into the room, just as Franka appeared through the kitchen door. I stretched out my hand to him. "Congratulations on your engagement and much happiness to you!"

"My engagement?" He did a double take.

That's when Franka chimed in, "Yes, yours and mine."

The poor man looked from me to her in consternation, as she flung herself into his arms. Obviously she had not told him he was her intended, and all I could do was to beat a hasty retreat to the kitchen to give them a chance to be alone. You know, I have witnessed any number of engagements by now. It seems that everyone is rushing toward some union to run away from loneliness, to start a new life with a partner. But I have not heard of or seen any engagement as peculiar as this one between Franka and her startled beau.

I leave on the early train for Munich, and what awaits me there is a renewed search for a consul: American, Swiss, or French. But instead of getting into my complaining mode, I must share with you my thoughts about a concert I attended last week.

I don't recall the composer, but the music was very strange. It consisted of a series of Chinese songs. The beginning of it set a strange, disquieting, haunting mood, but unfortunately the woman singer, a contralto, was about as wonderful as spinach with cold tea. What was supposed to be the song of a nightingale sounded much more like the growling of a bear! There was an incredible song by a male singer, rendered briskly, in a clear, pearl-like voice. The lyrics went like this: "In a small pavilion stands a castle of green and white porcelain /And toward the castle arches, like the back of a tiger, a bridge of jade."* Do you know it? I'm sure you do, because you know everything when it comes to music. You know what happens to me? When I hear music, I put some of my own words to it, my own rhymes and stories.

Oh, I forgot to tell you: Have you heard that Knappertsbusch† committed suicide? Seems his Nazi past was brought to light, and he didn't want to deal with the consequences.

It just occurred to me that none of those newly married and engaged people here have to send their kisses on such a long journey as we do ours.

Gerda

---

*Gustav Mahler's *Das Lied von der Erde* ("Song of the Earth").
†Hans Knappertsbusch, the well-known conductor in Munich, whom we had heard.

My beloved Kurt,

What do you think of me now? I wanted to surprise you, dearest, but unfortunately, it did not turn out as I thought it would. Nothing was happening in Germany, and no information was available about the opening of the American consulate. On top of that, the Swiss had refused my transit visa. When you wrote that Mr. Louis would be in Paris, I foolishly took the first opportunity that presented itself to join him, and here I am. How? Don't even ask! I hope to be able to tell you about it in person. I got here in two days, but Mr. Louis is still not here and the banker, whose name and address Uncle Leo had given me, didn't know whether or when he would arrive.

Kurt, I must tell you the entire truth; the situation I find myself in is terrible. I was told in Munich that there is a way of going to Paris, provided you have the right connections. So, based on my uncle's offer to put his Swiss bank account at my disposal, I promised a man who was allegedly a friend of the French consul that if he would take me to Paris, as promised, I would pay him once we got there. What I did *not* know, or maybe in my desperate state of mind did not *want* to know, was that this individual was not honest. He and his sister told me that the money they were requesting was needed to speed up the granting of a visa.

Please don't be angry with me. I was so euphoric for a little while to see my most ardent wish fulfilled and to have Germany disappear behind me that I paid scant attention to the "how" of my journey. Now I'm almost sorry that I didn't stay in Munich to wait it out longer. Please forgive me. Why were we told that Mr. Louis would be in Paris? The people who took me here promised to cable you and Uncle Leo, so I am writing this letter in order to explain the situation more fully.

I wanted only the best for both of us but could not foresee the consequences of my folly. I am beside myself, irrational, after days of sleeplessness and remorse. If only I will get word from you soon. Please think of me, so that I won't feel so alone.

Yours,
Gerda

Paris, March 28, 1946

Dearest,

This is my second letter to you from Paris. I'm sure you don't understand what has happened and why I am here. I hardly know it myself. All I can say is, please understand that I wanted to come to you as soon as I could and to leave that inferno behind. I cabled Uncle Leo in the hope that he would travel here or send Mr. Louis to my rescue. Imagine my disappointment at not finding him here. I am without direction, without advice. What shall I do?

Kurt, I have so much to tell you, and my heart is so full of the experiences of the last few days. I fell into the hands of horrible characters and in that regard I guess I am not without blame. I was told in Landsberg that people were freely traveling from Bavaria to France. How? Well, there was someone who allegedly had an "in" with the French consulate and who could facilitate the obtaining of a visa in short order. You can imagine how delirious I was at that promise. For months now everything I had tried had turned into failure. I didn't even tell you that I encountered not only walls of indifference but rude insults and hostility. So I went to see the man with the alleged connection to the French consul and did consider it a little fishy when he told me that he could get me a visa for two hundred dollars. I didn't have the money, of course, but Uncle Leo had offered to put funds at my disposal, both in France and in Switzerland. So, when the man said I could go to Paris the next day, I lost my head and abandoned all reason, even though I had an inkling that the money would end up in his pocket. After all, I had waited so long and was desperate. Getting out of hell the next day, after almost seven years, was all I needed to hear.

How could I know that I was letting myself in for something illegal? I have never done anything illegal in my life. I realized too late what was happening, that I was traveling under a fake identity, as Gerda Zalesky. I really panicked when I realized the train would stop for visa control at the French border, in Strasbourg, and so I took all the documents bearing my real identification—and that included your affidavits and those your family had furnished—and threw them out of the window of the speeding train. I feared that if they caught me—as I was certain they would—I would go to jail.

At the border stop, however, nobody checked any papers, no one even came to our compartment, because it was basically a troop train for American GIs. Arriving in Paris, where Mr. Lewis was to have met me, I found that he was not expected for another month. Uncle Leo's banker friend was very suspicious and did not believe that I was my uncle's niece. I can't blame him, considering the company I was in. I could only use my halting school French, and the creep, accompanied by his sister, didn't know that language either. They wouldn't let me out of their sight because they wanted to make sure they would get the money I had promised them. I didn't have a cent. In my hasty flight from Munich, I forgot to take along the envelope with the money you gave me before your departure. I had kept it in a special hiding place.

Now I can't go to the consulate here because I threw the papers away. I did hear in this awful place where I am staying that the Polish quota is closed at the moment and that now it's Germany from which people will be leaving. What am I to do? Kurt, please forgive me; I lost my head. I was so frantic. I abhor the thought of going back to Germany, but the creep is pressing me, threatening he'll take me back there. If that's my only option, then I will go back. But am I to be spared nothing? I'm stalling for time and want to wait for Uncle Leopold's answer. I'll have to think of something.

All my love,
Gerda

Paris, March 30, 1946

Dearest,

I have no recollection what I wrote you in my previous letter, I was simply too upset at the time. So forgive me if I am repeating myself. I ran away from those awful characters during the night. I'll have to tell you about those desperate hours in person, and you'll have to hold me tight when I relate the experience. It was nearly as bad as some of my days in the camps. But all is well now.

Where did I go? Thank God for my love of history and a little imagination. Do you remember in the hospital in Volary, when I asked you to forward some of the letters given to me by my friends who had relatives in other countries? You mailed several letters for a girl named Ronka. I remembered that her sister lived in Paris. What also came back to me was the fact that there was something about the address that had fired my imagination. It had something to do with my memory of a royal blacksmith, and that I had imagined how the royals sent their horses to a smithy to be shod. When I needed it so desperately, it virtually jumped out at me: rue de la Forge Royale! It took a good part of the night and most of the day and all of my poor knowledge of French to follow directions, after my lame *"Pardon, madame . . . écoutez . . . rue de la Forge Royale?"* And then the endless, confusing descriptions to keep *à droite* and *á gauche* and what have you. And yes, I did find it after crisscrossing what seemed like all of France. Ronka's sister, Suma, took me in, lent me money for cables to you and Uncle Leo, and today I already had a wired answer from my uncle.*

As you can see, everything is turning out okay. The second cable informed me that the creep will be paid off. He had my uncle's address from my first cable and then must have approached him on his own to get some money.

Please forgive me if I gave you a bad fright, and the concern and worry I put you through. My only hope is that both Uncle Leo's cable and mine reached you before my desperate letters did.

Now I truly believe that the pain and suffering of the last days has paid off. Uncle Leo has been fantastic; he seems ready to perform miracles and will help me to finally get my heart's desire: YOU!

Many kisses,
Gerda

Buffalo, March 31, 1946

Gerda, my very dearest,

The last few hours rank among the most dramatic I have lived through. Early in the evening a cable arrived from Uncle Leo, stating how happy he is to have heard from you and that he arranged for everything necessary that would be of help to you. Then he indicated an address, that is, Gerda Zalesky, 18 rue Botzaris, Paris 19, which at first didn't arouse any suspicion whatsoever, because it appeared as though he had merely furnished it so you could avail yourself of it in case your way out of Europe would have to be via Paris. I was just in the process of writing to him when his cable arrived and so was able to acknowledge a bit of wonderful news that had really created a lot of excitement here earlier

---

*In it, he repeated the message he had wired to the address provided by the smuggler. It read: HAPPY TO KNOW YOU ARE IN PARIS. CONTACT [Leo's banking connection]. HAVE GIVEN INSTRUCTIONS TO DO ALL NECESSARY. ARE ADVISING LOUIS IN LONDON. [He] WILL ARRIVE IN PARIS VERY SOON. WE EMBRACE YOU. CONFIRM RECEIPT. LEO

in the day. I'm talking about receipt of a wire from the Sigaloffs that your entry into Switzerland had finally been approved. You may not even be aware yet that, after endless efforts, Mr. Sigaloff just succeeded in obtaining the forever-longed-for permission.

So much for that, but I haven't even mentioned yet how the events developed later in the day. I happened to attend a marvelous concert tonight and on my return home in festive high spirits, Art greets me by handing me your cable—from Paris! That puts me in such a state of euphoria that I feel like doing somersaults! Of course I'm totally befuddled, inasmuch as your last few letters, dating back to the beginning of this month, gave no indication of anything of the sort. Moreover, I was quite certain you'd be on your way to Switzerland, if anywhere. Although I haven't the foggiest notion how you managed to get to Paris instead, the "how" is of secondary importance right now. The main thing is: You're on your way to me! Please don't expect to make any sense of these lines; I'm totally beside myself and find it impossible to keep a clear head vis-à-vis such an onslaught of emotions.

Thousands of questions run through my mind in that connection: I come up with endless speculations: for example, Mr. Louis succeeded in getting you to Paris, or perhaps it was one of the aid societies, and so you went to Ronka's sister's family. A total puzzle is your "Will *remain* in Paris, after all." Apparently you weren't sure whether it would be that city—or perhaps Marseilles or Lisbon? You must have assumed I'm informed about your trip to France.*

As difficult as it is, I guess I'll have to keep my impatience under control for a while. Good gosh, if I imagine how soon you might be here!! Perhaps you've even seen the American consul by now, and while that might take awhile yet, it could be accomplished within a few days, at least in theory. After that, perhaps a flight . . . I don't dare imagine it!

Please write or wire immediately—now that you can finally do so yourself—what you need, for what date I can make flight or ship's reservations, providing you already know it. Also, what other needs you might have (none, I hope, as far as the American consulate is concerned). How can I possibly go to sleep now? I'm going to explode any minute!

I'm so immensely grateful to see the mists of separation gradually lifting, while at the same time freedom casts its rays toward you in ever rosier radiance. Soon now, my little Gerda, all this will come true, how-

*The first cable to me was never sent by the smuggler.

ever many formalities may still await us. I know how easy it is for me to say that, while you're doing the running from one bureaucratic office to another.

Do give my very best regards to Ronka's sister, and please express my thanks to her. Looking forward to being able to firmly take you in my embrace and once again show you my love in person,

Your Kurt

P.S. I could shout with joy—it's the first time I'm permitted to write your name on an envelope.* What better proof is there that you're definitively moving toward unfettered freedom!

Paris, April 4, 1946

Dearest Kurt,

Today is a solemn day for me; I could almost call it a holy day: Papa's birthday. For the very first time, I will be observing it in freedom without him. Oh, Kurt, so many different thoughts crossed my mind since I awoke at dawn. I see Papa in front of me, much closer and more alive than in Germany. Although the memory is more painful, the picture is clearer, and the thought of you makes me want to dry my tears and find my balance. What helps perhaps is that I know the period remaining for me in Europe is dwindling; these are the final days of that phase of my life. I need to leave behind the shackles that bind me to my past, to the three people I loved most. They will have to stay here in death, although they will continue to live within me. I know I can count on you to understand how I feel, my love.

This morning, as every morning since I contacted him from here, I got Uncle Leopold's cabled greeting. At the same time a wire came from Mr. Louis in London with these words: "Am arriving in Paris on Saturday. Be patient till then, dear child, and comforted that all will turn out well. Louis."

You can imagine how soothing that is. The day after tomorrow I will see someone from my family after four years. Imagine, the day after tomorrow! Uncle Leopold is lavishing his love and concern on me with

---

*Instead of having to address it to an army go-between, because no international civilian mail service existed in Germany during that time.

his daily telegrams, with money, such as I received yesterday, with a note urging me to buy myself anything I want or need. He obviously wants to take the place of my parents. I told you how he adored Mama.

I do hope that my cables to you clarified the first days of my situation here and you will come to understand my thinking still better through the letters that followed and, later, in person. I think that my frantic excitement was justifiable. I deeply regret what chaos my impulsive decision caused you and my uncle, but I confess that despite it all I am elated to be out of Germany.

Soon more, much more. Am in a rush to post this letter.

With much love and kisses, yours,
Gerda

Paris, April 7, 1946

My beloved Kurt,

I can't even attempt to tell you everything that happened during the last few hours. I feel as if I had awakened, at long last, from a nightmare to an incredibly happy reality. Yesterday your cable arrived, outlining some suggested plans which in the light of what came up since, should please you even more. On the heels of your cable came one from Mr. Louis, announcing his arrival at 4 P.M. yesterday. And there were the usual two cables from Uncle Leopold, again showing overwhelming concern. He, too, is brimming with a variety of plans. The early morning mail brought an invitation to visit one of Paris's exclusive fashion houses, Agnès Drécole, on the Place Vendôme. This was in response to a cable from Istanbul, instructing them to outfit me completely. Imagine, from rags to Paris fashions!

As announced, Mr. Louis arrived in the afternoon, reclining luxuriously in a huge car that barely squeezed through the narrow, dilapidated street. He gave the appearance of being every inch an English lord, including a bowler hat and rolled-up umbrella. He brought wonderful gifts for Ronka's family and whisked me away to a very elegant restaurant for a most delicious feast and conversation.

To begin with, he explained why my uncle had not come. What a terrible story. You see, Uncle Leo is really stateless, has no passport. The place where he and my mother were born, Bielitz, was then a part of the Austro-Hungarian empire. After World War I, it became Bielsko,

Poland. My uncle left home soon thereafter and never became a Polish citizen. He also was never able to gain Turkish citizenship, despite the fact that he lived there for so many years and was married to a Turkish citizen. Therefore he can't travel right now. However, it is his dearest wish to see me and to meet you. Briefly the plan is this: As an American citizen, you will be able to travel freely. Therefore you should come to Paris by the fastest route. We would then be married here in a civil ceremony, and as your wife, I should have no difficulty traveling to Turkey. Once there, we would be married in the temple where Uncle Leo was married, my father having represented that side of the family on that occasion. In our case Leo will be taking Papa's place. Imagine what that would mean to me! Oh, please, please, say YES! Moreover, they already secured reservations on a new airline for both of us: Paris–Rome–Athens–Istanbul. We will stay there for a while before going on to New York. I am in such a tizzy; my head is swirling and I can't believe that it's real and should soon come true.

I do have to come down to earth to discuss one issue which, knowing you, might spoil this plan. It's your reluctance to accept financial help in connection with all this. I know your pride, and my uncle is aware of it too, since you apparently refused it flatly when he offered it in order to get me out of Germany. I thank you for that. Acting on my uncle's instructions, Mr. Louis proposed that if it made you happier to come to Paris on your own, you should do so. But once we are married, he feels that as my husband you should be able to accept a wedding gift from my family, without it hurting your pride. That would be our trip to Istanbul, thus fulfilling my uncle's keenest dream to see the only surviving member of his family. I will abide by your decision of course, but please, Kurt, please, help make it possible.

It's Sunday morning now, and Mr. Louis is coming to pick me up for lunch and goodness knows what other diversions. The boulevards of Paris are suffused with sunshine, or could it be from the radiance in my heart? I'm dreaming of walking with you here—soon, I pray.

Just got a three-page telegram from my uncle. Will write later; am in a hurry, but never too hurried to kiss you many times.

Yours,
Gerda

My dearest Gerda,

Our cables cross each other so fast and furiously that it's nearly impossible to come up with anything new to report. I do, however, want to further elaborate on my latest answer to Mr. Louis's inquiry regarding an accelerated crossing for me.

It goes without saying that I'm going to grasp the first opportunity that comes along. Unfortunately it will take a few weeks until I can get a passport. At the same time I have to rely on a favorable answer on the part of the steamship companies or airlines, something that's in the works through Max at his travel agency. I would have liked to furnish more exact details today; however, I couldn't get them yet. I tried in vain to reach Max by phone tonight, but will try again later.

It's a tremendous load off my mind to know that you are in good hands now. I can say that your cable contributed a lot toward calming me down. How fabulous of Mr. Louis and Uncle Leo to contribute to your well-being to such an extent. I want to thank them over and over for that and feel very much indebted to them.

There's one more thing you could try if you think it's apropos. The American Red Cross may be able to furnish such information as you might still need. Meanwhile I'm also doing some research on this end, mainly into the question: Will they permit you to travel from Paris to Istanbul as long as you're not an American citizen yet, even after our marriage? It's possible that there are still certain travel restrictions.

One more "big" request, whose importance I shouldn't have to stress in this case: Is there a way in which you can send me the exact size of your ring finger? In that connection, it'll probably make little difference, but I do want to prepare you for the fact that wedding rings are worn on the ring finger of the *left* hand here. You'll get used to the idea that, according to European thinking, everything is turned on its head here. To which I can only add, thank goodness!

The enclosed photos are brand new, taken only two days ago. There's nothing to be done about *how* I look, but if you're going to insist that I don't look well, it's going to get my dander up. I hope to be able to convince you soon of my "splendid" appearance in person.

Good night, Dimples. I'm as good as with you now!

All my love,
Kurt

My beloved Kurt,

I am in a very strange, pensive mood and will explain the reason for it immediately. I don't know, dearest, how one reacts to that sort of thing, particularly when viewed in sober daylight, while a host of happenings lay claim to my every moment. Yet, I can't shake off the spell of last night. To begin with, I must explain that for the first time in my life I find I have trouble sleeping. I think I can count the hours of sleep since I came to Paris two weeks ago on the fingers of one hand.

Last night I went to bed, for me rather early, around midnight, and promptly fell asleep. You have to understand that I dream very seldom, but this time I did dream about my parents. Still, I can't recall what it was about. Then came this dream about Artur. I have not dreamed about him for years, but last night I saw him quite clearly. He looked so strange, older and haggard, only his beautiful, warm, brown eyes were the same. He was exhausted and bent over, so that his dark, soft hair lay on my hands. He said that the road to me had been very difficult and that he still had to go to you, to thank you. I can't explain my feelings. There was the sound of his voice, the tenderness in his eyes, and, finally, his long, mute embrace. Artur's appearance was not in the form of an icy, ghostly apparition, rather in the nature of a painful reunion and tender farewell all in one.

Back to the present. I expect Mr. Louis momentarily, and we want to see what we can accomplish today. We will be visiting a French attorney who will help us with our case. Mr. Louis will leave on Monday; his visa for France is only valid for ten days each time. He will be going to Italy and Switzerland, where he will visit your family and return to Paris, hopefully to await your arrival. Then we should all travel together to Istanbul. I had a most joyful cable from Uncle Leo; he can't wait to meet "our dear Kurt."

A thousand kisses, yours,
Gerda

P.S. Mr. Louis just brought me your wire, announcing that you will try to get here sooner. A million thanks and kisses!

Paris, April 16, 1946

My dearest Kurt,

You probably think, and rightly so, that Paris has gone to my head. Perhaps I don't make sense at all because everything is so new, unexpected, and fantastic that I have no handle on it myself yet. Above all my greatest joy lies in the fact that you really are coming. I say it to myself at least fifty times every hour and grin from ear to ear.

Unfortunately things will not go as smoothly as we had hoped. The question of my residency is not resolved as yet, but Mr. Louis got a firm promise from some high official that I will be getting the necessary permit. We will not need any affidavits because I will be able to travel as your wife, but not on your passport, as most European countries permit. Rather, it has to be on my own Polish papers, which are not considered a passport because they are temporary. Meanwhile Mr. Louis canceled our tickets to Istanbul. He feels that was best, and they can always be reinstated as soon as you come and we are married.

I am sorry for the turmoil in which we find ourselves. I can well imagine all that you have to do before your departure. The thing that causes me a great deal of worry is that your family will be angry at me for dragging you to Europe again, thus complicating your life. I am writing to Gerdi how much both my uncle and I hope that she will understand and forgive.

Yesterday Mr. Louis came over, accompanied by a Mario Sarino, a young man from Turkey whose father is a friend of Uncle Leopold's. He is the epitome of a carefree Parisian man-about-town. By the way, there was an instant transformation in Louis as well, from the typical Englishman, as I described him to you, to a French boulevardier. Suddenly he looks like Maurice Chevalier, and needless to say, his French is impeccable. Anyway, we drove to Enghien, about eleven miles from Paris. In the course of the two weeks of Paris traffic I've experienced, I had forgotten how calm, peaceful, and quiet the countryside can be, so I enjoyed every moment of this wonderful drive. Mario took us to what looked like an ancient farmhouse that these days has been turned into a rather posh inn. He is on friendly terms with the proprietor, and soon a meal appeared such as I had never seen or eaten before, each dish a gourmet's delight. Naturally I ate too much. At this rate I will be getting as fat as a wine barrel. The trouble is that lunches take between two and three hours. The consultation over the wines and the ensuing tasting of them are dead serious concerns. After that, there is the savoring of a *bon café,* out comes the fragrant cigar, the cognac, and so on. I think of the hungry people all over Europe and feel ashamed.

Following that we went to the races at Longchamps, and I put a bet on a horse because I liked the name and promptly lost my money. My fortunes turned once Mario gave me a tip on the next race. Result: I won seven thousand francs!

Today I went to the Louvre. How is it possible for one place on earth to have such an incredible wealth of treasures? I am beside myself and can hardly believe what I saw. I will be able to go there often, inasmuch as it is within walking distance from where I'm going to live. You see, I am about to move to the home of a relative of Uncle Leopold's secretary. Madame Flore is a Jewish lady, originally from Greece, a young widow who lost her husband in a concentration camp during the war. My uncle insists that I have a chaperone because, after all, "What would Kurt's family think of a young lady alone in Paris?" His caring for me is touching, and I am deeply grateful. I truly love the idea of being thought of as a young, helpless child who needs to be protected. On the other hand, do you remember the statement I made to you in a letter written one Friday night in Freising, when I said that going to Turkey might be "like living in a gilded cage?" It appears to be just that, and the bars are of pure gold. I hope that I'm not ungrateful, but I'm not used to all that abundance and don't want it. I just enjoy my uncle's wonderfully caring, loving words, "Rest my child, smile, laugh, be happy!" That leads me to the questions, Why do I deserve all that? How can I repay him? I do know this: The more food, clothes, and luxury items are thrust at me, the more I miss you, the deeper the desire to share such abundance with you, and the more certain the knowledge that we do not need much to be happy. I just want to be with you.

One more request, and I feel funny to have to ask you for it. You should bring along some sort of paper from a synagogue or other Jewish organization stating that you are not married. I am truly embarrassed about it, but I, too, will have to have some paper attesting to that. My uncle promised to take care of my certificate along those lines, so that we can be married by a rabbi. In Munich all this was only a distant dream, way off in some nebulous future. Now I really believe that it's coming true, that our reunion can be measured in weeks, perhaps even days, and that we will really get married. Please don't change your mind. I love you so!

An avalanche of kisses from your
Gerda

Kurt dearest,

Where should I start? With an apology, I guess. I have not written to you in two days, an unheard-of happening, and I could easily say that it was done on purpose because I am soon going to have to wean myself from writing to you. Imagine, no more letters! I seem to be running from place to place, trying to get my life in order. I was told that anybody wanting to get married has to have proof of birth! Fortunately Uncle Leo does have a copy of my birth certificate. God bless my father for the foresight to have sent those to Turkey before the war. It's being forwarded to me by registered mail, but that will take at least another week.

Now to your letters. Thanks, my love, for all your words and deeds and the narrow strip in your last letter, which you explained I should wind around my ring finger for the measure of my wedding ring. Needless to say, I was moved to tears, and would happily wear the paper. You are saying—and I wholeheartedly agree—that it should be an American ring, not one bought in Europe. You get extra kisses for that. Also, thanks for telling me—because I didn't know—that it's the *left* hand in America. Things are getting serious now; it looks as if we really are going to get married. I glanced at your picture and practiced saying, "My husband." Strange, but very nice.

I have to share something with you that is a bit disturbing. I asked Mr. Louis how long he thinks we should be planning to stay in Turkey, because you must secure a difficult passage and make arrangements regarding your job. He seemed evasive about it, and Uncle Leo did not give me an answer either when I inquired. Finally Mr. Louis told me to advise you to give up your job, that we should plan on a lengthy stay. I know this is not what you would want, and neither do I. I know your pride and love of independence, though at the moment I confess it is a wonderful feeling to be spoiled and indulged after so many years. You, and only you, can chart our future. I love my uncle very much, but know that he can be very authoritarian and can see where some of his ideas would not agree with yours.

To give you an example, I mentioned to Mr. Louis that you had indicated I would have to learn to drive to fit in with the life in Buffalo. That seemed to shock him and he remarked, "Your uncle would never agree to that." What's funny about that is that Uncle Leo, who looks a lot like Rudolph Valentino, had quite a reputation as a Don Juan, and as a child, I overheard many "scandalous" tales about his romantic exploits. I was always nosy about these things, and the adults didn't think I understood what they were talking about. These days, and in this world, my uncle comes up with such archaic ideas as far as women are concerned. Living in Turkey, perhaps something has rubbed off from the life of the sultans. He must have calmed down considerably now that he is elderly, either forty-six or forty-eight. I just felt that I should alert you to some of the plans that are being hatched.

My impatience is growing daily. I do fervently hope for May 7, when, reunited, we simply *must* celebrate the first anniversary of our meeting.

All my love and tons of kisses (wonder whether Uncle Leo suspects that I have kissed you?).

Yours,
Gerda

Paris, April 21, 1946

Kurt, my beloved,

Many hours have passed since the morning, and now it's quite late again. There is always so much to say, so much to explain. Please forgive my jumping from subject to subject and that some of my actions seem to defy logical explanations. Please be patient, if possible, for I do find things difficult, while everything should really be so simple. For months we have been trying to get married, yet one obstacle after another is thrown into our path. Each day that should bring us closer together only adds up to a new detour. Mr. Louis is looking into the situation in Switzerland again, to see whether it would be easier to get married there. I'm hoping that once you are here, perhaps that might work. At one point we were told that if two foreign citizens want to marry here, one has to be a resident for a year. My heart dropped when I heard that, but I was soon comforted by what an attorney told me; that is, that things *are* possible in France. You can draw your own conclusions. If only you'll get your visa soon and come.

I have met a number of people and am often invited to their homes, but to tell the truth, the conversations tend to be most disappointing. People want to know where I spent the war years and when I tell them, the advice is, "Just forget about it. Forget it." Easy for them to say! Something triggered a memory of the past, and I started to cry, and Mr. Louis reported it to Uncle Leo, who in turn passed the word that I shouldn't cry. Instead he suggested that I go out and buy myself a new dress. It would help me keep my composure, he told his father-in-law. What about my need to cry sometimes? You have always understood that and let me cry in your arms. Our relationship evolved mainly through understanding each other's grief. I shall never forget those occasions when your face reflected bitter pain, and pray that I may never see that expression on your face again. One question has tormented me a great deal: Am I the person you think I am? Will I be able to give you the happiness that you deserve? I pray that it may be so, for you deserve all the love I have to give.

Just one other request, and I've wanted to ask you about it for a long time. When you come here, please bring photos of your dear parents. Because, you see, I do love them very much and want them, together with mine, to be with us in spirit when we marry. I embrace you with countless kisses.

Yours,
Gerda

Paris, April 23, 1946

You, my beloved,

Thank you for sending me the birth certificate Uncle Leo forwarded to you. It's hard to tell how much good it will do, but perhaps it'll help secure more than a "temporary" Polish passport and will let me establish my legal residence here. Mr. Louis is having difficulty getting a Turkish visa for me. Yours would be no problem because of your American citizenship, but inasmuch as we found out that I will not be able to travel on your passport, I'll need a separate visa. Both he and the authorities seem hopeful, however, that once we are married, that requirement might change. Another thing: We are not to tell the Turks that we are Jewish. That is a bitter blow; I thought the war was over.

I had a wonderfully kind letter from Gerdi, and as you predicted, she absolutely understands our situation and is not at all angry that I'm dragging you to Europe again. In his daily cables and letters, Uncle Leopold is truly incredible. Being most reassuring about our difficulties, he is convinced we will overcome them. Then there's the subject of our wedding. I told him how moved I am by the thought that we will be married in the sanctuary where my beloved Papa once stood. It is terribly good of you to say that you think every girl is entitled to the pomp of a formal wedding. I know you well enough to be certain that you abhor it and will go along only to please me.

Let me explain. I dislike the idea very much myself. I witnessed a few of those "spectacles" in Germany. They turned me off and made me sad. Were these normal times, I would have loved all of it: gown, veil, train, etc. But without my parents, yours, and our families? No, my love, it would only make me sad, so I am writing to my uncle accordingly and as delicately as I can phrase it. He has always been so good to me. When I was a little girl, my tears could always be wiped away by a piece of chocolate or a doll that came from him. He still seems to think that a new dress from a Paris fashion house can do the same. I hate to hurt him and hesitate to tell him that I can only find peace and healing in your arms. I pray that will be soon.

As ever yours,
Gerda

Paris, April 28, 1946

My Dearest,

It is so strange, the hours fly by swiftly, but the days drag on so slowly that it becomes nearly unbearable. If only April were over. I don't like that month, but do love May, with all its promise. You must have so much to do in connection with your coming. How I wish I could help you, but then you wouldn't need to come here.

Had a wonderful letter from Gerdi and photos of Barbara and Larry. I can't get over the pleasure and delight of being an aunt. The children are adorable, and Gerdi writes that Larry looks like you did as a baby. But wait till you see my baby pictures. Uncle Leo must have tons of them in Turkey. He wrote that he kept all the family letters, so there must be a treasure trove of family memorabilia. I feel so fortunate about that. Most of my friends have nothing from their childhood home, not a broken saucer or a photograph. How tragic that is. I will be able to get the photos, or at least copies of them.

What I am most eagerly looking forward to seeing again is the wedding gift Mama gave to her brother. She had a real talent for needlework and did the most exquisite, intricate tapestry for him. It depicts a biblical scene of Eliezer and Rebecca at the well and is at least five feet wide. More than five years of my childhood memories are stitched into it.

That's how long I remember Mama working on it diligently, on a daily basis. She would finish a section, then would carefully fold it and stitch it before going on to the next part. It also comes back to me how she did the fine shadings that gave the faces character. On that she would usually work at high noon, when the light was best. She exhibited infinite patience, a trait I unfortunately did not inherit from her. I can't wait to see it again. I am so grateful it survived.

Now, my love, one request I know you will be reluctant to grant me. Knowing how you used to surprise me by your arrival, please grant me the joy of anticipation. Penelope was never more patient when it came to waiting for Ulysses. Let me have the joy of counting your arrival in terms of hours, instead of weeks and months. After all, you were an officer and (I hope) a gentleman, so I trust that chivalry has not deserted you.

Love and kisses,
Gerda

Buffalo, April 29, 1946

Hello Darling,

My mail to you has never been as sparse as right now, and I do have a real guilty conscience because of it. I expect from one day to the next to be able to give you the news we have longed for. My passport should arrive any day now; then just another day or two in Buffalo, a few more in New York, and—presto—I'll be with you!!! How nice to dream of that, day and night.

Mr. Louis's recent letter cleared up diverse matters. Now I am much better acquainted with the formalities and will prepare them accordingly. I can only hope that you were able meanwhile to register officially, because, as you know, it will still require another thirty days for us to go on record about our intent to marry. I'm certain I'll be with you by that time. Still no answer from Washington; on the other hand, I didn't expect one that quickly. Well, another week or two, I think. By the way, did you receive the birth certificate I sent? Can you inquire at the American consulate whether they'll add you on my passport or ask what else needs to be done?

There's no news here other than that I'm up to my neck in travel preparations. I no longer have any patience for mundane matters, and am totally useless, inasmuch as I'm here only in body. You'll have to make do meanwhile with only that other half, won't you? And for that, you'll get a dozen "spirited" kisses. Balance to follow with interest!

How are things going at Madame Flore's? I'll soon be there to help you talk with my hands. Poor lady doesn't know what's in store for her.

Have quite a bit to report yet, but will have to postpone it until tomorrow or the day after.

Lots and lots of love,
Kurt

Paris, May 1, 1946

Good morning, Kurt—*bon jour*!

It's a beautiful morning, as exquisite as only a morning in May can be. The first of May, the sound alone is full of exalted promise. I love this month, because it always meant a month of joy, and everything wonderful that's ever happened to me took place during that period, quite aside from the fact that it's also my birth month. And just a year ago, it held the happiest day of my life, my freedom, and YOU!

So much lies between yesterday and today. Even the fact that it rained yesterday and there is golden sunshine today, as if nature wanted to draw a heavy dividing line between April and May, between sorrow and joy.

Yes, on April 29 I had *yahrzeit** for Ilse. She was the most painful loss that I sustained a year ago. I still see it all so clearly in front of me. Oh, I can't have grown so shallow and callous, but when I think of her, of her last days, last hours, it is as if I read it in a book or saw it in a film. It somehow has no reality, I don't feel it in my being. I was looking into the glow of the memorial candle I lit for her and wanted to retreat to the hopeless gray pain of the time when I lost my dearest friend. I felt the tie, the bond I had with her, I was there with her, but something broke through that pain, a shaft of light, a bright beam, prying me loose from dark thoughts. And I confronted her remembered image, as we stand in reverence before heroes who fought for our freedom. I will be eternally grateful, but cannot be totally connected. Please tell me, my dearest, tell me, have I grown to be uncaring? I don't think that I am of a fickle nature, but something, some power is dragging me away, taking the weight off my soul. Now in this new spring, in our spring, I would like to cry my sorrow away in your arms and change the tears into tears of joy.

---

*Jewish memorial day of death anniversary.

All Paris is adorned with flowers so typical of May: lilies of the valley, your mother's favorite flowers and mine. The first flowers you brought me last May. I'm sending you this spray in her blessed memory with my gratitude and love for her.

I couldn't send the letter because the post office is closed, May Day being a holiday. It seems the entire population of Paris has taken to the streets. A throng of thousands of people is milling about, many of them singing. There are marching bands, and the streets are festooned with flags. Everyone is in a festive mood. I have never seen anything quite like that before. So much exuberance and patriotism. I hope the entire world will always live in peace and mutual understanding, giving us cause for even greater celebration. I went to the Place de la République, thinking how much of France's history played out there, and trying to remember the little that I knew about it.

I spent an absolutely delightful evening recently in the home of Uncle Leo's friends. The guest list was truly an array of international person-alities. There was a lady from Palestine, another from Spain, a young doctor from Poland, one from Italy, and, finally, one from Turkey. We had a lot of fun with the Turk, who speaks his native tongue only, except for a few words of English, even fewer than I. He knows my uncle and couldn't get over the fact that I was his niece, though he had heard of my existence. To him it was a source of never-ending wonder that I had been in Germany until recently. He was constantly shaking his head and invoking the name of Allah. It so happened he was my dinner part-ner and so kept putting food on my plate, saying, "You makes me happy!" And seeing me eat ravenously made him beam all over and repeat how happy I "makes" him. The evening was a veritable Tower of Babel: French, English, Hebrew, German, Turkish, and, thank goodness, Polish as well.

The trouble is that in general I eat too much. I love all the food and every conceivable type of fresh fruit that's available on the streets. I don't seem to be able to stop. I'm afraid that when we get to Turkey you will sell me into a sultan's harem. I hear they prefer hefty women!

Good night, my love.

Many "weighty" kisses from your "voluptuous"
Parisian

My Dearest,

Have you already forgotten that you were a soldier not long ago, a hero who liberated people? In five short days, it will be May 7, the day on which you liberated a certain girl you later called Dimples. You can't simply write one of those *adieu, ma petite* letters. How long do you think I can stand this loveless existence?

Uncle Leo's daily letters and cables continue to arrive. Today I got photos of his family, and they are fabulous. My aunt is exquisitely beautiful. I'm afraid you will fall in love with her, and I couldn't blame you. Unfortunately my uncle complains that we, you and I, don't write often enough. I write to him every day. I'm amazed by his concern and his actions and the amount of time he devotes to us. After all, he is a very busy *homme des affaires*. As you must have seen, all his letters are written by him personally, not by his secretary. It almost seems like an obsession, as though he is making up for the lack of contact during the war. I told you how my mother was in the habit of writing to her brother daily before the war. That is to say, she had a sheet of paper at the ready any time, much like a diary, and that's how she would report to him. I can't recall whether he responded in kind, but his letters, bearing all those exotic stamps, seemed to come all the time.

Mama and her brother adored each other, though you could hardly find two more divergent people. He, a man of the world, roaming all over the globe, while Mama's horizon barely went higher than the rooftops of Bielsko. I'm afraid he will be disappointed in me. He probably thinks of me as the image of my mother, when in most respects I take after my father. He seems to hunger for every detail of my present life but does not want to hear anything about the past.

No mail from you today, but a package of sweets arrived. Thank you for your goodness, but please, no more. I have gained an awful lot of weight.

Tons of kisses from
Your "Elephant"

Buffalo, May 2, 1946

My dearest Gerda,

I want to get this letter going and will presumably finish it tonight. Unfortunately I can't yet confirm the news you're waiting for most. No word from Washington so far. It ought to happen very soon now.

Even a tyrant like me can hardly resist your fervent pleas. Therefore, once I get an inkling of being able to leave here within a few days, you'll get a cable. It'll be impossible to fix the date of my arrival with certainty too far in advance, inasmuch as Max clued me in that I'll have to be at the airport each day until somebody doesn't show whose seat I can take over.

Meanwhile Mr. Louis cabled from Italy, wanting to know how long he should expect to stay there, because he'd like to synchronize his return to Paris with my arrival. I could reply only that I have no passport so far, and that, conservatively speaking, I estimate the time of my arrival to be in about three weeks. That means, unfortunately, that we probably won't be able to spend the two most important days of the year in each other's company. We'll make up for it, though. You will have to give me a detailed report on how you spent May 7 and 8* and whether you were able to contain your feminine curiosity sufficiently so as not to open my letters prematurely, if indeed they arrived on time. It goes without saying that I know the answer, but feel like irritating you a little, otherwise you'll think I no longer love you!

My travel preparations are nearly complete, my bags are packed (including the requested photos), and only a few inconsequential things are missing. It occurs to me you don't actually know why I'm marrying you. Simple. I need somebody who will straighten up the mess I'm leaving behind.

Do take huge birthday kisses—or would you prefer to cash them in according to your age? Better not; you might run out of breath. Impertinent? Of course; after all, it's

Your Kurt

Buffalo, May 5, 1946

Gerda dearest,

Writing was never as difficult as it is right now. On one hand, I certainly don't want to evoke more disappointment every time, by telling you there's still no word from Washington. On the other hand, everything I'm doing at the moment has lost its meaning in view of our impending reunion. It's not right to offer you trivial details of my daily routine as long as I can't furnish the much-longed-for news. I depend so much

*May 7, 1945, our first meeting. May 8, Gerda's birthday.

on your mail that the best and nicest moments happen when I get home at the end of my workday and find the hungrily awaited "Par Avion" envelope. That way I have a real inkling of what it will mean to be together, and everything looks a lot more cheerful. Just now, when our reunion is so imminent, it's harder than ever to be forced to spend the days without you.

It's not at all nice of Dimples to arouse my curiosity to such an extent that I'm close to snapping from suspense over the mysterious allusions to those "surprises" you are hatching. You must labor under the mistaken impression that because you succeeded in enchanting the French police with your charms, I will deal with you equally as gently. Just wait until I hold you in my arms. I'll instill the requisite respect, have no doubt! I won't let you get away with a simple ransom either. You won't be free again with fewer than two million kisses.

What you mention about our honeymoon trip to Turkey sounds fantastic, and you'll have to slap my face to make me realize I'm not dreaming. You deserve it, of course, but what am I doing there? Seriously, it somehow doesn't seem right to me—those matters are simply not done that way.* I don't really know how to express it without offending you; you do already know my misgivings. How can I accept something like that, which I myself have not worked for?

Gerdi and Gunther told me they had a terribly nice letter from you and say there's only one thing wrong with it; that is, that you constantly apologize unnecessarily for everything. Gerdi thinks the whole world ought to apologize to you! Yes, Gerda, that's something that'll never come up between us; you see, it isn't at all compatible with my perception of life. Every individual has an equal right to happiness, and no one is any more important than another at birth. It's strictly a matter of what you make of your life. Somehow or other I can't imagine that this spark has been breathed into us, only to let it be extinguished in useless or wasteful endeavors. I prefer to believe that we all have a mission, if nothing else than to make another person happy. That's why I don't like to listen to such apologies. To negate our existence in that manner means to deprive life of its meaning. I don't know another human being who has scaled the highest summits or been flung to the lowest depths, such as you experienced in your life. Was all that in vain? Nobody and nothing can compensate you for all the horror that has touched you. Aware

*I was reluctant to accept a gift of such magnitude.

of this fact, we want to build our happiness so that a firm foundation will be created from the debris of the past. That is my most fervent wish for both of us.

Gerda, if there exists a more selfless person than you, I can't imagine who it would be. You must be able to feel that the voices from the past cannot lay claim on your happiness (and through that on ours). Only by making something of ourselves can we show our reverence for those who left such a vast void in our lives. It is up to us, the survivors, to give expression to the beauty of being, thereby underscoring the heritage of goodness they have left in us.

All too often the word "mourning" is interpreted only through tears and the wearing of somber clothing. The latter, in particular, is only an outward manifestation of our grief. Tears? Yes, but not in every instance are they the expression of our pain, nor should they be. Believe me, Gerda, I shall never ask you why. Rather I shall try to understand you.

I love you,
Kurt

Paris, May 7, 1946

Kurt, my love, my Kurt,

So you were here during the night! But why, why, didn't you stay? How else would that enormous bouquet of white roses have gotten to my night table? I buried my face in their delicate fragrance and tenderly kissed their soft petals.

I had so hoped that you would reappear on this special day on which you came into my life a year ago. But no matter, we'll have another special date to celebrate in the future, the date of our upcoming reunion, after which, in the normal course of events, we should not have to separate again.

I do have to make a confession. That mysterious blue envelope arrived the day before yesterday, bearing its stern warning, *Défense d'ouvrir avant de . . .* * I turned it over and over numerous times, and guess what? The glue must have been brittle from all the handling and—it just "fell" open. Honestly, how can one resist looking at what's inside? I think even

*Don't open before . . .

an iceberg like you couldn't do that! I laughed no end about that delightful poem and all the artwork you created. There is no limit to your talents, it seems. I, too, wrote you a poem, but am really embarrassed to send it. My efforts are so lame, so amateurish compared to your accomplishments. Please forgive all its flaws, but I do think that the love with which it comes is without blemish.

A million liberated kisses and thanks,
Gerda

Paris, May 9, 1946

Kurt dearest,

While I wait for mail from you, what do you think I'm doing? To dispel my loneliness, I'm sweetening the hours by eating the delicious candy you continue to send. It's therefore you, and only you, who are to blame for the loss of my svelte figure. And now that I've reached the ancient age of twenty-two, I can only bury my sorrow in sweets and in the fragrant beauty of your white roses that came two days ago, only to be followed by yesterday's flaming red ones. All of them do help me to forget that I'm an old spinster and remind me that I will be a young wife as soon as you marry me. What a wonderful, comforting thought. I inhale the fragrance and feel your nearness, sending all my loving thoughts to you, with my thanks.

Kurt, my love, I sense something in your last letters that disturbs me. Certainly not in the expression of your love, but some slight hesitation, some unspoken concern. It is not defined, but I feel it and hope that I'm mistaken. Please, for my sake, let me respond to something that has not been uttered and if it is not expressed, I think I know why.

It has to do with Uncle Leo. I have gushed about his lavish gifts, perhaps foolishly and without giving it too much thought. It's just that his plans sound so exciting and hint of undreamed of luxuries. Perhaps you are concerned that I might get used to all that and will feel deprived if you cannot provide a similar lifestyle. Knowing your pride, you will not accept anything from him. Please let me go on. To begin with, my uncle is not as rich as his unrestrained generosity might reflect. He is undoubtedly very affluent. Our family was always known to go overboard when it came to generosity among its members.

Whenever he came to visit us, my uncle always had an aura of true magic about him, like a character out of *Tales of 1001 Nights*. His visits usually came twice a year until he gave up his bachelorhood in 1937. I regarded him as a pasha, who came on a magic carpet, baggage bulging with a plethora of gifts. I remember one year—I must have been about eight or nine—replying to his prompting as to what special wishes I had, and writing him that I would love to have a Persian cat. I had heard those were available in Turkey. Would you believe then that he promptly appeared at our train station, cage in hand, holding none other than an Angora cat? It had traveled with him on the Orient Express by way of Vienna, then by ordinary train to Bielsko. My grandmother was scandalized, if not outraged, by that gift and remarked how easily taken in her son was, inasmuch as each of the cat's eyes was of a different color, despite the valued pedigree. Furthermore, my thrifty Omama was incensed on learning of the cat's diet, which was supposed to contain fresh fish that she felt should be reserved for making gefilte fish for the Sabbath. Come to think of it, I don't recall what finally happened to that cat.

This might give you some insight into my family's idiosyncrasies and perhaps explain the root of some of our excesses. In light of that it is not so strange that my uncle wants to make up to me some of the things I lost—or never had—during my teenage years. It's obvious he wants to be a part of my happy reentry into a normal life—and yours, as far as that goes. For now he wants to give us a wonderful, memorable honeymoon. Can't you accept that?

As far as I am concerned, the trappings may have changed, but I am the same person that you found in Volary. I have only one desire, and that is to share your life, whatever it will be, whatever you want it to be. I have no wish to live in the style of my family in Turkey. I remember my father's stories about the time he was there in 1937. He and my mother lived a good, decent, simple life, as you told me your family did, and I want to emulate that. I often think of my love for you and am astonished that a feeling of that intensity can exist. Perhaps it might seem oppressive that I center everything on you, but you have confessed to similar feelings about me.

I will make one statement and swear it to be true. You know how much I hate to be in Germany, but if you decided to go and live there, I would go with you. I don't think that I need to say anything else.

Back for a moment to our wedding. It is my wish to have a small, religious ceremony by adhering to all that ties us to our parents, who died for our faith. I would like to start our life together in their spirit, knowing we would have had their blessings. I hope that this is what you, too, desire and I'd like very much to convey that to Uncle Leo. Please come soon so that I can convince you that I can only be happy if you are.

As ever yours,
Gerda

Paris, May 11, 1946

Hello, Monsieur, are you still in Buffalo?

What a stupid question, and I should know better. I also know how frustrated you must be. But cheer up, there are other ways, I hear, if all else fails. I had a cable from Mr. Louis in Basel, and he is having a lovely time with your family. Everybody seems to be able to get together but you and I. He is coming back to Paris tomorrow, and he usually gets things moving. I don't want to dwell on our problems all the time, so let me tell you something amusing.

As I mentioned, Madame Flore does not speak a word of German or Polish. My French leaves much to be desired, so we have very strange conversations. "Gerdika, *ma petite*," she calls me. Well, I am not so *petite*; she, on the other hand, is tiny. She asked my advice which dress she should wear, a one- or two-piece one. I completely misunderstood her when she used the word *pièce*, pronouncing it in French as *pyess,* which in Polish means dog. I must have been preoccupied because I responded to it with *chien,* the French word for dog, which she in turn interpreted as meaning that a dog had gotten into the apartment, because the door was wide open. So she started to look around for the nonexistent dog.

I have been spending my time in the Louvre, where many masterpieces are coming back from their hiding places and are being restored. I'm awed by so much beauty having been created throughout the ages and all over the world. I look at the paintings, wondering what they have witnessed, and wish they could talk. But they reveal nothing except their own significance. I feel so small, forlorn, and lonely. I need to share it with someone I have not seen in eight months. Do you think that today is the last Sunday without him? With that thought and hope in mind, lots and lots of kisses,

Gerda

Buffalo, May 11, 1946

My very dearest Gerda,

A few days have gone by without bringing the longed-for news. I've made an attempt to expedite the matter by urgently wiring the State Department about it. No response to that either so far. I really could use some proof of how urgent the matter is on your end. That's why it would be best if you could send me a cable stating the following: "Will have to return to Germany or Poland if you cannot come within two weeks."

I have no idea whether it'll become necessary to make use of such a cable, but I'd like to have it on hand if worse comes to worst. Meanwhile there are a few other things I'm also going to try. I was informed at the time I applied for my passport that it could take this long, but I had hoped that instead of four weeks, it would only be two, as is sometimes the case.

Apparently you never received the hundred dollars I sent you. In case the money still hasn't arrived by the time you get this, please advise, so that I can put in a claim. As to Mr. Louis, I suppose the time is drawing close when he will return to Paris, and I'm still not there! As depressing as all this waiting around is, it could conceivably change in a jiffy. But frankly the uncertainty gets on my nerves at the moment, and I can well imagine how you must feel about it. Our patience is really being tested to the limit, and I hope never again to have to wait for anything in this manner! It's only when I hold you in my arms that everything will be compensated for and we'll be able to put it behind us, Gerda.

My cousin from England finally arrived last Wednesday. All this time she was waiting in vain for a ship for herself and her two young children. Finally she succeeded in getting airline reservations. She spent a few days in New York, but I'm expecting to speak to her either today or tomorrow, at which time I'll get a direct report on Mr. Louis's visit at her home. I'm so glad that she still made it here before I have to leave, because it should be highly interesting to find out what happened in her life since the time I last saw her. You know, she and her husband treated me wonderfully well when I was in England during the war. I like both of them a lot. Their home has become a clearinghouse for all sorts of international visitors. I heard that my cousin, who is in the Palestine Brigade of the British Army along with his wife, recently paid a visit there. That's how it went with many relatives and acquaintances who found themselves in the British Isles during the war years.

So much for my report today. Meanwhile, a thousand kisses and the hope of holding you in my arms soon,

Kurt

Buffalo, May 13, 1946

My dearest Gerda,

Just today, when my thoughts harked back to that other May 13—when you were so critically ill in the hospital and I could at last see you again—your three wonderful and content-heavy letters of early May arrived, along with your poetic declaration of why and how it came about that at your instigation my heart became the target of a certain archer named Cupid. He may well gloat over his success, but believe me, so do I. That should teach you that "he who sets a trap for someone else, is likely to fall into it himself."* I think you really outsmarted yourself on that one.

I want to give you a status report. I called the Passport Division in Washington today. You can't ever pin them down on anything, of course, but I was advised that I can either expect an answer within two to three days, or I'll get the passport within that time. That'll make it over four weeks since I applied; they have been the longest four weeks of my life. It might work out to the twenty-second, although I hesitate to set any more dates.

All my love,
Kurt

Buffalo, May 16, 1946

My very dearest Gerda,

All that I can tell you today is already summarized in the cable I sent earlier, notifying you that my passport came through! The tension will be lifted only when I hold you securely in my arms and determine whether it's really you. Whatever still lies between then and now will pass like a dream, at the end of which I will behold your beloved face and, united with you, will face a sunny future.

*German proverb.

256

Apparently my phone call to Washington helped after all. I received a call at work, apprising me in the most dramatic fashion that the passport had arrived. And that's the only thing I could grasp coherently. My duds are packed, a few more good-byes, and then it's off to New York tomorrow. There the formalities should take only about two or three days. Then I ought to be able to catch a flight anytime after that.

Above all I want to avoid having to disappoint you again, so why don't you pretend that I won't get a seat on a flight right away. Should it go faster, well, all the better! I am going to try to let you know my exact arrival by cable, but it's always possible that I won't have sufficient time to do that, depending on developments. If I then stand in front of you, you'll be justified to be angry at me and you can vent your entire rage on me—okay?

By the way I will also keep Mr. Louis up-to-date. So far my passport has not been issued to include travel to Turkey. The answer I got was that that has to be taken care of in France. So let's hope!

I'm incapable now of writing a lot of trivia. You'll be hearing from me once I'm in New York. Everything else "orally," even without words. Just be sure to leave the door open, because if by chance nobody should be there when I arrive, I'd only have to turn around and go back. Or is it possible you're going to make an exception in this case by staying home?

Until I press that bell then, I am, with a real passionate kiss,

Your happy
Kurt

New York City, May 18, 1946

My very dearest Gerda,

I hope you correctly understood the cable I sent today and that you didn't encounter too many obstacles in trying to follow my directions. So let me give you a brief recap of the last few hours.

I arrived in New York last night and paid a visit to the various authorities this morning. At the French consulate I was convinced that I practically had the visa in hand, only to find that there is a new regulation, according to which you have to apply at the Paris city hall for a certificate, which you will have to send to me, providing proof of the

257

fact that our banns have been posted.* I realize that you once mentioned you could do nothing of the sort without my presence there. The claim here is, however, that all those who have the intent to marry have to go through the same procedure. I can only hope that your authorities over there are as well informed as their representatives here like to create the impression *they* are.

This danged hitch will cost us at least one week, quite aside from the apprehension of whether they will actually issue such a certificate, etc. With some luck I could still be with you by next weekend. As to the airline seat, things appear somewhat better. I'm being waitlisted and have to be ready to go at any moment. But the travel agent didn't think it would take longer than three days for me to get on a flight. Perhaps it'll go even faster. Should Mr. Louis have returned to Paris by now, please tell him that I unfortunately won't be able to make it by May 22.

I did get a transit visa for England from the British consulate, but Palestine is out of the question due to the current friction. The same holds true for Egypt, so we have to put our faith in the fact that nothing further lies in the path of a trip to Turkey, once I'm in France. As mentioned, we'll have to attempt those steps through the American embassy in Paris. Kisses until next week,

Kurt

Paris, May 20, 1946

My Dearest,

I find it very difficult to start this letter and with it a new phase of our correspondence. Unfortunately, as we both know so well, things in life don't always go as we want them to go.

Received your cable today that states that the news from Washington condemns us to two more weeks of waiting. I just feel so badly that you have left your job and have to stay in New York for the duration of that time. But being with the family, and especially with the children, should make you happy.

Your message came like an ice-cold shower, dashing our hopes again. The first thing I did was to try to get an SOS to Mr. Louis in Switzerland.

*The European custom of posting notices of intent to marry, giving others the chance to object to any impending marriage for valid reasons.

I called the Hôtel Metropol, only to be told that he had checked out. I knew that he was going on to London but didn't know where he was staying there. As soon as I put the phone down in dismay, it rang. Imagine my surprise and delight to hear Mr. Louis's voice! Where was he calling from? Paris! He decided to stop over here for a day to see how I was doing. Can you imagine that?

So you see, we are no longer alone in our battle. An hour later he was with me, and since then we've spent the entire time in taxis, running from office to office, to the Préfecture again and again, trying above all to put my papers in order. What I can't understand regarding my papers is this: The officials certainly know that there was a war, that most people are DP's, unable to get documents from their largely destroyed communities. I must be one of very few who has her original birth certificate. Still, you can't imagine what difficulties I run into.

One plan we came up with would have you trying to get a visa for England, Switzerland, or Germany, with a transit visa through France. You could stop here then and we could get married. The French consulate in New York might get suspicious, however, and deny your visa completely, instead of merely delaying it. Mr. Louis says that we have to go about it in the most cautious manner. One misstep, and we will have to start all over again.

I'm so desperately sorry that you have to go through all that on my account and that I have to write in this vein. It will all work out, I'm sure. But I know how difficult it is to be confronted by a rigid and final "no." I have faced it so many times in my life, never as bitterly as when I was confronted with it most recently in Germany, always accompanied by the officials' derision. If only I could talk to you, if only I could call America and hear your voice. If we could reassure each other, it wouldn't seem so bad. You must take comfort from the thought that I am no longer alone here, as I was in Germany. I have my uncle's father-in-law, through whom he is accessible, though there is no phone service with Turkey yet. How I would love to hear my uncle's voice after nine years!

Please, my love, you will see that something good will happen, perhaps sooner than we expect. Nobody in this world can say "no" to us, as long as we have said "yes" to each other. With that thought in mind we must go on. I'm grateful to God for having your love and I embrace you with many kisses.

Yours,
Gerda

It's now a day later, and Mr. Louis delayed his journey to London to take care of some matters for Leo. Here is what he instructed me to tell you. He will wire you, but wants me to put it in a letter anyway.

Please have two copies made, certifying that you are single and will marry me. We have gone through all that, but now another agency wants it. On a separate paper, please give the names of your parents, with birth dates, etc.

Your most recent happy letter from Buffalo arrived, superseded now by your being in New York. I am convinced that all will turn out well in the end. In the process of waiting, I turned twenty-two last week. That means, if I could wait for you for twenty-two years, I certainly can wait a few more weeks. But you know, what really upsets me no end is that as soon as the French authorities hear that my fiancé is American, they come up with the nastiest remarks. That really hurts; I remember, on the other hand, your reports of the reception you Americans got when you liberated France! What a short memory those people have! When Mr. Louis saw me on the verge of tears on one occasion, he whispered in my ear, "You will see Kurt soon."

I'll leave you with that thought.

All my love,
Gerda

⬥   ⬥   ⬥   ⬥   ⬥   ⬥   ⬥   ⬥   ⬥   ⬥   ⬥   ⬥

The most difficult aspect of my encounters with bureaucracy, especially when it came to the authorities in Germany, were the sneers and doubts implicit in the officials' voices when I told them that my fiancé was an American who would marry me as soon as I could make it to the United States. I was up against such remarks as, "If your friend wanted to marry you, why didn't he do so when he was here?" There would be a wealth of additional gratuitous advice, recommending that I stop deluding myself about this relationship. And other indignities were voiced after I would offer to show some of Kurt's letters stating his intent to marry me. It would prompt the retort—in the words of a well-known German proverb—that "paper is patient," or it would be pointed out that Kurt had probably found an American girl by now.

The worst part was that I couldn't tell Kurt about those sneers. It would only have reinforced his resolve to sign up for another two-year stint in the army, which he was suggesting around that time. It was something I

felt I must prevent at all costs, and it made my dealings with officialdom
sheer agony.

I had imagined that once I left Germany I would never encounter such
high-handed attitudes again, only to find that I was confronted by similar
derision among French officials.

ༀ   ༀ   ༀ   ༀ   ༀ   ༀ   ༀ   ༀ   ༀ   ༀ   ༀ   ༀ

Paris, May 21, 1946

My beloved Kurt,

It is impossible to go to bed, because I know I won't be able to sleep. I
know how upset you are about the latest difficulties. I have cabled and
written to Uncle Leo, because he too is terribly concerned, although
fully confident—as I am—that all will work out. I am sorry that you
apparently consider it an additional burden that Mr. Louis and my uncle
are doing so much here in Paris. That's ridiculous. Everyone who cares
for us is helping. Your family certainly would do so if they could. Please
don't make it any harder on yourself. We have had a very rough time to
get this far, but will overcome all obstacles, I am sure. I have never
been stronger than now, really. If someone had told me when I arrived
in France two months ago, after that terrible experience you still don't
know about in its entirety, that I would see you within three months'
time, I would have done cartwheels. So this is really no great tragedy.

There is one other possibility for us that I think you might find amusing. Mr. Louis is looking into it in London right now. It would be very
good if you could get a visa for England; you can then either come with
him to Paris or listen to this possibility.

There appears to be a blacksmith in Gretna Green, Scotland, whose
ancestor, also a blacksmith, agreed to perform a marriage between an
English prince and his ladylove when others had refused to do so. Once
the prince became king, he granted this blacksmith and his descendants
the right to marry lovers in distress.

Mr. Louis has already discussed the matter with your cousin in England, and she would be quite willing to get me there as a domestic.
That seems to be the only way they would admit me to that country. It
might take a little time, because we'll have to wait until Trude returns
from her visit to the U.S., but as you see, there are all kinds of possibilities. So please don't despair.

Oh, yes, something very important: In case you should be questioned as to how I got to France and why I did not go with you to America when you went back home, you'll have to be prepared to come up with the same answers I gave. They are as follows: I came to France with a displaced persons' transport, part of a military convoy. As to why we didn't get married in Germany, it was because you got your orders to go home quite suddenly, at a time when I had no papers to prove my identity. It's true that I received them only months later. I was not aware at the time that my uncle in Turkey was in possession of my birth certificate. Further, after everything that happened to me in Germany, it is not surprising that I did not want to start my new life there. That, too, is true, Kurt. I would not have married you in Germany, so please stop agonizing about that and blaming yourself. Just remember, there is nobody I care for more than you, nobody I love and respect more than you. Doesn't that make you feel a little better?

Millions of kisses. (How long will that take to accomplish?)

Yours,
Gerda

New York City, May 21, 1946

Gerda, my love,

I'm in possession of Mr. Louis's cable, which states that it will take another three weeks until the certificate can be issued. I can hardly give proper expression to my disappointment; it really looks as though everything that could conceivably block our way is in fact doing so.

I'm going to have another go at seeing the French vice-consul tomorrow, but don't know how successful that will be, inasmuch as my passport unfortunately wasn't issued in the manner I had requested. In it France is given as my final destination. Therefore nothing will probably come of the transit visa.

You'll hear tomorrow how things progressed here, and I will also cable the outcome, so that you'll know either way. My current stay in New York is like a nightmare. Every step I take turns out totally discouraging, and yet it would be so easy to come to you! Oh, Gerda, it's time we got together!

Kurt

Dearest Kurt,

Just a few words. We had a very busy but most productive day. Early in the morning I went to the city hall with Mr. Louis and met two distinguished high officials who had seen my papers and fully understood what happened in this case. They were willing to act as my witnesses to expedite matters regarding my residency permit. It normally takes upward of three weeks to get it, but I was assured it will take *only* three days in this instance. With the document of their approval in hand, we went directly to the Préfecture de Police, and suddenly, magically, all doors were open. The chief of police himself took matters in hand. It will not be issued until the day after tomorrow, because right now it still lacks a few signatures; a mere formality, I was told. They assured me that by next week I would have my residency papers, in other words, official permission to be in France.

Can you imagine how much has changed since yesterday! I am not cabling this news, but when I get the residency permit, the wires between Paris and New York will buzz!

I am going to accompany poor, tired Mr. Louis to the Gare du Nord, because he is going back to England today. He still thinks it would be good if you could meet him there. On his last trip to London your cousin gave him a picture of you that promptly went to Istanbul. Your family sang your praises, and now mine wants to claim you as their own. I have seen to that already. In haste, but still enough time for a kiss,

Gerda

New York City, May 22, 1946

My dearest Gerda,

By now I should be with you but instead can only report failure after failure. You wrote to Gerdi today in such a state of exhilaration, and now I can imagine you before me, the consequences of this latest delay engraved on your face. And what can I say about it? When I think of what these obstacles must be doing to you, I could jump out of my skin!

As per my cable to you, I went to the French consulate once more today. Absolutely nothing to be achieved there, not even a transit visa (which incidentally would only be valid for a few days), inasmuch as my passport unfortunately shows my final destination as France. To have it changed over, such as to Switzerland, for example, would require more time than will the certificate you are trying to get, provided the authorities would even approve that. I received that information from the Passport Division here.

Don't ask how I'm spending my time here—or rather will still be spending it. It's almost degenerated to a state of catatonia. The slightest provocation can make me flare up and brings out impossible behavior. I'd really be interested to know whether you consider me good-natured. If so, then be prepared for some unpleasant surprises that'll serve you right.

I do want you to know, though, that I *can* be receptive to the right attire. I will let the cat out of the bag by telling you that I recently acquired a dressing gown, typically American, like those screaming loud ties! One thing I can already predict at this point: Either you'll adjust your taste or I'll never take you to Fifth Avenue, where all the elegant stores and personalities can be seen. If you're all riled up by now, I propose a state of truce. And I promise to completely smudge your carefully applied lipstick—okay?

Kurt

Paris, May 27, 1946

My Beloved,

I am at the Préfecture de Police and *I got it*! Must let you know without a minute's delay that I got my residency permit for a two-month stay, with all the trimmings. Because we have excellent connections now, we will be able to obtain permission to marry as soon as you get here. I'm also cabling you the joyous news.

Can't put the document in the envelope without a few more words. Everyone here—especially me—is overjoyed that you are coming! You *are* coming, it's true, it's really true. I am trying to imagine when you will arrive. Will it be morning, afternoon, or evening? Where will we see each other first? My love, if you could only know how happy I am. I dream of our future: Paris, Istanbul, New York, Buffalo. But the most beautiful of all thoughts is the one that I will enter your beloved America with you, that we will go home together.

I embrace you with all my love.

Yours,
Gerda

CERTIFICAT DE DOMICILE

Je soussigné, M _Barrière_

Concierge de l'Immeuble, sis _Rue Saulnier_ Nº _26-23_

certifie que M _lle Gerda Weissmann_

est domicilié ___ dans le dit Immeuble depuis le _18 Avril 1946_

le _27 Mai_ 194_6_

Vu, soussigné pour

Visa du Commissaire de Police
mat.

Paris

Signature :
Barrière

⁷ MAI 1946

Police

New York City, May 27, 1946

Gerda, my beloved,

I'm trying to commit some thoughts to paper while Barby is wriggling around on my knees. I'm still in a state of ecstasy that nothing can diminish; in retrospect, not even your confirmation of our worst fears regarding any potential obstacles that were thrown across our path. All those complications are as if wiped away, hopefully forever, now that I'm in possession of your cabled joyful message!

As you will have gathered from my various missives meanwhile, this is definitively the happiest solution to our problems. Everything else, even if it had been possible to achieve, would have used up more precious time.

Although I can hardly contain my impatience, I'm gratefully awaiting receipt of the papers, and in that connection my guess is that, if all goes well, they'll arrive two days from now, on Wednesday. After all those disappointments, I hardly dare express what shapes up as an enchanting image in my mind. Only one thing I can say with certainty: My peace of mind has been restored, thanks to your incomparably beautiful and brave words, penned with the selfless eloquence that only *you* can rise to. I read them over and over again, each time gaining new strength from them, because the spark of this tremendous fortitude is contagious and moved me profoundly and miraculously. I was able to sense your nearness and can hardly determine how such riches of feelings and emotions became a part of my life.

Gerda, my beloved, you offer such manifold gifts, while at the same time demanding nothing for yourself. And yet you were spared nothing. What can I possibly do in order to compensate you? Even if it were possible to bring you the stars from the sky, it would be woefully inadequate.

You've hinted variously at some of the dangers you were exposed to since our separation, and I don't claim to be able to measure their full extent. I've refrained thus far from asking for further details, because I realize that the details may not be suitable for correspondence. But because I know you, I can picture even from what little you mention, and without knowing the full story, what the true extent of your physical and psychological torment must have been. Certainly it's been my perception at times that in the light of the actual cruelties humans are capable of inflicting on others, my imagination fails me. I can only say that these experiences, even if I have had them indirectly, are less of a surprise than they are the cause of great pain. But we ought to go into that another time. Today your lines made me so happy that I feel like going up to the top of the Empire State Building and shouting to the world how magnificent it is to be connected with a human being like you!

I *will* be able to show you my love soon.

Kurt

Epilogue

It was June 18, 1946, a glorious spring morning in Paris, the day of our wedding. I now have the luxury of looking back with joy on my happy marriage of more than half a century, but the memory of that particular day fills me with poignant sadness.

I see myself alone in Madame Flore's apartment, which had become my temporary abode. I dress slowly in my new, elegant, white Agnès Drécole suit, a generous gift from my uncle in Turkey. I place my small white straw hat on my dark curls with infinite care and adjust the short veil. My image in the mirror is wistful and forlorn. If only someone were here to tell me that I am a pretty bride, someone who cares and who loves me: Mama, Papa, my brother, relatives, and friends. But I am alone.

The doorbell rings, and there is Kurt, looking very handsome in a dark suit and an elegant blue tie. With a smile he hands me a florist's box that yields white orchids and lilies of the valley, his mother's favorite flowers and—as he knows—mine as well. I too am clutching a small parcel.

A taxi is waiting downstairs, ready to take us to a destination we had decided on a few days earlier. Before proceeding to the civil ceremony at the Ninth Arrondissement city hall, we plan to visit a synagogue. Once there, we have to make our way slowly over the debris that litters the courtyard, coming to a door that creaks as we open it. We see that although the interior is run-down and neglected, it somehow has survived the war intact. I unwrap my parcel and take out several memorial candles, which we proceed to light. We stand in silence, our hands linked. From my bowed head I can see swirls of dust floating on a few feeble rays of sunlight streaming through the stained-glass window, touching us as if in benediction. At that very same instant we turn to each other and embrace. We understand that we have just taken our vows.

Arriving at the *mairie*, we find the air charged with noisy exuberance, a hubbub of voices rising from the crowd of young couples, their families, and well-wishers. Mr. Louis, quite formal in a homburg, has been transformed back into his English lord guise. The other witness is Mario Sarino, playboy son of one of Uncle Leo's friends, a bit pudgy, with bright, fun-loving eyes and a weak chin.

The presiding official, in a formal black suit and *tricolore* sash, looks daunting and officious. A stream of words issues from his lips, a litany he must have recited hundreds of times before, very little of which I manage to comprehend. My mind is not on his words, but suddenly it is our turn to appear before him. Addressing me as *mademoiselle*, he poses a few questions I understand sufficiently to breathe a low *oui*. After Kurt's more audible affirmation, it is *"félicitations, madame et monsieur,"* and now, as far as the French authorities are concerned, this is it. For good measure the *justice* hands us a license, accompanied by a *livrette de famille*,* with sufficient room for the names of twelve children and a wealth of advice, including breast-feeding instructions.

After kisses and warm embraces from Mr. Louis and an embrace and a hand kiss from Mario Sarino, we repair to the Café de la Paix, but Kurt and I scarcely touch our lunch. After a while it is clear that Mario is eager to get away to watch his horse running an important race at Longchamps, while Mr. Louis is obviously tired, exhausted after the days and weeks of endless bouts with French officialdom. We plead with him to go back to the George V, his first priority presumably to cable Uncle Leo the successful accomplishment of his mission.

That leaves Kurt and me to walk back to his hotel. He asks for the guest register, properly bringing it up-to-date as "Monsieur et Madame." I hold on to the reality of Kurt and think: I'm married, I'm really married! Yes, it's true: The agony of waiting, the dashed hopes, and the uncertainty of that long, fateful year are over.

In our desperation we had conjured up a host of diverse plans in case all else failed. The most romantic of those—which I loved—hardly mattered now. We would somehow get to Scotland, to Gretna Green, and be married in an ancient smithy, lucky horseshoes scattered all around. The famed blacksmith who had the authority to marry lovers in distress

*A booklet that might be entitled *Steps to a Successful Marriage*.

would hear our vows. We would emerge in a shower of apple blossoms: a fairy-tale ending.

But I had my fairy-tale ending. I was just married here, in romantic Paris in the springtime, and would be able to stay with Kurt forever! The plain golden circlet on my finger is more precious to me than a crown.

Now that we were married everything seemed possible, and the trip to Istanbul became our first priority. However, we hadn't counted on the rigidity of the Turkish authorities. We found ourselves in limbo for weeks on end while the consulate awaited a decision from Ankara. When it finally came two months later, Kurt's visa for Turkey was approved because he was an American citizen, while mine was rejected despite the fact that I was now his wife. Kurt consoled me that there would be other opportunities later. I suspect that he felt a measure of relief, because he had been somewhat reluctant to accept the offered hospitality. I did not know then, however, that Kurt and my uncle would never meet.

In the months ahead Uncle Leo's life would change dramatically. I was to find out that he had concealed the disastrous state of his marriage from me. Then it became clear why he so desperately wanted us to come to Turkey right away. He was to go through a bitter divorce, in the course of which he sustained great financial losses, and ultimately settled in Paris with his children in 1949. But a greater catastrophe was to befall him. Even then he was ill with throat cancer, and I was with him in Paris in 1950, when it became obvious that no cure was possible. I was able to be at his side at his death in April 1951. Once again I saw Paris, this time through the rain-washed window of the hearse that took my last remaining close relative to his final resting place. Summing up the bitter irony, the undertaker told me that Père Lachaise Cemetery was *plus chic* than another that had been suggested by Uncle Leo's staff.

The long period of waiting had depleted our resources. We had spent most of the money Kurt had saved for years, so he was anxious to get back home and back to work. Transatlantic transportation still being a problem in those days, we were fortunate to be able to book a flight that would depart in a few days' time and that led us to roam the now-familiar streets of Paris to bid them farewell.

It was our last night in Paris, the last night on the Continent. I remember walking for hours, finally stopping on a bridge, leaning over its parapet, looking down on the flow of the Seine below, taking in the magnificent sights all around us. Tomorrow I would be leaving this soil forever. I had no desire to return to those accursed sites on the map of Europe where all the horror had played out. I would leave behind the pain, the hunger, the sorrow of parting from those I had loved. I am going home with Kurt, I thought, never to return. I stood next to him now, feeling his hand touching mine on the ancient stones of the bridge. I recalled how he had entered my life at its lowest point and from then on had reversed the downward spiral. There was this extraordinary sensation from the earliest days of our meeting, one of closeness and familiarity, the inexplicable flash of happiness whenever I would see him, which would blot out my loneliness and sense of isolation; then, later, the ecstasy when he would hold me in his arms. Now we would never part again. I am leaving here forever! I exulted.

Suddenly, tiny barbs—sharp, spiky, like a million poisonous insects—invaded the idyllic serenity of my happiness. Could I really leave the soil of this continent, could I abandon my parents' and brother's unmarked graves? Everything I had known and loved during my untroubled childhood was here in Europe.

I had no real idea of the place I was going to, only what I was able to create in my imagination. I knew no one in that distant land, didn't know the language. Would Kurt's family really accept me? Would I have friends? Would I ever learn English? I only knew Kurt. Would he always love me? Always—even if—? Now the poisonous barbs struck home with force. Would he love me even if—even if I couldn't have children? The children that were my sacred debt to my family's past and future.

Something Kurt was saying penetrated my consciousness; it had to do with how we would look back on this day in a year's time; yes, even after an unimaginable period of ten years. Of course there would be peace. The world would surely learn, and there would never be another war after this one. A peace conference was being held right here in Paris at the Palais de Luxembourg. Kurt made me turn around to the other side of the bridge to see the imposing building. There it was, massive and majestic, with an enormous August moon rising behind it. My gaze traveled to its clock tower. The hands on the illuminated dial stood at 9:10.

At precisely 9:10 A.M., on Sunday, September 3, 1939, my brother's watch had fallen from his trembling fingers onto the green carpet of my childhood home. Its hands stopped at the moment in time when the first German motorcycles roared down the streets of my hometown.

There it was again: 9:10. How eerie that on my very last day in Europe I should be facing the clock tower of the Palais de Luxembourg, where the conclusion of the bitter war was being transmuted into peace. I took that as a positive omen. Tomorrow at dawn I would be leaving the Continent for the New World, for a new life.

I had fallen in love with America at the moment I saw the white star of its army shining through the mud-splattered hood of a Jeep on the day of my liberation. Now, a year later, stepping on U.S. soil with Kurt's arm around me, I felt I truly had come home.

Every discovery I made was new and bright, ringing with freedom. The soil of this vibrant land was mercifully unsullied by the blood of those I loved. Here I could look at the people I encountered without the ever-present question of where they had been and what they had done during the twelve years of the "Thousand-Year Reich."

Intoxicated by my discoveries, I was perhaps blinded by the brightness that engulfed me, oblivious to any flaws, even when they were pointed out to me. In my urgent desire to belong, I would defend those shortcomings even to myself, and I find that now, more than half a century later, I still can't bear criticisms leveled against this country.

There were many puzzling aspects to the intricacies of the English language as I slowly became acquainted with some of its nuances. But first I had to concern myself with basics. I remember well the panic when the phone would ring and I would strain to understand what was being said and, eventually, the relief when I realized that I could carry on a limited conversation.

In my eagerness to become a part of this country, I probably overdid a lot of things. That first fall, with Thanksgiving just around the corner, I flung myself with zeal into all the holiday preparations, feeling as committed and proud as if I had arrived at these shores on the *Mayflower*. Cooking, baking, and homemaking in general were skills I was able to manage. They connected me with the role model I wanted to emulate, my mother. In other areas I felt hopelessly inadequate. Although I was definitely making progress with the language, I was far from fluent in it. And I had not caught on to the rhythm of the city, didn't know my way around, usually depending on Kurt to solve everyday problems. On the other hand, that was comfortable and soothing. It was like being a child at home again, under the authority of my parents who had made most decisions for me. This was the safety that I craved ever since I had been so brutally uprooted and had to bear the burden of a role for which I was unprepared. Other young women my age whom I met had no point of reference to anything I stood for. Most of them, married to Kurt's friends, had just graduated college. I could not really converse with them the way I would have liked, nor did I understand anything about their education or what they had been reading and were discussing. My development had been arrested, yet I had gained knowledge of life's experiences way beyond my years.

To Kurt's eternal credit it must be stated that he let me grow at my own pace. As I realized later, he watched me with tolerant, amused indulgence. He seemed to delight with me at the wondrous discovery of riches to be found in such places as the five-and-dime stores, then displayed infinite patience with my fascination for tinsel and glitter. It was a way of making up for some of the pursuits that had been altogether absent from my teenage years. I would come home in great triumph, bearing the fruits of my latest explorations, which might range from drinking glasses adorned with poodles to artificial daisies that I would promptly stick into vases in the shape of ducks.

There was only one matter on which Kurt stood firm and unbending: He insisted that for the most part he would speak only English to me. Once I had surmounted the initial obstacles along that road, I threw myself into the new language with impetuous fervor. I sensed that it was the key to all things American, and knew how liberating it would be to pour out my thoughts and emotions in the language of my environment. Gradually I got a feel for English, for its light and darkness, for its manifold subtle shadings. A rush of elation would sweep through me whenever I realized that I was harnessing some part of what I felt. I was trying to whip feelings into form, and in a welter of emotions was groping for words that would set me free from the shackles of my limited language ability. And when I succeeded, it took me back to the ecstasy that had taken hold when I had first learned to read, to the wonder of discovery when suddenly those strange black configurations assembled themselves and spoke to me. I could still see it: *Ul, w ulu jest miód.* "Beehive. In the beehive is honey." Those were the first words in my Polish elementary-school primer that I understood, and after that, I simply devoured books and eventually found release in what seemed a flair for writing. When the war came I had to learn the rudiments of German, although it had been my mother tongue. At that point I could neither read nor write it, and my father set out to teach me.

Now it was English that gave me that kind of release and intoxicated me with its vibrant beauty. Musicians and painters can express themselves in a universal language that needs no words, whereas a writer's task is far more complex. I would get frustrated when people spoke louder to me or would use simpler words, assuming that because I had an accent I could not understand the language. Occasionally that still happens, but these days it is a source of amusement. Though I was aware of the difficulty of truly mastering a language, English appeared to me to offer the richest and finest distinctions to anyone attuned to words.

My first attempt at writing the story of my life, only a few months after coming to this country, was done in German, but in short order I had the good sense to abandon the effort. Instead I consoled myself with the idea that someday I would have the capability to resume it in English, which indeed turned out to be the case. Thus *All But My Life* was published in 1957, and writing it in my new language was a healing experience. I love English for all it has given me in so many ways, and above all for setting me free.

The greatest relief from the burdens of my past came a little over two years after our wedding, with the birth of our first daughter. That was when death truly turned into life and the ultimate question was answered: Yes, I could have a healthy, normal child. In each case the birth of our children and grandchildren imbued me with a feeling of awe bordering on holiness. The fears that enter my being before such momentous events always overwhelm my emotions. Those tiny pinpricks of doubt that I have come to regard as both my friends and my enemies return each time, reminders of the vagaries of life, preventing me from being swept away in a flood of ecstasy or pain. I love and hate them at the same time, knowing that they are sharpening my perception of potential dangers that could block fulfillment; they are, so to speak, guardians of the gates of paradise.

Holding my first child in my arms, I overflowed with gratitude that such a treasure was given to me, that my body could house such a miracle. For years I longed to hold, to embrace, to touch my mother, my father, and my brother. Now, through my child's tiny heart pulsed their blood. Her skin was soft, warm, and fragrant under my lips. They had returned.

In 1952, four years after our first daughter, we had a second, and in 1957 a son. Each time I held one of our newborn children in my arms, the feeling would return that I had been entrusted with a sacred legacy from those in my family who had been deprived of life. Overcome by an awed gratitude, I felt anointed by the privilege of being a conduit, a link between the past and the future.

Becoming a mother yielded many other benefits. It allowed me to enter the mainstream of the life around me, put me on an equal footing with my contemporaries, closing the chasm that had existed between us. The routine of caring for babies became the great equalizer. At last I could speak the same language in every respect, could share and express similar concerns. As my children developed, so did my personal growth, instilling a sense of security in the rebuilding of family and giving me a place in the community as well.

That is not to say that our lives were free of problems. We had our share of disappointments, particularly painful when it concerned people we trusted and regarded as friends. There were times of economic insecurity, pain, and illness, but the resilience of youth helped us to overcome them. And always the bonds of our love and trust in each other were the shield against many obstacles.

Each of our three children married exceptionally fine and caring partners and had children. They have redeemed our highest hopes and are the source of our greatest happiness. In the fullness of years we have watched with pride how our grandchildren have grown, eventually towering over us, filling us in on their technology-assisted plans, undreamed of in our youth. They are able to travel the globe much as we did childhood haunts that merely spanned a few miles. Every so often Kurt and I resolve to retire, to devote more time to watching those glorious Arizona sunsets, but our resolutions have as yet proved elusive, if not delusive.

I have learned that we must occasionally pause on that steep climb to whatever summit we are seeking, take a backward glance, and be grateful for how far we have come. I have found that for me the meaning of life was not gained at a summit, whatever the achievement might be. Summits tend to be windy, cold, and lonely. Nor have I found the answer to the meaning of life in the abyss of hunger, abuse, and pain. The crest of my dreams during the years of slavery in the camps were thoughts of an evening at home with my family. That vision has served me well. No matter how enviable or luxurious my surroundings as a visitor, there is always that ever-present yearning of wanting to go home, a feeling that has never disappointed me. I can recall with crystal clarity a scene from the icy, windswept twilight of the death march during the last stages of the war. Close to the limits of our physical endurance, we were trudging through the snow outside Dresden, as a light was going on in a humble abode some distance from the road. I envisioned a family sitting down to supper and would gladly have renounced all that the future might hold for me, if I were permitted to enter that hovel, warm myself by the fire, and be given something to eat.

Early one morning many years ago, Kurt and I stood at the rim of the Grand Canyon waiting for the sun to rise. Gradually and majestically the darkness lifted on the horizon, and we stood in awe, watching the birth of a new day. Birds arose from the chasm, sweeping over the canyon, screeching their haunting greetings to the dawn. A pink hue was spreading toward the rim as flickering golden tongues of light licked and probed the depth of the earth. We stood mesmerized, numb, feeling somehow that we were witnessing the dawn of creation. A strident voice cut into the mood of the moment. "Damn it, that coffee is cold!" The new sunlight was reflected on the silver surface of the woman's thermos, and a thought came to me. It was a picture of myself, on an early winter morning in Buffalo, standing outside the house in front of our car. I, too, had exclaimed, "Damn it, that lock is frozen!" And there I was, pouring scalding water from a teakettle onto the frozen lock of my car. Was the dawn also breaking at that very moment? Each day begins with a sunrise and will continue to do so long after all our concerns and disappointments have been lost in the sands of time. The rising of the sun will not help to unfreeze the lock of my car, but the memory of that daily miracle might nonetheless take the edge off my irritation.

One magic July night we again found ourselves in Paris, the City of Light. The whole family was there to celebrate Kurt's birthday and that of our daughter Leslie, just one day apart. No one wanted the enchantment of the evening to end. A full moon hung in a brilliantly star-studded sky as we strolled with our children and their spouses over the near-empty boulevards of the sleeping city. Walking at first as one group, then breaking up into clusters of two and three, we were held by the spell that united us. We were loath to let go of it, wanting to hold on to the magic of the night as long as we could. A bridge arched over the Seine just ahead of us, and we proceeded to cross it, pausing to take in the view. Kurt's voice, deep and tinged with awe, reached me. "Turn around," he urged. "Do you know where we are?" There, ahead, over the molten gold of the moonlit Seine, outlined against the night sky, stood a tower, on it the illuminated dial of its clock.

So much had transpired since we stood on that very spot decades earlier. What then had been only dreams was now reality. We were here with our children and had grandchildren at home. Prayers I had never dared to pray were fulfilled; dreams I never knew to dream had turned into reality. Gifts and honors have been heaped on me from around the world, while all I have ever prayed for was freedom, a family, a home, and never to be hungry again. We have the blessing of our love, but also the freedom that allows it to flourish.

My eyes traveled to the clock on the tower of the building silhouetted against the velvety sky. No, it was not 9:10; it was much, much later.

Gerda Weissmann Klein